Managing the Digital Transformation

Thomas Hess

Managing the Digital Transformation

A Guide to Successful Organizational Change

Springer Gabler

Thomas Hess
Institute for Digital Management
and New Media (DMM@LMU)
LMU Munich
Munich, Germany

ISBN 978-3-658-38423-4 ISBN 978-3-658-38424-1 (eBook)
https://doi.org/10.1007/978-3-658-38424-1

Responsible Editor: Barbara Roscher
This Springer Gabler imprint is published by the registered company Springer Fachmedien Wiesbaden GmbH, part of Springer Nature.
The registered company address is: Abraham-Lincoln-Str. 46, 65189 Wiesbaden, Germany

Preface to the 1st English Edition

Digitalization and digital transformation are important topics, especially for companies. These topics are still relatively new for many people and they are certainly complex and multi-faceted. The latter explains why the discussion is often dominated by catchy slogans and seemingly alternative recipes. This gets attention for the topic and thus the entry into many companies. But this is not enough for the implementation of projects—specific frameworks, methods and instruments are required. These have been developed and tested in recent years, but have not yet been brought together and embedded in an overall concept. This book aims to close this gap. It focuses on the management of digital transformation and is specifically aimed at managers and digitalization experts who want to deal with this issue systematically and with a scientifically proven background.

The first edition of this book, presented in German, was very well received, which of course pleasead me and motivated me to publish a new edition. The basic concept of the book has remained unchanged. Nevertheless, the topic of transformation management continues to enjoy uninterrupted attention in research. The most important findings have been incorporated into the revision, which consists of three focus areas. A first focus was on organizational aspects, in particular the role of start-ups for digital transformation, the design of so-called Digital Innovation Units and the role of the Chief Digital Officer in digital transformation. The second focus of the revision was a much more differentiated view of the design and management of digitalization projects. The third focus of the revision was the further specification and delimitation of the concept of digital transformation. In addition, account was taken of the ongoing technological development. This edition represents the English translation of the second German edition.

The second edition was also significantly carried by the research group "Digital Management" at my institute at LMU Munich. I would like to express my special thanks to Philipp Barthel. Philipp Barthel has coordinated the revision process with foresight and deep understanding of the topic, brought in his special topics comprehensively, and suggested many updates. I would also like to thank Christian Sciuk, Janine Hagen and Simon Engert. They also engaged in the revision of individual passages. Julia Schulmeyer supported Philipp Barthel in the coordination of the second revision and in finalizing the first English version, my thanks also go to her. And—last but not least—my thanks go to Barbara Roscher and her team for their usual efficient support of the project on the publisher's side.

For the sake of better readability, the simultaneous use of the language forms male, female and diverse (m/w/d) is dispensed with. All terms and expressions apply equally to all genders.

Munich, Germany
August 2022

Thomas Hess

Contents

1

Challenge of Digital Transformation

Many companies have already started a number of digitalization projects, some are still facing their first major project. The question that always arises is how to approach the topic of digitalization systematically. Should a company appoint a Chief Digital Officer or not? For example, how must the IT landscape and corporate culture be prepared so that the actual digitalization projects are successful? Isn't a transformation strategy ultimately just a classic IT strategy? What is actually a digitalization project? This chapter presents the Three-Layer Model of digital transformation *which provides a framework for digital change in a company and ensures that no important topic related to digital innovation is overlooked.*

1.1 Three Insights into Digital Transformation

Digitalization and the resulting digital transformation are omnipresent topics in the media. Almost everyday there are reports of new business models, new products or new processes, initiatives to promote start-ups or digitalization in school education, the new role of robots, the risks of cybercrime or the danger of data giants such as Google.

Of course, digitization and digital transformation are taking place not only in the media, but also in companies in the real world. Three things become clear quite quickly to every manager and every entrepreneur who deals with the topic:

T. Hess, *Managing the Digital Transformation*,
https://doi.org/10.1007/978-3-658-38424-1_1

- First of all, you can't just ignore the topic. The digital change seems to affect the most diverse areas in the company, from procurement to sales and from organization to strategy development. It also seems pointless to simply delegate the topic to the IT department, as was perhaps still possible with the topic of enterprise resource planning systems (ERP systems) a few years ago.
- Secondly, there does not seem to be a patent solution for the topic—the questions and possibilities raised as well as the conditions existing in the companies are too different.
- And thirdly, it must not remain the case that the topic is only dealt with on the initiative of individual persons—the priorities are too erratic, the processes are too inefficient.

This book specifically deals with the third topic area. It would like to help managers and entrepreneurs set up specific structures in their organization that allow them to approach the digital transformation in a systematic way and to be less dependent on chance. It is not explicitly about a rough overview of the topic of digitization, nor about the potentials of individual technologies or individual product ideas. Rather, the focus is on the process of digital transformation of a company. The book would like to show ways in which a company can organize this process effectively and efficiently—as far as this is already known and can be seen today. It is aimed at practitioners, whether they are line managers, staff in staffs or digitalization experts. The entrepreneurial perspective on the topic is deliberately chosen, i.e. the company with its products and processes is in the focus; other things like structures or technical solutions are primarily seen as means to an end.

1.2 The Two Levels of Digital Transformation

When you talk to companies in the German-speaking world about how intensively they have already dealt with digitalization and the digital transformation based on it, you get a divided picture (etventure, 2019; Telekom, 2020).

A first group of companies in Germany has already started a large number of digitalization projects. For example, many large retail banks are currently dealing with new online offerings and the dismantling of the branch business. Large retailers are trying to make up for lost ground with online shops in order to be able to compete with Amazon and other "born digitals". Television stations are currently exploring how they can stand up to Netflix and Co. Typically, such companies already have a large number of digitalization initiatives underway. Often these projects run largely uncoordinated alongside each other. Sometimes they even overlap. Due to the sole focus on these projects, important new developments are often overlooked. "We're already dealing with digital transformation" is a typical statement you hear in these companies again and again. Such companies urgently need a systematic coordination of their digitalization initiatives.

The second group of companies in Germany is still facing the first substantial digitalization project. In these companies, the topic of digital change has certainly arrived. Typically, it has been discussed once before. For example, you have invited an external speaker to a meeting of the supervisory board or advisory board. Individual ideas have also been developed, such as an innovative app for marketing or a completely new, data-based approach for the evaluation of production data. In addition, consultants are always offering to support you. There are also cooperation requests from Internet start-ups, but without concrete digitalization projects you can't really do anything with them. In companies of this second group, the awareness of the challenge is present. But the next step is missing—and time is pressing.

The starting point in the two groups of companies mentioned is different at first glance. On closer inspection, however, an important similarity becomes apparent. Namely, in both cases a systematic and cross-project approach is required to the question of how the process of digital transformation is to be organized. Should the responsibility for digital transformation lie with the Chief Executive Officer (CEO)[1] or should he delegate it, for example, to a Chief Digital Officer (CDO) or the Chief Information Officer (CIO)? Is a transformation strategy necessary even though the company has an accepted and current IT strategy? What role does the HR department play in the context of digital transformation? What tools support the development of digital products, for example? Should the topic be delegated to the IT department? How often should top management deal with the topic of digital transformation?

In all these questions it is important to approach the process of digital transformation systematically and not randomly, unstructured and uncoordinated. In essence, it is about creating the conditions so that the opportunities and risks of digital change can be recognized, the right priorities can be set, the right projects can be prioritized and structural conditions can be

[1] There is a wide range of management positions in the German-speaking world. For the sake of simplicity, this book uses the internationally accepted terms.

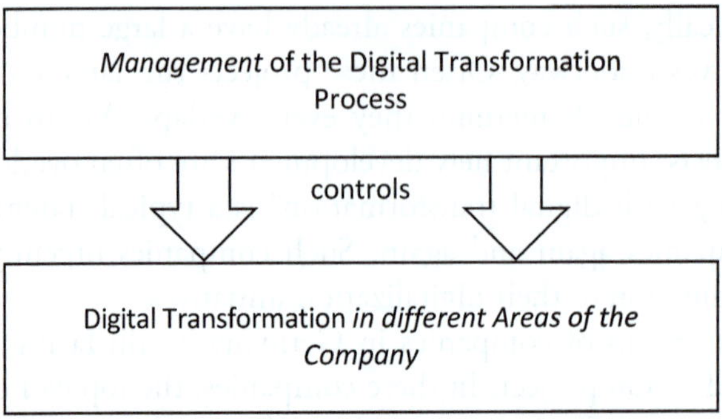

Fig. 1.1 Two Levels of Digital Transformation (Hess & Barthel, 2017)

created. This is to be referred to here as the **management level of digital transformation** (Hess & Barthel, 2017). Only this level creates the conditions for the **operational level of digital transformation**—just as a management system is required in other parts of the company so that operational action is effective and efficient.

So far, the management of digital transformation has been neglected to a large extent in many companies. Many companies were previously satisfied that the issue had been identified at all. This is no longer enough today. A systematic examination of how the process of digital transformation can be controlled in one's own company is required (Fig. 1.1).

1.3 New Technologies as Drivers of Digital Innovation

At the center of the digital transformation of companies are **"digital innovations"** (Nambisan et al., 2017; Wiesböck & Hess, 2020). Digital innovations arise from the innovative use of digital technologies. The central feature of digital innovations is that they comprise two components, a technical and a professional (content-related, application-specific) solution (see Fig. 1.2). An example of this is the combination of an online news service (innovative professional solution) with a machine-learning-based recommendation system (innovative technical solution). However, these components must be coordinated ("integrated"), and are therefore like the two sides of a coin. Traditionally, the impetus for a digital innovation comes from new professional requirements, e.g. from a changed sales or controlling concept. These new requirements are implemented in a technical solution ("Technology Pull"). However, this is no longer enough today. Today,

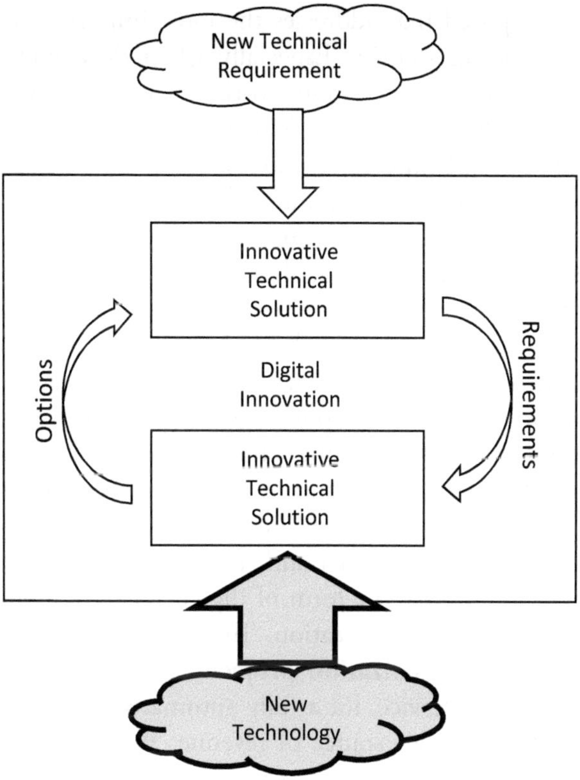

Fig. 1.2 "Technology Push" in the basic model of digital innovation (Wiesböck & Hess, 2020)

technical developments are very often the drivers for digital innovations, i.e. the impetus often comes from the technology ("Technology Push"). In Fig. 1.2 this special "entry point" is particularly pronounced.

The integrated consideration of a digital innovation and in particular the today dominant role of the technical drivers will occupy us in this book at many points.

1.4 The Three-Layer Framework of Digital Transformation

The need to establish a management structure in order to exploit the potential of digital technologies and thus realize digital innovations is obvious. However, this insight is not enough for practical implementation. Rather, a framework is required that addresses the most important issues and thus provides corresponding security. Especially when developing an approach for one's own company, such a framework can help to approach the project systematically. Of course, such a framework cannot be implemented in a one-size-fits-all approach in every company. Industry, size, age and the level of engagement with digitalization and digital transformation decide which tasks should be given priority in a company.

The "Three-Layer Model of Digital Transformation" (3LDT-Framework) is such a framework. It was developed in cooperation between science and practice over the past years (Wiesböck & Hess, 2020) and further developed for this book. This framework considers digital transformation from a holistic perspective for a company and puts digital innovations at the center.

The core of the 3LDT-Framework is the change in value creation through the **development and implementation of digital innovations**. These digital innovations can be oriented towards an internal (digital process innovation) or external (digital product and service innovation) change in value creation. They can also take the form of digital business model innovations that affect all aspects of value creation. These changes are implemented by means of **"original" digitalization projects**, such as by means of a project for a new Internet service, for a fully automated business process or for exploiting a completely new source of revenue. We also refer to these projects as digital transformation projects in the **narrower** sense, because they directly change the value creation of the company.

However, products, processes and business models can only be changed if a **number of conditions in the company** are met. These conditions include, for example, the company's organization. For example, an organization promoting innovation must be in place. This cannot be achieved with an original digitalization project. The same is true, for example, of corporate culture. Typically, this can only be changed, if at all, over a longer period of time. Similarly, such **"support projects"** follow a completely different logic and, unlike original transformation projects, only lead to new applications in exceptional cases. We also refer to these projects as digital transformation projects in the **broader** sense because they only contribute indirectly to changing value creation. Creating conditions is therefore the second layer of the LSDT framework. This essentially affects the company's IT landscape, competencies and formal and informal structures. Typical projects here are, for example, the flexibility of the IT landscape for the adaptation of product features or the setting up of special organizational units that promote the emergence of new business ideas. In a company, this typically leads to a large

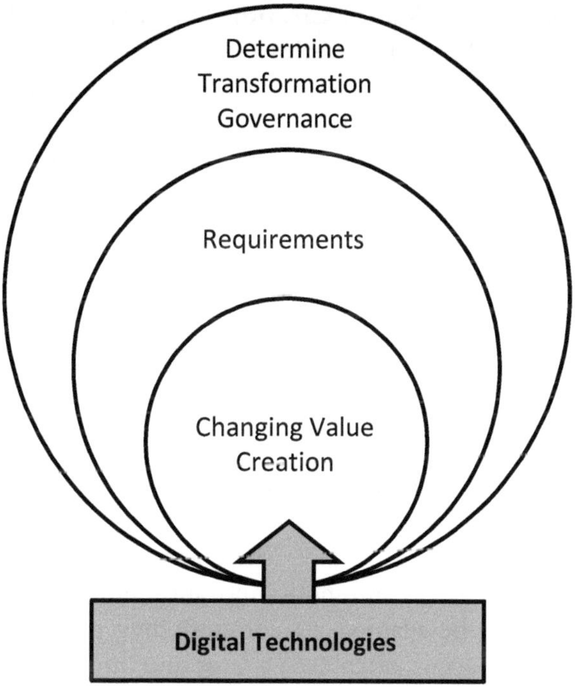

Fig. 1.3 The Three-Layer Framework of Digital Transformation (based on Wiesböck & Hess, 2020)

number of ideas for new products and processes. This also leads to the adaptation of structures, systems and cultures.

Therefore, a **transformation governance** is required that ensures the successful implementation and embedding of digital innovations. A key component of this governance is the **transformation strategy** that sets priorities and takes into account the context of the financial framework and technological possibilities. It is not to be confused with an IT strategy and also creates the connection to the corporate strategy and possibly other "guidelines". Furthermore, the question must also be answered here as to which **management position** is primarily responsible for the transformation process in the company. Projects that are based on this third layer, such as pure strategy development projects, can also be counted as digital transformation projects in the **broader** sense, as they can play a key role in the success of the transformation, but not directly change value creation. The development of a transformation governance thus forms the third and outermost layer of the 3LDT framework.

Fig. 1.3 shows the 3LDT framework. The three layers and the associated topic areas are presented in detail below.

Topic 1: Change in Value Creation through Development and Implementation of Digital Innovations

Original digitalization projects change value creation through the development and implementation of digital innovations. They call into question existing products, customer interfaces, processes and business models. But they also open up the opportunity for new products, customer interfaces, processes and business models that have not yet existed in the company or in general. There are specific approaches, instruments and concepts for each of the mentioned points. For example, products can be developed in an agile way, but this is rarely the case for processes. Specifics must also be taken into account, e.g. new players such as Google or Facebook at the interface between customers and established companies.

Topic 2: Creating the Conditions for Digital Transformation

Digital transformation only succeeds if the necessary conditions have been created in a forward-looking manner. These are in the IT landscape, in the workforce, in structures that promote innovation and in corporate culture. Often, these have to be adapted via corresponding projects (support projects). They are also part of, often even a large and important part, of a digital transformation.

Topic 3: Defining Transformation Governance

Transformation governance, in particular, includes the development of a transformation strategy that, as already mentioned, sets the essential guidelines for a company's digital transformation. It describes the central steps a company takes as part of digital transformation. This results in numerous interfaces to other areas, in particular to corporate strategy and IT strategy. These interfaces need to be clarified in the context of developing a transformation strategy. Once a transformation strategy has been defined in the sense described above, it is essential to communicate it to all employees in the company. This point is particularly critical because it decides whether the planned change will be accepted by the employees or resistance will form. Different groups in the company may need to be addressed individually. It is important that not only is it communicated *what* will change, but also *why* and why *in this way.* Another guideline is set by defining management roles. Specifically, it needs to be decided who drives digital transformation, who controls implementation, and who creates important preconditions.

Table 1.1 Management Tasks in the Context of Digital Transformation. (Wiesböck & Hess, 2020)

Topic	Tasks
Change in value creation through development and implementation of digital innovations	Development and implementation of digital innovations in the area of: – Products and services – Customer interfaces – Business processes – Business models
Create conditions for digital transformation	Prepare IT landscape Build structures that promote innovation Change corporate culture Build competence
Define transformation governance	Include ideas and impulses for transformation strategy Define interfaces to other strategies Fix and communicate transformation strategy Define roles for digital transformation

In Table 1.1 the tasks in the three topic areas are summarized in the context of digital transformation. In this overview it becomes clear that such a management structure is only meaningful if it is about changes that affect a company's competitive position. The 3SDT framework is specifically designed to deal with such changes. Of course, there are also smaller "digitalizations", for example in individual functional areas such as accounting or human resources. But these usually come with a less comprehensive management approach.

Table 1.1 also makes it visible that the management of digital transformation is something new. The management of digital transformation has hardly anything to do with IT management. In IT management, it is about the IT landscape of a company and sometimes about gradual changes in business processes. The scope of IT management therefore ranges from the operation and maintenance of individual systems and their interaction to the networking of computers to the outsourcing of entire parts to service providers. In the course of the steadily increasing importance of IT, the factors of security and availability have gained significantly in importance in recent years. In addition, the cost pressure on IT has increased steadily. The operation and further development of IT, as well as the gradual change of processes as a result of the introduction of new IT systems, are challenging management issues. However, they are clearly to be distinguished from the management of digital change.

1.5 Structure of this Book

The structure of the book follows the 3LDT framework. Chapter 2 first provides the "basics" on the topic of digitalization and digital transformation. Chapter 3 deals with the change in value creation, in particular with the management of digitalization projects, as well as innovation in the area of products, customer interfaces, processes and business models. Chapter 4 is dedicated to the requirements for digital transformation, such as those to be created in the areas of IT landscape and organizational structure. In Chapter 5 finally, transformation governance is at the center. Transformation strategies and structures are discussed. In Chap. 6 the procedure is summarized briefly and a way to get started is shown.

The best way to get a comprehensive understanding is to work through Chaps. 2, 3, 4, 5 and 6 successively—Chapter 2 can be skipped if you are already familiar with the topics of digitalization and digital transformation. However, it is also possible to start with Chapter 6. From there you can jump into the details in Chapters 3, 4 and 5.

References

Deutsche Telekom. (2020). *Digitalisierungsindex Mittelstand 2020/2021 – Der digitale Status quo des deutschen Mittelstands.* https://www.digitalisierungsindex.de/studie/gesamtbericht-2021/. Accessed 7 Sept 2021.

etventure. (2019). *Studie Digitale Transformation 2019: Die Zukunftsfähigkeit der deutschen Unternehmen.* https://service.etventure.de/digitale-transformation-2019. Accessed 7 Sept 2021.

Hess, T., & Barthel, P. (2017). Wieviel digitale Transformation steckt im Informationsmanagement? Zum Zusammenspiel eines etablierten und eines neuen Managementkonzepts. *HMD Praxis der Wirtschaftsinformatik, 54*(3), 313–323.

Nambisan, S., Lyytinen, K., Majchrzak, A., & Song, M. (2017). Digital innovation management: Reinventing innovation management research in a digital world. *MIS Quarterly, 41*(1), 223–238.

Wiesböck, F., & Hess, T. (2020). Digital innovations – Embedding in organizations. *Electronic Markets, 30*(2), 75–86.

2

Welcome to the Digital Business World

Digital disruption, Industry 4.0, Social Media Marketing—one could almost endlessly extend and constantly expand the list of terms and concepts used in the context of digital transformation. This chapter should bring some order to the hardly comprehensible set of terms. The two central features of digital transformation will be highlighted. Furthermore, the terms digitalization and digital transformation will be embedded in the logic of digital innovations. For the basic understanding of the topic, however, it is just as important to take a look at the current technological developments and the resulting basic questions for companies. An overview of this will also be given .

2.1 Potential of Digital Technologies: From Automated Accounting to the Self-Driving Car

For a long time now, new digital technologies have led to new business concepts. Below we show the development in two industries as an example and present a general model with which the effects of new digital technologies can be recorded.

T. Hess, *Managing the Digital Transformation*,
https://doi.org/10.1007/978-3-658-38424-1_2

2.1.1 Music Industry: The Napster Shock and its Consequences

For a long time, the sale of music has been a lucrative business. The profits were considerable and the central challenge for the music industry was to reliably identify the next top sellers. Until the end of the 1990s, four internationally active publishers divided the market among themselves (one of which belonged to the German Bertelsmann group), and smaller regional players occupied the niche markets. At this time, IT was only used to increase efficiency in the so-called back office.

But suddenly everything changed. The start-up Napster came to the market. Napster was the first to use the potential of "peer-to-peer technology" for the exchange of music files. The decisive factor is that this now takes place directly between the computers and not via a central unit. Figure 2.1 shows the basic principle of networking, as it is also used for the exchange of music files.

Although this obviously violated existing copyrights, the service quickly gained popularity, which was reflected in the rapidly increasing number of users. Napster, in its original form, was shut down a few years after its launch as a result of numerous lawsuits initiated by the music industry. However, together with other music sharing sites, the service had already caused significant sales loss for the major music labels in this relatively short period of time. IT was no longer exclusively a back-office issue for music publishers, but was on the strategic agenda of all music publishers overnight.

As a result of this development, the music industry was forced to rethink and began testing digital distribution concepts in the early 2000s.

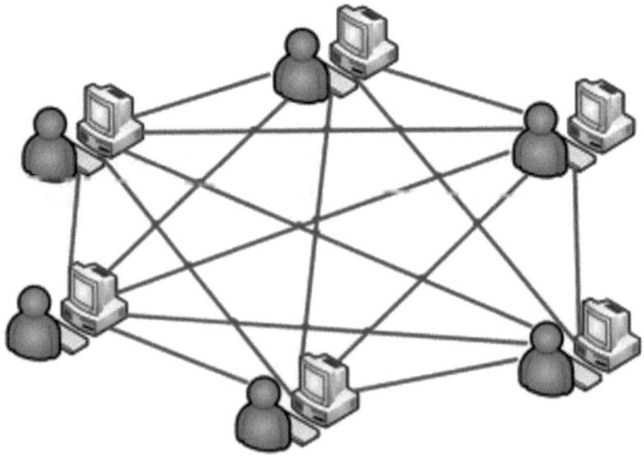

Fig. 2.1 Peer-to-Peer Music Exchange Network

One of the first forms of these new distribution methods was the concept of "download-to-own", i.e. a form of one-time purchase of downloads for entire albums or individual songs. At first, the music publishers tried to sell their available albums and songs via their own websites—but the success remained largely absent.

The music industry was more successful when cooperating with Apple. In 2001, Apple launched its iTunes internet service. For the first time, consumers could easily buy and download music files. The so-called rights protection systems ensured that consumers could not freely share a music file they had purchased. The music publishers receive a share of the profits from the sales of the files, the rest goes to the platform operator Apple. Thanks to a special storage format, the files could only be used on Apple devices. With this, Apple had found an important entry point to support the sale of its own hardware. Later, more providers of download services were added, and eventually Apple also allowed users to play the files on other devices.

Today, music is consumed increasingly via streaming. With streaming, a new distribution method has been added, in which the music files are only transmitted over the (mobile) internet for the moment of use and are no longer stored locally on the computer or on mobile devices. One of the best-known streaming providers in Germany is Spotify. Streaming services like Spotify are typically paid through a monthly fee. Some providers also follow a so-called "freemium" revenue model, which in addition to selling subscriptions as part of a premium version of the service also includes a free but limited offer. Some providers even try to integrate their content into new usage contexts such as connected homes or connected cars. Today, the music industry in Germany already generates around two-thirds of its sales through online channels, with a trend towards growth (Bundesverband der Musikindustrie, 2021).

Within 20 years, the music industry has changed fundamentally. The formerly dominant CD has become a niche product. Music is now offered as a file or as a service, embedded in a technical context. The fundamental change is also in the sources of revenue. The music publishers now receive revenue for songs sold or played on streaming services and have therefore significantly expanded their competence in the areas of IT and digitization. The attractive bundle offers that are found, for example, on CDs are thus largely gone. For music publishers, the market power of platform operators such as Apple and Spotify is risky because they occupy the interface to the customer and are active worldwide—something that the music or media industry has not been able to do. This gives them a good negotiating position vis-à-vis the publishers and allows them to invest more in technological innovation, for example in better systems that offer the customer the most suitable content.

2.1.2 Automotive Industry: From Process Optimization in Production to New Mobility and New Vehicle Architecture

The automotive industry is one of the pillars of the German economy. In recent years, it has greatly increased its global market share and celebrated success after success. Nevertheless, there is no company in the automotive industry that has not yet written digitalization and digital transformation on its flag, both among vehicle manufacturers and among suppliers. This can be surprising at first glance—because unlike a piece of music, a car cannot be digitized at its core. But even here, the industry is currently undergoing a fundamental change.

The digitalization also started with the vehicle manufacturers in the administrative area. The topic of digitalization gained more attention when digital technologies became the lever for changing value-added processes. The focus was on improvements in product development and, in particular, in the management of supply chains. The efficient exchange of data with suppliers is a central requirement for the functionality of the multi-tier supplier networks set up by the vehicle manufacturers. The Internet quickly became the technical basis for this exchange. Operatively, these networks allow for the coordinated planning across the boundaries of the individual company. With specific investments, they bind the suppliers to the vehicle manufacturers. Together with the cross-site optimization of production and logistics, digitalization thus became a step-by-step strategically important topic for vehicle manufacturers. In parts, the Internet offer for customers was also extended in this phase and thus the monopoly of the classical distribution was questioned.

The topic of digital transformation has recently gained considerable importance, because now it is closer to the product. Under the keyword "Connected Car", all major automobile manufacturers are striving to integrate the vehicles into the Internet; digital technologies thus provide an important supplement to the core product. However, creating such a "Connected Car" is a great technical challenge, because it requires significantly increased computing power. While it was previously sufficient to provide this in the up to 100 distributed control units ("mini-computers") in the vehicle, the next generation of vehicles will require one or more central high-performance computers. This in turn requires a complete change in the entire electrical and electronic architecture—the "nervous system"—of the vehicle. The manufacturers are moving away from independent components to a central architecture. Figure 2.2 shows an example of BMW's approach to the Connected Car.

The topic is now no longer in the classical IT departments, but in product development and in the strategy departments as well as in the newly founded digitalization units. Many manufacturers are trying to provide attractive additional services, such as specific suspension settings or an intelligent headlight assistant, and thus to generate additional revenue after the purchase of a car and even during the operation of cars. It is precisely at this point that new players enter the market. Some of them, like Tesla, want to produce cars themselves and differentiate themselves both through digital services and through a new drive technology. Others, like Google, rely more on their multiple relevance to customers and the knowledge they have gathered about customers through various application areas.

A connected car, in turn, is the basis for two scenarios with which vehicle manufacturers are currently dealing. It is foreseeable that the role of the human driver will be gradually replaced by the computer using so-called assistance systems. When such systems can completely replace the driver, when this will be accepted and honored by the customer and when the

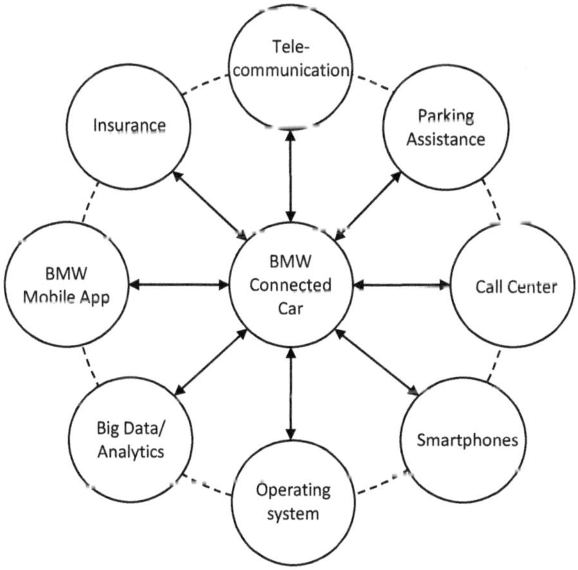

Fig. 2.2 "Connected Car" at BMW (2018)

legal framework will be created for this, this is not foreseeable today. In any case, this scenario requires to further equipping the car with digital technologies—digital technologies become a central element of the product, the product becomes hybrid.

In parallel to autonomous driving, the automotive industry is still dealing with a second scenario. So far, the automotive industry has produced products (cars) that essentially support the individual mobility of a person or a small group of people. However, these use the car relatively rarely, i.e. the car is unused for a long time. In addition, it can be observed that younger generations in general and also specifically assign less importance to the ownership of a car. In addition, the car is losing its status as a status symbol. Both together lead to the testing of so-called car-sharing concepts. The basic idea of car-sharing is that manufacturers no longer sell a car, but become providers of mobility solutions. Carsharing users do not buy the car, but pay essentially for the kilometers traveled by a car.

The efforts of the major vehicle manufacturers to adapt their organizational structures are also noteworthy. For this one must know that vehicle manufacturers are traditionally very hierarchical and centralized—for an efficient mass production in a stable environment this is certainly also the right organizational form. But this stable environment does not exist anymore—many manufacturers want and have to take this into account.

If you compare a vehicle manufacturer 20 years ago with a vehicle manufacturer today, digital technologies have so far caused gradual changes, especially in processes. The networking of vehicles and even more the concepts of car sharing based on this are presenting vehicle manufacturers with completely new challenges today, both in terms of products, processes and organizational structures. The networking makes digital technologies part of the actually analog product. Car-sharing concepts—if they are accepted by the general public—would call the traditional self-image of a vehicle manufacturer fundamentally into question.

2.1.3 The Five Stages of Digital Transformation

Venkatraman (1994) has early on presented a systematization of the stages of change of companies through digital transformation. Venkatraman distinguishes five stages of digital transformation (see Fig. 2.3). He refers to changes in the local area (e.g. through a software solution in a single department) and also to the company-wide integration (e.g. through uniform

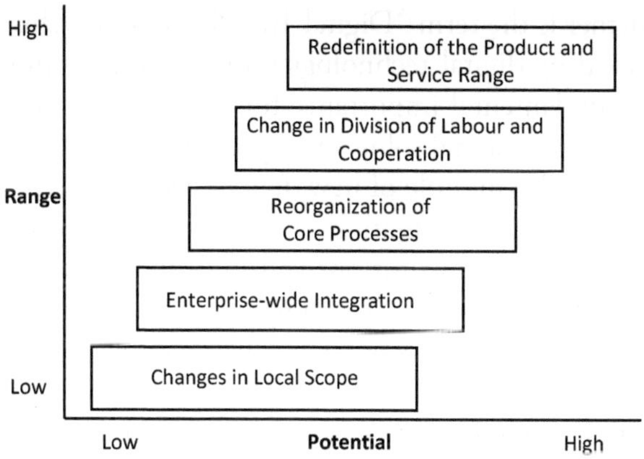

Fig. 2.3 Five Stages of the Scope of Digital Transformation (based on Venkatraman, 1994)

commercial systems) as evolutionary (stage 1 and 2). He refers to the changes driven by digital technologies in the area of important processes, the division of labor between companies and the product and service range of a company as revolutionary (stages 3 to 5). Revolutionary changes undoubtedly have a significant impact on the competitive position of a company. These are typically in the focus of digital transformation.

2.2 Important Terms and Concepts

In the context of our topic, there is an almost unmanageable number of terms. If one were to create one of the word clouds commonly used today, it could quickly fill several pages. This diversity often leads to uncertainty and possibly even confusion. The following should therefore shed some light on the amount of terms (Hess, 2019).

2.2.1 Digitalization and Digital Transformation

"Digitalization" describes the introduction of new, digitally based solutions. "Digitalization" can be easily confused with "Digitization"; the latter refers to the transfer of information from an analog to a digital storage form and thus a very specific form of "Digitalization".

One step further is the term "Digital Transformation". This term describes the change caused by digital technologies and the digital innovations based on them, with fundamental importance for the company. It emphasizes the introduction of a professional solution (e.g. a new sales control concept), but also emphasizes the driving role of new digital technologies.

Examples of digital transformation can be found in almost all areas of life, i.e. in companies, in state institutions and in private households—although in very different manifestations. In companies, for example, products and processes change. Governments adapt regulations (e.g. in the form of new regulations on internet crime in criminal law) and also simplify their processes. A private household, for example, increasingly buys online and submits its tax return online. The Corona crisis has intensified the pressure for digital transformation and has led to an additional digitalization boost in both companies and private households. All of this is only possible with the digital storage of information and its processing by machines and thus by digitalization. Nevertheless, in all of the examples just mentioned, the professional solutions are the focus, the technology is a means to an end.

The focus of this book is on the perspective of a company, i.e. it is about the **digital transformation *of companies*** (Vial, 2019). Of course, this includes how customers and other business partners as well as the state are digitized, but the view is always from the perspective of a company. Österle was the first to introduce this perspective into the German-speaking world under the term **"information-based corporate management"** (Österle, 1987).

Digital transformation includes fundamental changes that are caused by digital technologies in companies. Accordingly, it should also be approached as a strategic issue, which requires the development of cross-cutting governance structures and the creation of conditions across the company. Some authors even go so far as to only speak of digital transformation if the identity and value creation process of a company changes completely (e.g. Wessel et al., 2021). What is right about this perspective is that it emphasizes the far-reaching consequences of digital transformation. However, it does partly go past the lived reality of digital transformation. This book therefore also takes into account far-reaching changes that do not lead to a completely new company identity and a completely new value proposition.

2.2.2 Digital Transformation as a Specific Management Concept

In the two cases introduced at the beginning of this section, new digital technologies were and are the drivers of development. In the case of the music industry, it is about the availability of consumers via the Internet, supplemented by specific technological solutions such as peer-to-peer networks, shop systems, rights systems and streaming. In the case of vehicle manufacturers, it is about the Internet as a tool for networking cars and companies, for driver assistance systems or for platforms for transport services. This means: Digitization and digital transformation are **"technology-driven".** Technology as a starting point is therefore the first characteristic.

At first glance, this is hardly surprising. However, a perspective originating from technology is by no means as self-evident as it may sound at first, because it is not a question of simply digitizing existing solutions. From an inefficient analog process, only an inefficient digital process results. It was also rarely convincing to simply transfer an existing product, e.g. in the media sector, to a new medium. Rather, it is about exploiting new technologies to create new approaches. The term "Techno-Change" is occasionally used in the literature for this technology-driven change (Markus, 2004)—this brings the idea clearly to the point without, of course, postulating the omnipotence of technologies in a naive way.

A second attribute is also characteristic. In Chap. 1 it was shown that the digital transformation must be controlled and flanked. Controlled means that a company must approach the digital transformation systematically, e.g. by introducing new management roles or formulating special strategies for the digital transformation. Flanked means that a company's focus must not only be on transformation projects. Rather, a complete adaptation of the management structures or a new orientation of important resources is required. In this sense, for example, automobile manufacturers have introduced more flexible organizational structures and music publishers have significantly expanded their competencies in the field of digital technologies. Digital transformation is driven by technological development, but goes far beyond the introduction of new IT systems. The digital transformation is therefore a **broad management approach**—this is the second characteristic.

A third, equally important characteristic lies in the importance of change for the organization. For many years, digital technologies have been gradually changing the organization, but this is often no longer the case. We therefore speak of digital transformation when the IT-induced change is fundamental for the company. This is particularly evident in the fact that the attention of top management is required. **Fundamental importance** is therefore the third characteristic.

The effects of digital technologies are very different in this context. In the two cases considered above, in the case of music publishers and automobile manufacturers, it was initially—as in almost all industries—only about efficiency gains in the administrative area. These are undoubtedly desirable, but for the competitiveness of a company they are only rarely really decisive. At the beginning, digitalization and the digital transformation based on it were therefore not a topic for general management. However, the two cases mentioned above also show that this has changed in the meantime. In the case of the media industry, it is today essentially about the product itself, in the case of automobile manufacturers at least about important product features.

Around the year 2000, the term "E-Business" was particularly popular. From the perspective of the terminology just presented, this also meant the digital transformation of companies, but with a very strong focus on the Internet as a driver of change and with a much narrower understanding of the range of possible impacts.

2.2.3 Digital Innovations and Disruptive Innovations

Digital innovation and digital disruption are terms that are also often used in the context of digital change. The term digital innovation was already introduced in Sect. 1.3. Digital innovations arise from new digital technologies. To understand and implement them, an integrated, i.e. coordinated view of the technical and the subject-specific aspects of an innovation is essential (Wiesböck & Hess, 2020). So it is—to take an example from sales—not "just" about the app and its user interface, but also about its integration into a new sales concept.

A special form of (digital) innovation is disruption, more precisely disruptive (digital) product innovation. According to Christensen (1997), who introduced this term, it is a special form of technology-driven product innovation. This product innovation is characterized by offering new product features that the customer has not yet considered relevant. A typical example of such a digital product innovation was the smartphone. Although users cannot make phone calls much better with a smartphone than with a mobile phone, a smartphone has features that are interesting for mobile users, such as easy access to many interesting Internet services.

Occasionally, the term disruption is also equated with radicality. This is intended to highlight the high degree of change—but this does not correspond to Christensen's original intention.

2.2.4 Industry 4.0, Social Media Marketing and Similar Concepts

"Social Media Marketing" and "Industry 4.0" are new professional concepts that are embedded in digital innovation. A central theme of social media marketing, for example, is the inclusion of the previously purely passive, receptive customer as a source of ideas for the development of products. Presentation models and success indicators are also presented. An industrial company in the mode 4.0 is characterized by the close integration of customers and other business partners into its own business processes. Drivers include, for example, the improved possibilities for networking of machines and companies as well as other special solutions, e.g. in production control and data acquisition.

At this point, one could still present at least ten comparable concepts that have individual aspects of the technology-induced change of companies as their subject. But often they are difficult to delimit and, as the two examples above have already shown, serve more to transport an idea than to precisely describe a concept. For example, in Table 2.1 a few selected professional concepts are presented, which have arisen in the last 25 years.

2.2.5 Add-on: Theoretical Classification of Digital Transformation

A specific branch of research deals with the interaction between an organization (and thus a company as a special variant of an organization) and technology. The basic approaches (Orlikowski, 1992) were the **organizational imperative,** the **technological imperative** and an **integrative approach** worked out. The first approach emphasizes the dominant role of the human being in the decision-making process on the use of technology. The second approach emphasizes the role of technology as a driver of change in organizations. The third approach, often anchored in "structuration theory", tries to connect the two approaches.

With the emphasis on the role of new digital technologies as drivers, the concept of digital transformation is certainly primarily attributable to the

Table 2.1 Specific Concepts for Digital Change

Concept	Business Process Optimization	Mass Customization	Social Media Marketing	Industry 4.0
Relevant business area	Core processes of a company	Marketing and production	Marketing	Production
Core idea	Processes as "forgotten" dimension that can only be unfolded through new potentials of technology	Individualized production at low costs	Activation of the previously passive user	Networking of all devices and systems
Technical Drivers	Basically all, with a focus on ERP systems	Customer internet access, flexible production systems	Social media platforms on the internet	Networking of machines and possibly smaller devices based on the Internet
Origin	Around 1995	Around 2000	Around 2005	Around 2010

second approach. This does not in any way question the mutual influence of specialist and technical solutions—the starting point is simply the new technology.

2.3 Digitalization: How Digital Innovations Arise Today

In the sections 2.1 and 2.2 ,the most important conceptual and conceptual basics were presented. But just as important for a basic understanding are also the relevant "contents", i.e. the most important technological trends and the resulting changes in the environment of companies and the options for their structuring. The technological trends begin.

For this, a step back is required. In essence, a computer can only do one thing: it can process information. But it can do it well, especially much faster than the human being. Over the years, this skill has gradually and sometimes abruptly improved. Step by step he replaces the human brain—just as the machine can replace the human muscle power.

A computer consists of three components at its core (Mertens et al., 2017; see Fig. 2.4). The **hardware** refers to all those parts that can be touched. The **software** contains the commands that tell the hardware what to do. A special role is played by the way a computer interacts with a human and with its

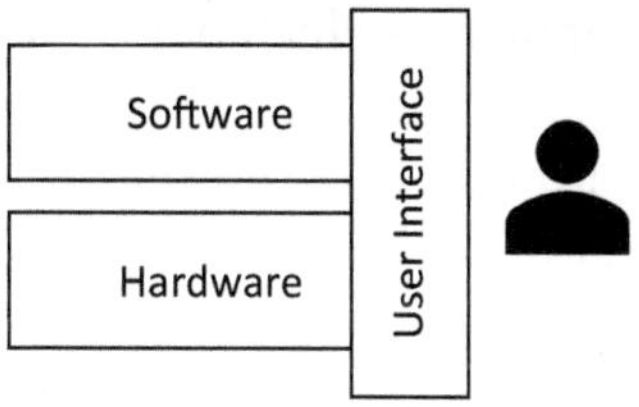

Fig. 2.4 The Three Logical Components of a Single Computer

environment in general, the so-called **user interface.** Specific combinations of hardware (such as a screen or a sensor) and software (for controlling the screen and sensors) are used at the user interface. The following describes the basic developments in hardware, software and user interface.

2.3.1 Trends in Hardware

It all started with a single computer. This was still very limited in its processing speed—every calculator can process more information today. In addition, the computers were not connected, i.e. each computer worked independent from others.

Huge advances in information technology have greatly improved a computer's processing capacity over the past few decades. Moore's Law is still in effect here. It states that the processing speed of an integrated circuit in a computer, and thus the **computational speed** of a computer, will double at least every two years. If we go back just 20 years, it becomes clear how much faster a computer has become. There have also been significant advances in the technologies used to **store** data. All data that is not currently being processed and that is to be kept long-term is stored in memory.

The advances made in networking computers over the past few decades are at least as important. Today, almost every computer can be reached by another computer via the Internet. This became possible because the Internet found a standard in the 80s that made exchanging information between any two computers much simpler. The importance of this infrastructure progress cannot be overestimated. Once the necessary conditions were in place, the physical networks were expanded. The **transmission capacity** was increased year after year. In addition, more and more private households were connected—which was not so long ago still an exception, today is self-evident. A second major breakthrough was the expansion and, above all, the opening of the **mobile networks.** Originally, these were only intended for telephone calls. Today, mobile networks are also used primarily for network computers—which of course do not always have to be stationary.

The development of hardware is by no means already completed. There will be noticeable progress in both computing power and the capacity and availability of networks in the coming years. One important development in recent years has been the so-called **"cloud computing".** Cloud computing means that the data or software required is no longer on the user's own computer, but on another person's computer. For example, if a doctor wants to use complex software to analyze medical images, the software and data required for this are usually stored on his or her local computer. With cloud computing, both the data and the software would be stored on another computer. The doctor accesses this via the Internet and the networks above it, his or her own computer is largely "stupid". This reduces the technical complexity on his or her terminal considerably. On the other hand, his or her data is no longer under his or her control. He or she is also dependent on the availability of a connection to the Internet.

A second current development is the emergence of the **"Internet of Things"**. So far, the Internet and the networks below have served as a platform for the networking of a considerable number of terminals. However, these terminals, usually dedicated computers, are operated by a human being, ranging from the desktop PC to the tablet PC to the smartphone. The idea behind the Internet of Things is that it makes sense to connect a variety of technical devices beyond dedicated computers, and that a human being does not necessarily have to control these devices. "Candidates" for this can be found in both companies and in private households. In companies, this involves a variety of machines, possibly also mobile goods. In private households, the range extends from the most important household appliances such as heating, blinds and lamps to cars and fitness trackers. The necessary technical requirements are usually in place today, both for the terminals and for the organization of the Internet.

2.3.2 Trends in Software

System software coordinates the interaction of the individual components of a computer and takes over overarching, rather technical functions. For a long time, not much had happened in this area. However, in recent years there have been significant improvements in software for managing large amounts of data. For a long time there has been software that comprehensively supported the management of large amounts of data. However, these data had to be structured in the same way. In addition, the evaluation options were rather limited. Newer software allows, under the term **Big Data**, both the merging of heterogeneous data sets (for example, from the log files of a web shop, a customer database and a market research institute) and their comprehensive evaluation. The latter includes the construction of user-related profiles, the search for previously unknown relationships (for example, the drivers of the purchasing habits of consumers of a certain product) as well as the somewhat target-oriented prediction of the behavior of individual users or user groups. The latter mentioned systems are used, inter alia, to control police patrols in the context of the statistically determined risk of residential burglaries.

The **blockchain technology** can also be counted among the innovations in data management. The core idea is to distribute a data set as a linked list over a large number of computers. Blockchains are thus a completely new form of a distributed database. Whether and, if so, which applications beyond virtual currencies will prevail, is not yet foreseeable today.

Application software is directly important for digital transformation. It is developed specifically for a specific application area and relies on system software and hardware. It all started with software to support the administrative functions in a company, such as those found in accounting and payroll. Gradually, more and more tasks and processes were supported in companies, for example, the ERP systems mentioned above, supply chain management systems (SCM systems) or CRM systems.

With the increasing availability of inexpensive devices and their connection to the Internet, a second segment for software developed for applications in the private context. It started with simple, familiar from the business environment software, such as for e-mail or for word processing. Meanwhile, there are specific software, such as media consumption, for managing personal finances, or in the form of games. In addition, there are now some types of software that are used in both the professional and private context, such as various communication tools such as **social networks** or **messaging services** as well as the aforementioned word processing software.

In recent years, progress has also been observed in the field of **artificial intelligence**. Attempts to put a computer in a position to solve a problem not only by processing a clearly defined sequence have been made repeatedly. The often high expectations have been partially fulfilled so far. In some cases, for example in image recognition or prediction, remarkable success has been achieved. Based on the large amount of data available today, systems are currently being tested that learn constantly. In the field of image processing, first success has already been achieved. It is also possible to use computers as communication partners in simple dialogues without the human communication partner immediately recognizing the machine as such (social bots). These systems also learn constantly.

2.3.3 Trends at the User Interface

Until well into the 1980s, a computer's user interface was very similar to a typewriter's. The user had a classic keyboard available to enter commands into the system sequentially. On the screen, the user saw letters, numbers, and a few special characters. And that was it. A significant improvement was the **graphical interfaces,** which began appearing in the early 1990s. Instead of just simple letters and characters, the screen now also showes graphical symbols, and in color too. The mouse could now be used for navigation. Meanwhile, all computers have such interfaces.

In recent years, we've seen the addition of **touch-sensitive screens** and **specific glasses.** Also in practical use, a large number of **sensors** report environmental conditions back to a computer. Another typical application can be found in warehousing. In the connected home, sensors report room temperatures back to the user.

There have also been advances in user interfaces on the software side. Particularly important are advances in **speech recognition.** Today, for example, most smartphones have applications that allow for simple dialogues in natural language. For example, Amazon has brought the Alexa assistant system to market, which is designed to allow for the control of the home using natural language.

2.3.4 Conclusion

Computers can now be operated relatively intuitively and no longer require the study of extensive manuals—an important prerequisite, among other things, for the use of computers by private individuals.

The trends mentioned are summarized in Table 2.2.

If you take the trends in the three components of a computer together, then there is a general trend towards **autonomous systems** overall. Unlike with traditional IT systems, the behaviour of such systems is not fully defined in advance, i.e. the system further develops its internal logic based on the reception of the environment. The most tangible example of this are human-like robots, as they are at least already being tested today.

Table 2.2 Current Technical Trends at a Glance

Area	Trend
Hardware	Cloud computing: shifting of software components "into the cloud" Internet of Things: connection of various "things" to the internet
Software	Simplification of the merging and evaluation of large, heterogeneous data sets New forms of distributed databases in blockchains Use of newer methods of artificial intelligence (AI) in application systems
User Interface	Improved sensorics Improved interaction in human language based on methods of AI

2.4 Digital Transformation: Where Digital Innovations are Taking Place Today

Of course, every company has to find its own way for the digital transformation. This depends on the starting situation, the specific opportunities and risks of digital technologies in the particular case, the investment funds available, and many other factors. It can also take longer for basic innovations such as the Internet to be transferred into concrete solutions—social networks, for example, were not available when the Internet was created in the 1990s. Nevertheless, a few typical starting points can be worked out, which are currently relevant for a larger number of companies. These can be found in the market and value creation structure as well as in the individual companies.

2.4.1 Current Changes in the Company Environment

Intermediaries between suppliers and customers have always existed. Just think of retailers and banks. With the operators of **internet platforms**, a new class of intermediaries has arisen (Parker et al., 2017). They bring together suppliers and customers—just like a classic intermediary. However, such platforms do not require expensive sales rooms and thus also no large amounts of capital. Rather, they have relationships with customers and suppliers as well as a comprehensive database of their customers. The latter leads to high switching costs for customers who want to access products quickly and easily. The switching barriers are particularly high when the attractiveness of an offer of a platform increases not only with the number of suppliers, but also with the number of users.

Internet platforms are therefore something like huge department stores, but without the typical investment volumes and the typical costs of a department store, with efficient customer communication and very loyal customers. They position themselves between customers and producers and can play their market power both against producers and (!) against customers. The danger of monopoly formation is obvious. This is particularly true for communication-oriented platforms. Every additional user, e.g. of a social network, is potentially interesting for another user—the so-called direct network effects become virulent.

One of the first platforms of this kind was developed by Apple with the iTunes system for the online distribution of music in the form of music files. With this, Apple—as a company from another industry—has established an important position in the music business. Google, Uber, Amazon, eBay and Meta are other companies that have already positioned themselves as platforms for consumers. They all have a wide user base and position themselves between user and producers. This is exactly what is currently also occupied by the vehicle manufacturers. They want to avoid that a company like Google or Amazon is positioned between them and the vehicle user—a quite realistic danger.

In addition to establishing platforms, **cooperation** also plays an important role in the digitalizing world (Picot et al., 2003). This was not the case in the analog world. Typically, a company had market relationships with its customers and suppliers. If another company became interesting, it tried to buy and integrate it. Cooperation, on the other hand, is a hybrid construct: the actors remain independent, but at the same time work together in selected areas over a longer period of time.

Cooperation first gained greater importance in the automotive industry's supplier networks, and this was many years ago. In the classical industrial sector, inter-company optimization systems were also established. For example, some retailers report their sales figures early, which allows manufacturers more accurate production planning. There are also such cooperation in the air traffic. There the airlines have joined forces in two international alliances (Star Alliance and One World). In these alliances they coordinate flight plans, cooperate within frequent flyer programs and operationally provide increased comfort for travelers. The latter is unthinkable today without IT systems.

Currently, new forms of cooperation are emerging. One important manifestation of this are the so-called **ecosystems** (Moore, 1997). Ecosystems are often developed around a specific product and often form in the environment of the Internet platforms already outlined. All companies that can add value to the product at the center are included. They agree on a long-term cooperation. For example, the manufacturers of a heating system, the manufacturers of radiators, the operator of an app and possibly the operator of a home network must coordinate their solutions in order to offer an integrated solution for digital heating control. They cannot offer an attractive product on their own. But if they align their solutions with each other, then an offer that is interesting from the customer's point of view can arise. Such coordination is only possible on the basis of a long-term cooperation. The central subject is the agreement on a cross-system architecture as well as standards for the communication between the components of different manufacturers involved in the system. The so-called **"network effects"** (Shapiro & Varian, 1998) come into play here. Direct network effects arise when a customer has an advantage as soon as the number of customers using similar products increases. Indirect network effects arise when the consumer has an advantage because a complementary product is available.

However, new digital technologies such as the Internet of Things, blockchain or artificial intelligence are giving rise to ecosystems in which not only a product is at the center, but digital spaces with a variety of different actors who, depending on each other, nevertheless try to create, offer and exploit value independently. Such digital ecosystems are often characterized by a high rate of technical change, which sometimes brings radical uncertainty with it. Digital technologies enable the quick linking with a variety of actors, while at the same time the linking can be dissolved just as quickly. This trend is particularly important to consider in software development, as the technical possibilities are almost permanently changing. New tools, libraries, automation or interfaces enable the embedding of various applications and integration with solutions from other providers and thus form a far-reaching digital ecosystem. The potential possibilities of networking are so diverse that decision-makers actively limit and weigh them.

2.4.2 Typical Changes on the Market Side

In the analog world, a company usually had little direct contact with its customers. In addition, traditional industrial production required large quantities. Both have now changed. A company can now communicate extensively and for a long time directly with its (potential) customers via the Internet. The customer can thus express his preferences, or his preferences can be derived from his behavior. Based on these preferences, the customer can be provided with **individualized products** as a second approach.

This approach is used, for example, by the search engine provider Google. It collects information about the preferences of its customers and allows this to flow into the calculation of the relevance of websites. In addition, it uses this information to place advertising that best meets the user's preferences. Plakativ and strongly simplified this means: Whoever searches for cars in the search engine will also receive advertising for cars in a very short time. As a result, the scattering losses are reduced and the prices for placing the advertising go up. But even with material goods, individualization is now possible. For example, manufacturers of sports shoes offer the configuration of an individualized running shoe. Manufacturers of T-shirts make it possible to print any text. Flexible production systems up to 3-D printers make this possible. And the customer thanks him with a higher willingness to pay.

Insurance companies use a similar approach and are currently testing individualized tariffs for damage insurance. In these tariff models, for example, the customer of a car insurance receives a bonus if he does not exceed a certain driving performance or drives particularly defensively. However, such tiered tariffs require detailed information about the driving behavior.

In addition to adapting existing products and services, digital technologies are also **part of many analog products.** Examples can be found among both investment and consumer goods. In the field of investment goods, remote maintenance is a typical example. In this scenario, a classic machine is supplemented by specific software and equipped with a connection to the Internet (the Internet of Things mentioned above is created). The software recognizes when a defect is imminent or a consumable part needs to be replaced soon. Via the Internet connection, it sends a corresponding message to the manufacturer. In this way, the manufacturer of the machine can position itself as a service provider. He also learns something about the use of his machines in everyday work life. But there are also corresponding examples among consumer goods. Ravensburger, for example, is a successful manufacturer of classic children games. The company has now equipped its books with contact points and offers a pen for control. If a small child points to a spot in one of these books, he or she learns what kind of animal it is and what kind of sound is typical for the animal. Further examples can be found in the connected household. For example, by attaching a control module, a heating system can be better adapted to the needs, for example in the event of a delayed return.

2.4.3 Typical Changes in the Organization

The most classical starting point for the use of digital innovations in companies lies in the transfer of tasks to the computer that were previously carried out by a human—the third major area of digital technology within companies. Clearly structured tasks and processes can be described quite easily in software and transferred to the computer. This has happened to a large extent in recent years. For example, the complex task of payroll was almost completely transferred to the machine. In addition, companies can also use procedures that could not (or at least not at reasonable cost) be carried out by humans thanks to the computer. For example, modern sales support software allows the calculation of customer-specific coverage ratios. Just as modern optimization software can, for example, calculate the best possible routes in logistics.

The new artificial intelligence methods mentioned above now also make it possible to transfer less structured tasks to the computer. Typical examples can be found in customer dialogues or in the creation of texts in media companies. Interesting options also arise through the improvement of robots. Step by step, a robot can take over more complex tasks, for example in industrial production or in private households. However, computers and robots are still (so far) subject to clear limits. Tasks that require empathy can probably not be transferred to them for a long time. Another area of activity lies in the organizational structure of a company. Traditionally, companies have been more hierarchical and static in structure. For a classic industrialized production, be it in the processing industry or in the service sector, this is the most appropriate organizational form in many areas. If markets change due to digital technologies, to a very great or frequent extent, such structural organizations represent a barrier. That is why many companies are testing more flexible forms of cooperation within the company. The trend towards more flexible organizational forms also applies to cooperation with other companies. An extreme form are the so-called **virtual companies,** a special case of the company networks already mentioned above. For a virtual company, companies with complementary competencies and capacities join together. They agree on rules for cooperation in individual cases, as a rule on the basis of technically supported communication and coordination. However, they do not lose their independence.

Table 2.3 Current Economic Trends at a Glance

Starting point	Trend
Environment of companies	Industry platforms as a new business model More cooperation, also in innovative form, e.g. as ecosystems
Market side of companies	Individualization of customer approach and products Supplementing of analogue products by digital solutions
Organization of companies	Automation of less structured tasks More flexible company structures and cooperation

2.4.4 Conclusion

The current trends in the three areas just mentioned are summarized in Table 2.3.

2.4.5 Add-on: Data Economy as a Cross-Cutting Issue

Almost all of the approaches described previously have one thing in common: it is always about the improved **availability of data.** Platforms are based in particular on the data they have collected about their users. Cooperation only becomes attractive when data can be exchanged efficiently between the parties involved. Personalization of products, as well as a comprehensive view of the customer and further automation of processes, are based on improved data availability. The provision and use of data is therefore a cross-cutting issue. Companies are currently carrying out a number of projects to first identify existing data and to identify the opportunities for data consolidation. Many questions, such as the value of data or the benefits of data consolidation, are still largely unresolved. The focus is often strongly on personal data. The associated questions (for example in the context of social networks, but also simple e-mail newsletters) are interesting. But the processing of non-personal data, for example in the interaction of companies, is at least equally interesting.

2.5 When Digital Innovations Become Effective: Towards the Acceptance of New Systems

New technical solutions and the associated business concepts must be seen as interim results of transformation projects. In the end, what is of sole importance is how these technical and business innovations are accepted and thus used. **Acceptance models** show which factors have a major impact on the acceptance and thus the use of technical and business solutions. They also make it clear which levers companies can use to promote the acceptance of solutions by customers or employees. The following is an overview of the most important approaches. Unfortunately, the presentation is limited to new technical solutions. For new technical concepts (such as products, processes or business models), such models do not yet exist.

One of the best-known models for explaining the acceptance of new technical solutions is the **"Technology Acceptance Model"** (TAM), developed by Davis and colleagues (Davis et al., 1989). It is shown in Fig. 2.5.

The TAM is aimed at the actual use of new technical solutions in an organizational context and thus also within companies. A prerequisite for this actual use is a corresponding intention. This intention in turn requires a corresponding attitude. This attitude in turn results from a weighing up of the potential user between the perceived usefulness of a technical solution on the one hand and the perceived ease of use on the other. In other words: What is decisive is that a system is useful in the work context (for example, because tasks can be processed more quickly) and that the user comfort is high (for example, because the user interface is very intuitive). This leads to a positive attitude, which in turn leads to the intention to use and then to the use—almost automatically.

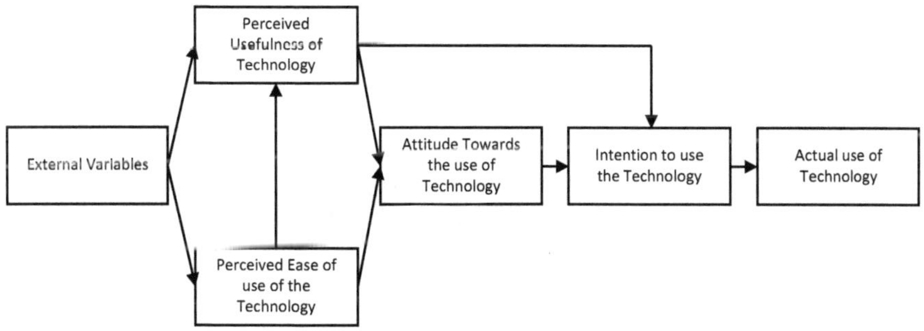

Fig. 2.5 Technology Acceptance Model (Davis et al., 1989)

The decisive levers for a company therefore lie in improving the usefulness perceived by the user and the perceived ease of use. This can of course be influenced in the development of the system, for example by taking strong account of the features of a system demanded by users or by an sophisticated design of the interface or by a strong involvement of the user in the development of the system (as demanded by newer proposals for the design of systems). In addition, there are a whole series of measures which can positively influence the usefulness perceived or the perceived ease of use of a given system. In Fig. 2.5 these factors are somewhat generally referred to as external factors. Thus, training, workshops and active user support help to positively influence the usefulness perceived or the ease of use of a new technical solution. By conveying an effective use of a new system and the communication of its added value in the work environment, the acceptance and use of a new technical solution in the company can also be promoted.

However, acceptance models do not only offer companies a suitable aid in the introduction of a new technical solution within their own company. In order to investigate user acceptance and thus the use of new technical solutions in the end consumer context, the **"Unified Theory of Acceptance and Use of Technology 2"** (UTAUT2, Venkatesh et al., 2012) was developed. UTAUT2 (see Fig. 2.6) thus has the determinant factors of the intention to use known from the TAM model. Thus, the perceived usefulness—here in the form of the expected performance of a technology—and the perceived

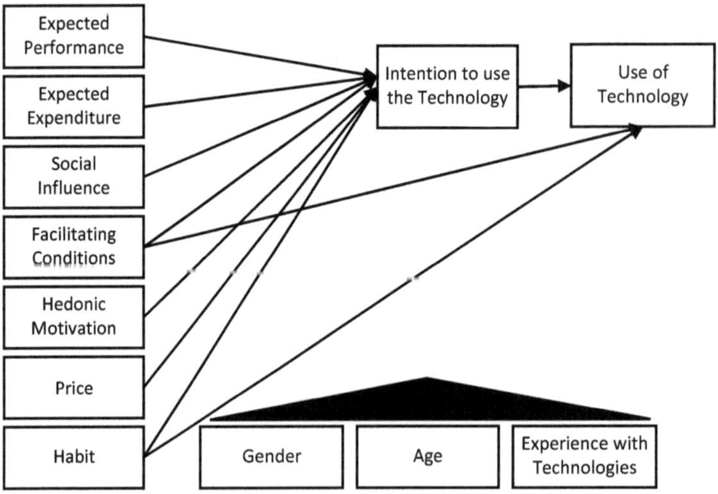

Fig. 2.6 Unified Theory of Acceptance and Use of Technology 2 (Venkatesh et al., 2012)

ease of use of a technology—represented in the model by the expected effort of using a technology—play an important role in the acceptance of a new technical solution. Furthermore, the social influence, that is, the degree to which an end user is influenced in his acceptance decision by his social environment, is taken into account. The fourth main determinant of the UTAUT2 model, the facilitating conditions, is new. These describe environmental factors that are perceived by consumers helpful in using a new technology, such as the technical support offered by the manufacturer for a new technology. UTAUT2 also includes factors that relate specifically to the consumer context. These include the hedonic motivation—that is, the pleasure of using a technology—and the cost-benefit ratio when using a technology. The perception that the use of a technology becomes a habit is also part of the model.

The already known determining factors allow the conclusion for companies that—not surprisingly—the expected added value of a new technical solution is also of great importance for the end user. Furthermore, the operation of the system should be as intuitive as possible in order to keep the initial effort low before the first use. In addition, good technical support from the manufacturer can also influence the users in their technology acceptance. However, it appears to be of particular importance that the customers have a positive cost-benefit perception in relation to the product and that the use is fun. Especially in connection with the relevance of the social influence, a positive as well as a negative attitude towards a technology can spread quickly among potential customers. Furthermore, targeted marketing campaigns can, for example, show different usage scenarios of a technology, which makes it easier to habituate the use of technology.

The UTAUT2 model also includes three so-called **moderator variables:** gender, age and (prior) experience with the solution (Venkatesh et al., 2012). Moderator variables amplify or reduce the effect of a relationship and are therefore particularly interesting for specific strategies. For example, it can be shown that the individual experience in dealing with technology reduces the influence of the expected effort when using a new technology on the intention to use it. It can also be shown that young men are mainly influenced by the fun of using technology. Older women, on the other hand, need continuous technology support in order to use a new technical solution permanently. Furthermore, older women are more price-sensitive than other user groups.

2.6 Is More Always Better? From the "Optimal" Degree of Digitalization

All the examples presented above are steps on the way to more digitalization, i.e. an increase in the transfer of tasks to the computer. A number of articles, studies and books convey the impression directly or indirectly that more digital change is always better. Of course this is wrong, and it can even be dangerous.

From a purely technical perspective, a digitalization rate of 100% would of course be fascinating. This would mean that a company has transferred all of its tasks, both value-creating (primary) and value-supporting (secondary) tasks as well as management tasks, completely to the computer. In extreme cases, there are already examples of this for primary tasks today—just think of the internet search engines. Each request is processed automatically, and the required data is also obtained automatically (by means of a continuously operating crawler). There are also individual examples of a fully automated factory in the processing industry. In this, machines produce the products. The procurement of raw materials and semi-finished products is also carried out completely automatically. However, it is not yet foreseeable to transfer the secondary activities completely to the computer. Even in the extreme case of the search engines, improvements in the algorithm are still being developed by humans today. Even the development of a product and the procurement of personnel or the further development of the IT infrastructure can only be partially transferred to computers. So far, it has also not been possible to completely transfer complex management tasks (such as the formulation of a strategy) to a computer.

From an economic perspective, the picture quickly relativizes itself, even if one only deals with the meaningfulness of an increase in the degree of digitalization, and not yet with the rather utopian goal of full automation. From the perspective of a single actor (a company, a private household), an investment in a digital technology is only then meaningful if its positive effects (e.g. in the form of reduced production costs) exceed its negative effects (such as the costs for the introduction and operation of a system). For example, a company only invests in a new solution for customer management if the attributable benefits (e.g. in the form of more customers or reduced process costs) exceed the attributable costs (e.g. for the development and operation of the system). It is obvious that this calculation does not always work out positively—practical problems of cost and benefit capture aside. Nor is it automatically meaningful for a company to transfer work from humans to machines. At a low wage level, it may make more sense to leave the work with humans. In addition, the cost structure of a company also changes with an increased degree of automation. The more tasks are transferred to machines, the less a company can flexibly adjust its costs to utilization.

Overall, it must be said that, from the perspective of a company, digitalization and the digital transformation based on it can only ever be about the question of to what extent the use of digital technologies leads to an improvement in the economic situation. By no means is this always the case with an increase in the degree of digitalization. No new insight—but still important!

References

BMW. (2018). *BMW connected drive – Digital services*. https://www.bmw.de/de/topics/faszination-bmw/connecteddrive/bmw-connected-drive.html. Accessed 27 Aug 2018.

Bundesverband der Musikindustrie. (2021). *Umsatz*. https://www.musikindustrie.de/markt-bestseller/musikindustrie-in-zahlen/umsatz-2020. Accessed 16 July 2021.

Christensen, C. M. (1997). *The innovator's dilemma: When new technologies cause great firms to fail*. Harvard Business School Press.

Davis, F. D., Bagozzi, R. P., & Warshaw, P. R. (1989). User acceptance of computer technology: A comparison of two theoretical models. *Management Science, 35*(8), 982–1003.

Hess, T. (2019). Digitalisierung, Digitale Unternehmung. In N. Gronau, J. Becker, N. Kliewer, J. M. Leimeister & S. Overhage (Eds.), *Enzyklopädie der Wirtschaftsinformatik* (11th ed.). GITO.

Markus, M. L. (2004). Technochange management: Using IT to drive organizational change. *Journal of Information Technology, 19*, 4–20.

Mertens, P., Bodendorf, F., König, W., Schumann, M., Hess, T., & Buxmann, P. (2017). *Grundzüge der Wirtschaftsinformatik* (12th ed.). Springer.

Moore, J. F. (1997). *The death of competition: Leadership and strategy in the age of business ecosystems*. Harper Paperbacks.

Orlikowski, W. J. (1992). The duality of technology: Rethinking the concept of technology in organizations. *Organization Science, 3*(3), 398–427.

Österle, H. (1987). Erfolgsfaktor Informatik – Umsetzung der Informationstechnik in Unternehmensführung. *Information Management, 2*(3), 24–31.

Parker, G. G., Van Alstyne, M. W., & Choudary, S. P. (2017). *Platform revolution: How networked markets are transforming the economy – And how to make them work for you*. Norton.

Picot, A., Reichwald, R., & Wigand, R. T. (2003). *Die grenzenlose Unternehmung*. Gabler.

Shapiro, C., & Varian, H. R. (1998). *Information rules: A strategic guide to the network economy*. Harvard Business Review Press.

Venkatesh, V., Thong, J. Y. L., & Xu, X. (2012). Consumer acceptance and use of information technology: Extending the unified theory of acceptance and use of technology. *MIS Quarterly, 36*(1), 157–178.

Venkatraman, N. (1994). IT-enabled business transformation: From automation to business scope redefinition. *Sloan Management Review, 35*(2), 73–87.

Vial, G. (2019). Understanding digital transformation: A review and a research agenda. *The Journal of Strategic Information Systems, 28*(2), 118–144.

Wessel, L., Baiyere, A., Ologeanu-Taddei, R., Cha, J., & Blegind Jensen, J. (2021). Unpacking the difference between digital transformation and IT-enabled organizational transformation. *Journal of the Association for Information Systems, 22*(1), 102–129.

Wiesböck, F., & Hess, T. (2020). Digital innovations – Embedding in organizations. *Electronic Markets, 30*(2), 75–86.

3

Changing Value Creation Structures through Digital Transformation

Digitalization can change products and services, the customer interface, business processes or the business model. In most cases, such innovations come into a company through projects. The question arises, therefore, how such original transformation projects should be designed, where they should start and how to proceed in the specific case. It is discussed, among other things, whether agile or rather the traditional approaches are suitable for transformation projects. In addition, specific instruments such as the customer journey analysis are presented.

3.1 What is Special About Digital Transformation Projects?

Digital innovations, which are the focus of this book, are usually carried out in a company through projects. Projects are therefore a central driver for the realization of digital transformation. Companies are quite willing to spend on their portfolio of transformation projects. The retail giant Walmart is putting 2 billion US$ on the table (approx. 0.4% of annual sales), General Electric is with 1 billion US$ (approx. 0.8% of annual sales) (Schadler, 2016). These sums show in which dimensions transformation project portfolios move. At the same time, studies come to the conclusion that 70% of all digitalization projects fail (Forbes, 2019). The urgent question therefore arises as to how transformation projects should be designed and how to successfully lead them. Both questions will be addressed below.

T. Hess, *Managing the Digital Transformation*,
https://doi.org/10.1007/978-3-658-38424-1_3

3.1.1 On the Structure of Original Transformation Projects: The Integration Paradigm of Digital Transformation

A characteristic of transformation projects is that they have two components: on the one hand the technical solution and on the other hand the functional solution built on it (Barthel & Hess, 2020). The integrated consideration of these two aspects, which is mandatory in the context of digital transformation, is referred to as the **integration paradigm of digital transformation**. As already described in Sect. 1.4, original digitalization projects, i.e. transformation projects in the narrower sense, always aim at the core of the 3LDT framework, the change of value creation through digital transformation. Projects that instead focus on the conditions (enabler projects) or the transformation governance (e.g. strategy development projects) are referred to as transformation projects in the wider sense.

A typical example of a project that complies with this paradigm is the supplementing of a traditional product with a service component, such as the apps of airlines, with which one can check in and obtain information about the status of the flight. On the one hand, this requires a technical implementation (a software solution with an app on the customer side and a server solution associated with it on the provider side) and on the other hand adapted business processes. Another example that also follows the integration paradigm is the provision of services via a platform for Internet of Things systems. The new service associated with this for B2B customers offers the company new opportunities for customer approach, marketing of products and services and ultimately also for price differentiation and thus represents the functional concept of the solution. The development, provision and operation of the platform itself represent the technical component of the solution, which is closely linked to the functional concept.

Companies carry out transformation projects in different contexts. This is partly done in reaction to dynamic market conditions or environmental changes such as the entry of new competitors, for example from the internet industry, or the introduction of new digital technologies. Transformation projects are often pioneer projects that are intended to test the use of digital technologies for the first time. Results of such projects can be starting points for the use of new digital technologies, concrete concepts for their use in process optimization or products or services made possible through digital technologies. Transformation projects usually involve the relevant department (e.g. sales, production, human resources), the IT department (either itself or using external service providers) and, if available, a digitalization unit.

Transformation projects contain a number of elements that are also found in other project types (Barthel & Hess, 2020). These elements are brought together anew in transformation projects and thus largely follow the Techno-Change approach already presented in Chap. 2 (Markus, 2004). This makes it possible to clearly distinguish them from other types of projects.

To Classical IT Projects Although the progress of digital technologies plays an indispensable role in transformation projects as a driver of digital innovation, these can be clearly distinguished from IT projects (Châlons & Dufft, 2016; Mertens & Wieczorrek, 2011). The focus of an IT project is always the introduction of a technical solution. Some IT projects are limited to the technical solution, others also include the effect of new systems. In the latter case, however, it is usually "only" about changed processes, hardly ever about product or service innovation and certainly not about new business models. IT projects therefore have a clearly different focus than transformation projects. The only overlap can sometimes be found in IT projects that are linked to projects for changing business processes.

The organizational scope of transformation projects and classical IT projects is fundamentally different. IT projects are usually inward-looking, i.e. external customers usually do not play a direct role. Also, behind the project are usually efforts to improve efficiency. In contrast, transformation projects can have an internal and an external focus, i.e. they can include both the development of new product, service and business model innovations and the optimization of business processes. Transformation projects are often also located at the interface of the company to external partners and customers. For example, companies want to create a new digital customer experience at the interface to the customer by means of transformation projects in order to realize a differentiation from the competition and new sources of revenue.

Another distinction can be found in the occupation of projects. IT projects are typically carried out by the IT department itself, possibly supplemented by external service providers. The specialized department is only involved to a limited extent. The configuration of transformation projects, as outlined above, is fundamentally different.

To Organizational Development Projects Organizational development projects deal with the change of the organization as a whole (Kanter et al., 1992; Majchrzak & Meshkati, 2007). The focus of organizational development projects is on the formal or informal regulations of an organization, i.e. for example the distribution of tasks, the scope of delegation, the values of an organization or also the handling of errors in an organization. Transformation projects, on the other hand, deal with concrete changes in products, processes and business models. The organizational structure, in particular its innovation capability, is the framework for the implementation of transformation projects, but not their subject.

Differences can also be seen in the composition of the projects. In transformation projects, employees of the department(s), IT and, if necessary, the digitalization unit work together. In organizational development projects, leadership is typically in the hands of specialists from the organizational department and HR.

In addition, organizational development projects and transformation projects differ clearly in a third dimension. What is constitutive for transformation projects is the development and implementation of digital innovations, i.e. a combination of technical and specialist solutions. In organizational development projects, technical solutions are at most a marginal issue. Table 3.1 compares the two project types mentioned with transformation projects again.

Table 3.1 Transformation Projects Compared to Other Project Types (Barthel & Hess, 2020; Markus, 2004)

Dimension	"Original" Digital Transformation Projects	Classic IT Projects	Organizational Development Projects
Subject	Develop and introduce a digital product, process or business model innovations (combination of expert and technical solutions)	Introduce a new IT solution based on derived requirements	Change the structure of an organization, possibly as a direct or indirect effect of the introduction of new systems
Examples	Introduction of a new digital sales platform while simultaneously restructuring existing internal sales processes and structures	Replacing outdated reporting software with data warehouse and analysis tools to speed up the creation of management reports	Transforming an established organization that is dependent on competition by strengthening the innovation power, customer focus and self-responsibility of employees
Involved	Equal cooperation of a specialist department, IT department, and digitalization unit	Primarily IT department, supplemented by a specialist department	Organizational department and a specialist department

3.1.2 Management of Transformation Projects

The selection of the right way of structuring is of course the central question for the management of transformation projects. But there are also other aspects to be considered in the management of such projects. The most important are briefly presented below (Barthel & Hess, 2020; Barthel et al., 2020, 2021; Weinreich, 2016).

3.1.2.1 Team Composition

Transformation projects are often characterized by new task profiles and thus differ significantly from the routine line tasks that most employees carry out on a daily basis. In addition, transformation projects often take place across departments and therefore require interdisciplinary knowledge. It is important that not regular coordination takes place between technical and specialist teams, but also continuous, integrated cooperation. This means that in transformation projects, in addition to IT experts and programmers, representatives of different business functions such as marketing or business development work together to form interdisciplinary and cross-functional digitalization teams. When assembling the team, in addition to the specialized expertise, particular attention must be paid to high self-motivation and independence as well as a high affinity for digitalization topics. A lack of these factors can lead to the failure of transformation projects, especially if projects are not carried out with the *right* people, but only with the *available* employees.

It should also be noted that team members not only work on the respective project, but also act as ambassadors of the project (and thus of digital transformation) in their line departments and in the company as a whole. In the best case, this can increase acceptance, awareness and understanding of digital transformation in the company. However, it should also be assumed that dissatisfied project employees will carry a negative attitude into large parts of the company.

3.1.2.2 Project Management Style and Methods

Transformation projects are mostly characterized by a horizontal distribution of responsibility for the project. While a traditionally strong hierarchical organization can be an efficient coordination form for the routine tasks of the core business, it is often not up to the requirements of digitization. Here, flexibility, agility and self-responsibility are needed to meet the rapid progress and short-term changes. This means that the project manager does not appear as a classic management figure and gives instructions, but rather supports the team as a mentor and coach and "empowers" the team to work on the projects independently. This avoids immense potential for conflict, as many managers are not willing to give up their accustomed leadership power and lead a digitization team as a coach or mentor, rather than leading it.

The interdisciplinary composition of the project teams also often results in different interests within the project; often corporate policy also plays a role. Overcoming internal conflicts between the various participants (people and departments) is one of the most important challenges in the context of digital transformation. Continuous internal communication, coordination and mediation by the project manager therefore play a key role. Here is a typical example of a team composition: the team of a transformation project is led by the digitization unit of the company, and two to three employees of the unit work directly on the project. In addition to employees from the digitization unit, members of the core organization also work on the project. Two employees from the affected department (e.g. from sales) bring the necessary specialist knowledge for the solution with them, two more employees from IT are responsible for the technical implementation. Since there are no qualified employees in the company for a specific project component, the team is also supplemented by external specialists from a technology consulting firm.

Closely linked to the design of the project management style is the selection of suitable project methods. Transformation projects are often carried out using agile methods. This is partly because the goals of transformation projects cannot be finally defined at the beginning of the project and kept open for a long time. Agile methods meet this imprecise target formulation by promoting iterative target concretisation during the course of the project. Transformation projects are sometimes never "finished", but can be continuously adapted and further developed. What is decisive here is the already mentioned integrated cooperation of IT and specialist departments, as only in this way can digital solutions be delivered and further developed continuously. The special features of agile project management are dealt with in more detail in Sect. 3.2.4.1.

3.1.2.3 Project Controlling and Evaluation

In the early phase of digital transformation, it was and is often the case in many companies that as many transformation projects as possible are given the green light and promoted. Companies hope in this way to get the transformation going and to gain momentum. This of course increases the complexity of the project's landscape, companies can quickly lose sight of the large number of projects and, above all, their value contribution. This makes it more difficult to make systematic and objective decisions about prioritisation, resource allocation or continuation of projects. However, this complexity should not tempt companies to rely solely on the subjective gut feeling of some managers when steering transformation projects. Instead, suitable forms of project controlling and project evaluation must be found.

The project controlling is supposed to support companies in gaining transparency concerning resources and processes in the project as well as in optimizing or steeringly intervening in decisions on this basis. Three essential aspects characterize the project controlling: progress control, quality control, and risk management. Traditionally, the project controlling relies very strongly on plan-actual comparisons and the observance of deadline, cost, and quality targets. However, also traditional methods of project evaluation usually rely very strongly on primarily financial KPIs. This approach is often not implementable in transformation projects however.

On one hand, this is because transformation projects are also innovation projects, whose goals or results partly do not concretize until the project runtime. Accordingly, the projects often run in iterative cycles according to the agile methodology, which makes it more difficult to compare interim results with plan data. Here, the satisfaction of the important stakeholders (in particular customers/users) can be a more suitable criterion for the quality of the output, because even a precise implementation of the formal requirements specification does not guarantee the fulfilment of the—possibly unspoken—expectations of the stakeholders (Gothelf & Seiden, 2017; Meyer & Reher, 2015).

On the other hand, the results of transformation projects are often not of a short-term, financial nature, but develop their effect through long-term, strategic advantages. It is also not always easy to attribute the indirect value contributions of transformation projects to them. Purely financial KPIs therefore fall short, instead a comprehensive consideration of several, also difficult to quantify criteria is required. These criteria can become more concrete over the course of the project. It is also important here who evaluates the value of transformation projects, that is, whose standards are used in the evaluation of the project. In practice, it has been shown that the assessments and evaluation criteria of digitalization units, departments and controlling can differ greatly. Accordingly, it is crucial that at the beginning of a project all stakeholders together decide according to which criteria the project is to be evaluated. These criteria can change over the course of the project, but this adaptation must then be carried by everyone involved. Overall, the "fair" evaluation of transformation projects is still a huge challenge for companies that has hardly been solved so far.

A first indication of a solution to the problem can be provided by a joint project of researchers from LMU Munich and TU Darmstadt, as well as innovation experts from a digitalization unit of the BMW Group IT (Barthel et al., 2021). The aim of this research project was to develop a method for evaluating digitalization projects. The digitalization unit's finding is that it is difficult for them to assess the value contributions of their projects appropriately was decisive for the project, which on one hand makes it more difficult to effectively control and prioritize projects and on the other hand makes it more difficult to demonstrate the unit's justification of existence to the core organization. Based on this problem, the goals of an appropriate evaluation method were defined, then developed in an iterative process, their applicability demonstrated and evaluated on the digitalization unit's project portfolio and then communicated more broadly in the company. The developed method builds on the so-called Digital Value Canvas (Anding, 2020). The basic idea is to capture all value contributions relevant to BMW and to back them up with corresponding KPIs. The value contributions are divided into three categories. The first category, "**iInnovation for profitability**", aims at cost reduction or revenue increase that are directly and measurable created by the projects. This can happen, for example, through the development of a digital service for which customers are willing to pay, or by optimizing a process through digital technologies to the extent that cost-intensive work steps are eliminated. This category is relatively unproblematic, as value contributions are usually easily measurable here and valued by all parties involved. The second category, "**iInnovation to promote the core business**", aims at indirect but well quantifiable value contributions of digitalization projects. This is about advantages that a project creates in the existing core business, for example by increasing customer satisfaction, plant utilization or revenue in the core business. Value contributions in this category are relatively easy to measure, but the challenge here is to correctly attribute them to the corresponding projects. The third category, "**Innovation for future success**", is the most difficult to measure. It is about the long-term, often strategic advantages that arise from digitalization projects, for example through the build-up of technology expertise. These value contributions are difficult to quantify, but suitable KPIs can still be found. In the area of technology expertise, this can be, for example, the number of registered patents or the number of employees who can use a new technology. Figure 3.1 shows an overview of the value contributions of the three categories.

As important as the selection of the right KPIs, the appropriate embedding of the evaluation method in the innovation process is of great importance. It is crucial here above all that the goals of a digitalization project are jointly set at the beginning by the digitalization unit and the department. This is done in the form of a "Definition of Good". So it should not be the case that the majority of projects are simply started into the blue, in order to then find some value contribution afterwards. The progress of the project is measured on the basis of the Definition of Good and at the end it is decided whether the project was successful and taken over by the department. The project goals can of course change, since these are dynamic innovation projects, but a change must be agreed on from all sides. Digitalization projects should therefore be carried out in a targeted manner without restricting their innovative power.

The developed evaluation method now creates an important basis for the perception of whether the digitalization unit and its projects are successful not to diverge too much between the core organization and the unit itself.

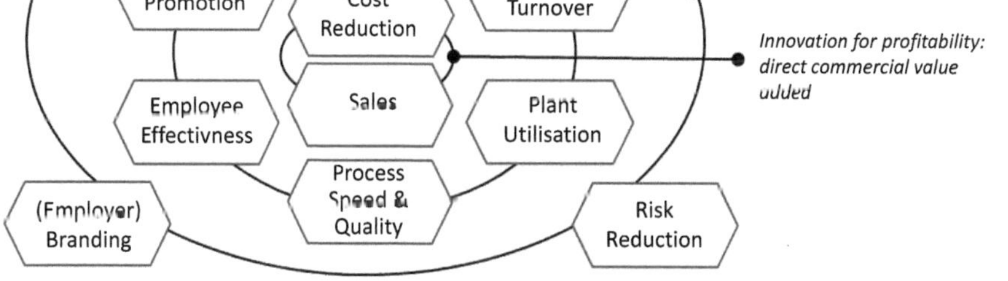

Fig. 3.1 Value Contributions of Transformation Projects (Barthel et al., 2021)

Overall, it is expected that the assessment of digitalization activities in general and digitalization projects in particular will become increasingly important in the coming years as many companies enter into more advanced phases of the transformation process. Here, it is important for digitalization responsible not to lose the connection.

3.1.2.4 Embedding in the Core Organization and Project Landscape

The continuous development of solutions is only possible if the project results can be sustainably embedded in the organization. Transformation projects are not isolated problem-solving projects, but part of a complex web of business and social relationships. Accordingly, the project work in cross-departmental transformation projects often exceeds the established formal organizational structure of a company, which is designed to efficiently carry out the recurring routine tasks of the core business. The members of the project teams usually work in parallel on the project and on their line tasks, sometimes they are also involved in several projects at the same time. In order to successfully carry out projects, a separate temporary project organization is therefore necessary within the core organization. Regardless of the chosen approach, it is important that the project organization is hung up at the right place, that is, at the relevant decision-makers of the core organization. Only in this way is a simple, flexible and fast procedure possible. One approach that can be chosen here is the creation of a digitalization unit that is responsible for the coordination of transformation projects.

However, transformation projects are not only embedded in a corporate context, but often also in a complex multi-project landscape. Digital transformation cannot be implemented with a single "big bang" project, but requires the cooperation of numerous projects in different areas and levels of a company. The resulting complex project landscape can quickly become overwhelming. It is more important that digitalization responsible persons apply appropriate approaches of program or project portfolio management here. The chosen management approaches must ensure that projects are systematically selected and prioritized, interdependencies and synergies between projects are correctly recorded and all projects are aligned with the overall goal of digital transformation. Otherwise, a company will quickly find itself with a bunch of isolated digitalization initiatives instead of a targeted transformation program. At the same time, however, the program and project portfolio management must be open and flexible enough not to excessively restrict the innovation of transformation projects. Therefore, methods from traditional IT management cannot simply be transferred to transformation projects, as these methods are oriented towards the much more predictable and linear IT projects.

3.2 Digital Products and Services

With the digital change, the competition has become more global and the customer requirements are changing more and more. Instead of simply transferring analog products and services unchanged into the digital world, many companies want to use the possibilities of digital technologies and open up new business areas. The following gives an overview of these products and services.

3.2.1 Three Variants of Digital Products and Services

Companies can integrate digital products and services into their business model in three ways:

- On the one hand, they can offer completely new and standalone digital products and services—such as a search service for the Internet.
- In addition, digitalization makes it possible to combine analog and digital products or services. For example, Ravensburger has created such a solution with Tiptoi. In the printed books, children can point to an animal or another object with a pen and thus retrieve the name.
- And thirdly, it is possible to supplement established products with digital value-added services.

The following describes these three variants in more detail.

New Digital Services The emergence of such services can be observed particularly well in the media industry. Traditionally, many content has been and is provided by authors or editors, such as the classic newspaper or a feature film. In this model, the user is passive. Something else was not possible with print media and radio/television. With the Internet, this has changed. Via the Internet, the consumer can still consume, but he or she can also create content him or herself, and in any format. Technical support is required for the exchange of this content. The so-called content platforms offer such support (Hess, 2014). Meanwhile, there are a variety of these platforms. Social networks (such as Facebook or Xing) and video platforms (such as Netflix or Amazon) are particularly well known.

These new services have little in common with the classical products of the media industry. They too support public communication, but in a completely different way than the classical products of the media industry. They also follow other market logics. Here, in particular, the high importance of network effects is to be mentioned. This central construct for the digital economy was already introduced in Sect. 2.4. It will be explained using the example of Facebook, which benefits from both indirect and direct network effects. Direct network effects lead to Facebook's perceived attractiveness and value increasing with the number of users. This means that the more users use Facebook, the higher the incentive for people outside the network to use the platform. Indirect network effects lead to the spread of complementary products having a positive effect on the value of the platform. This means that the more additional applications are offered on Facebook, the more additional users join the network, and vice versa. In addition, the number of advertisers who place ads on Facebook also increases with the number of users. Figure 3.2 shows this logic in a schematic representation, embedded in the flow of money and services.

In addition to the information-oriented services, there is a second group of also original Internet services. These support markets in a way that has not been possible before. The number of services in this segment is hardly manageable, because, unlike information-oriented services, there are no direct network effects here that quickly lead to polarization. Auction services were

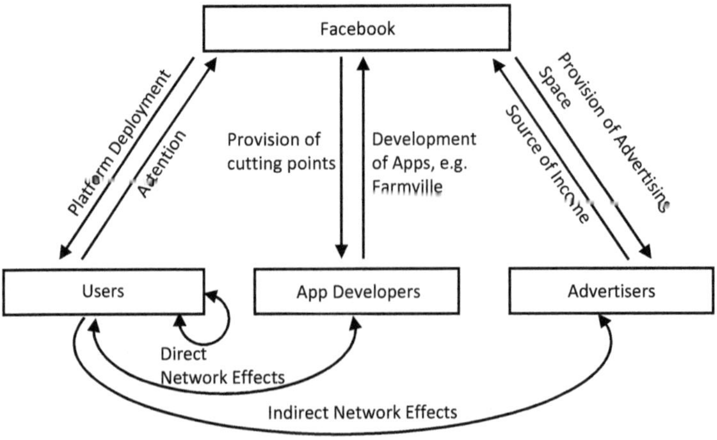

Fig. 3.2 Network Effects on The Example of Facebook

very early on the market. Due to the high transaction costs, auctions were previously only available to a few goods. With the auction platforms such as eBay, this has changed. Marketplaces were quick to follow, for example for travel platforms. There are also such marketplaces in the industrial sector; they are used, for example, for the purchase of B-parts by many companies.

Hybrid Products and Services As a second variant, companies can provide their established products via an online channel. A good example of the provision of classic products via the Internet is the currently observable digital transformation of the classic banking business. Online banking makes it possible to actively involve the customer in the service creation process. For example, the customer can make transfers, fill out forms and transactions online. Both the customer and the provider can benefit from this development. On the one hand, the financial institution can save costs that would arise from maintaining the branch and personal customer care. On the other hand, customers benefit from the flexibility and convenience that online banking offers. However, more complex businesses, such as concluding a larger credit agreement, cannot be handled via online banking. In sum, this creates a hybrid product that has online and offline components—if the bank does it right.

There is also a wide range of hybrid products and services in the much-cited media sector For example, many daily newspapers make their content available in both classical form (in printed editions) and via online services for access via stationary or mobile devices. In this constellation, the question of mutual displacement, i.e. the cannibalization of existing offers and services, arises very quickly. Cannibalization always occurs when the products provided via the different channels differ too little from each other. This was exactly the case at the beginning of the transfer of content to online channels in the media industry. Meanwhile, the online offerings of media companies differ significantly from the analog offerings.

Similar questions also arise in trade. For many years, traditional retailers have been reluctant to set up their own online offering for fear of cannibalizing the offering in the stores. New providers with Amazon at the top have successfully filled this gap. Traditional retailers are slowly beginning to think that they must set up an online offering, too.

Value-Added Services As a third variant, companies can use digital technologies to supplement their current offering. In this way, providers can differentiate themselves positively from competitors and increase the loyalty and willingness to pay of their customers. Such services can be based on the product itself, on the provision of the product or on the initiation of the purchase as well as on the service after the purchase. For example, many airlines now offer applications for smartphones that make the flying experience more pleasant and efficient. Customers can, for example, check in on their smartphone and retrieve current information about the flight status and boarding pass, i.e. the service covers both the initiation and the implementation phase. This allows airlines to extend and improve their service promise along all phases of the customer relationship. The core product, in this case the transport by airplane, remains the same, but digital services are added to it. Such services are offered today, for example, by many automobile manufacturers. Together with assistance systems, cars will probably soon become hybrid products.

Value-added services are also available in the industrial sector. A number of machine builders also offer such services. They equip machines with sensors, an additional application and a connection to their own company and can offer an improved form of "remote maintenance" on this basis. With such services they open up a new source of revenue and also gain interesting information about the operation of their machines. Table 3.2 shows the sketched types and subtypes of digital offers in a compact overview.

3.2.2 The Role of Ecosystems for Digital Products and Services

In the digital world, companies are particularly successful if they have been able to build a variety of complementary products around a core product and control the resulting overall system. Such an overall system is referred to as a (business) ecosystem. In Sect. 2.4 this construct had already been sketched, now it should be deepened.

Table 3.2 Types and Subtypes of Digital Offers

Standalone digital products and services	Hybrid products and services	Value-added services
Information services, e.g. search engines	Coordinated online-offline offers, e.g. at banks	Support for matchmaking, e.g. with product information
Market services, e.g. auctions	Competing offers, e.g. newspapers with various channels for largely the same content	Support for processing, e.g. at airlines Supplement to the classic product, e.g. digital services in the car

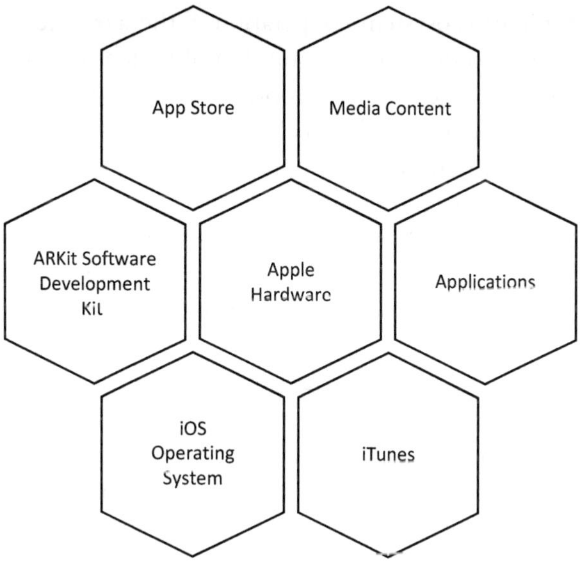

Fig. 3.3 The Ecosystem of Apple

Included in an ecosystem are all actors who can contribute with an added value to the product at the center. The connection to the elements of an ecosystem is made via the already mentioned network effects, specifically the indirect network effects. The concept of ecosystems is conceptually and terminologically based on ecosystems in nature—here, all actors are dependent on each other for their existence.

The value creation in ecosystems has a different, more complex structure than traditional value chains. The traditional value chain is linear. In ecosystems, both end customers and providers of complementary services and products each represent different market sides of the core product, which can each receive services and contribute to sales. The engagement of all participants is essential for the long-term survival of an ecosystem.

Different current examples show that ecosystems are particularly relevant in the context of online offerings. Apple with the core product iPhone is a very successful example (see also Fig. 3.3). For example, the operators of an app, the manufacturers of accessories and the suppliers of product parts have to coordinate in order to offer a customer-centered solution. As a lone fighter, Apple could not offer such an attractive product. Apple depends on developers developing interesting apps and thus creating additional customer value. If there is a large complementary offer, the core product is usually also more attractive to end customers.

The main topic of ecosystem cooperation is the agreement on a comprehensive system architecture, i.e. the question of which technical components the system comprises and—most importantly—how they interact. For the interaction, a standard is usually specified. This can serve to exchange data or to call functions in another component of the system via so-called APIs (Application Programming Interfaces).

Companies that want to offer the core product of an ecosystem (such as Apple in the example above) face the task of managing cooperation, i.e. the composition and control of cooperation (Benlian et al., 2015). As the initiator of the ecosystem, the provider of the core product must be careful with creating a balance of interests between the different groups of participants. In the phase of market introduction of an ecosystem, the danger exists that neither complementary manufacturers can be convinced to go into advance payment, nor end customers are willing to buy a product for which the necessary complementary offers (not yet) are not available. For this "chicken and egg problem" in the establishment of an ecosystem, a solution approach can be found in a corresponding pricing, by subsidizing one of the two groups involved in the ecosystem (complementary or end users) in the start phase in order to increase the attractiveness.

In addition to pricing, the degree of openness of the ecosystem is the second central control instrument. Providers must decide whether they want to open up to competing ecosystems and to what extent a vertical opening towards providers of complementary is desired. An opening leads to a greater diversity, but at the expense of the control options of the provider. So there are currently several (horizontal) competing providers of smart home platforms with proprietary standards and also different solutions with regard to the vertical opening, from open source to selected, licensed complementary providers. It remains to be seen which concept will prevail in the long term.

If different ecosystems are available, a complementary provider (in the example above, for example, a provider of content) must first decide whether he wants to join one or more ecosystems, because usually the entry into an ecosystem involves costs, because, for example, interfaces to the platform of the ecosystem have to be created. If high entry barriers have to be overcome or if there is already an established competition for similar offers, this can also lead to the selection of a less established ecosystem.

The networking of various actors, which is promoted by many digital technologies or even forms a core aspect (cf. the Internet of Things or data networks for artificial intelligence), also has decisive effects for digital transformation. While the company still remains at the center of consideration, the view increasingly extends beyond organizational boundaries. In ecosystems, the transformation of the company is to be understood in connection with linked partners, complementary providers and other providers. In the context of digital technologies, ecosystems are characterized in particular by the large number of involved heterogeneous actors and a certain degree of uncertainty caused by the constant technological change and the frequent entry and exit of actors. This has to be taken into account when digitizing a company that is embedded in an ecosystem.

In order to better understand the ecosystem of a company, to structure it in a structured way and to analyze the central collaborations but also dependencies on partners, it is necessary to describe the involved actors and their relationships. While there are a variety of different methodological approaches to visualize or model the networking and interlocking, a clear approach offers itself (see Fig. 3.4 for the description of the ecosystem of Apple using the example of the App Store), which focuses on the four central components of an ecosystem:

- **Actors**—which companies, organizations or customers play a role?
- **Activities**—which services, services or activities are provided by which of the actors for the ecosystem to function?
- **Positions**—how can the (power) positions of the actors be understood in relation to each other?
- **Relationships**—how are the actors interconnected and what kind of relationships do they maintain?

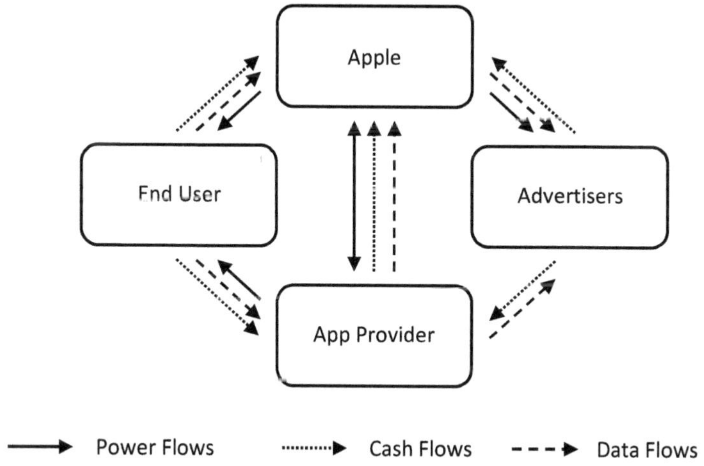

Fig. 3.4 Description of an Ecosystem Using the Example of the Apple App Store

3.2.3 Add-on: How much Privacy does the (German) Customer want from Digital Products and Services?

Data is already today a central "raw material" and an important business basis for many companies. Although companies differ in the degree of dependence on personal data, they all have the interest to use data to address their customers more specifically to individual customer groups or even customers and, if necessary, to differentiate their prices and—if possible—to adapt the product or service to customer groups or individual customers (Morlok et al., 2017). Examples include personalized movie suggestions on Netflix's video-on-demand service or the well-known recommendations in e-commerce ("customers who bought this item also bought …"). It is also known that users of Apple smartphones are given a higher price in online shops than users of other devices. In the extreme case, this development even leads to apparently free offers that the user has to pay for in other ways. Google's search service is probably the best-known example of the "paying the customer" by his data (Buxmann, 2018).

The Internet provides numerous new opportunities to gain information about the customer. The use of various Internet services expects from the user a number of details about the person, gender, age, etc. Such data has always been collected in principle, even if the self-descriptions found today in social networks were unimaginable a few years ago. What is new is the amount of data about the individual user behavior. These are found in log files of the application systems behind the online offers and in the system software of many mobile and stationary offers. This is implemented in an extreme form by the providers of some websites. If the respective page is called up via a browser, then small programs run in the background for the user (so-called plug-ins) which pass on information to third parties. Think also of the Internet of Things, that is the Internet connection of often equipped with sensors everyday objects (such as intelligent household appliances or the connected car), which creates new sources of information for manufacturers of mainly physical everyday objects.

But the possibilities for compressing and evaluating the collected data have also improved significantly. With the help of the latest database systems, large amounts of data can be brought together to form a profile of a user. In the extreme case, even predictions of behaviour can be derived from the data, either for an individual person (e.g. the likelihood of buying a product) or for a certain number of people.

But consumers do not immediately and unhesitatingly give away their data and thus the control over their so-called informational privacy. The topics of privacy and data protection have been brought more into the public consciousness by the NSA spying scandal, various attacks on sensitive customer data by companies and the modified data protection law. So 37% of the German population is concerned or very concerned about their privacy when using the Internet (Trepte & Masur, 2015). 61% of citizens fear that they do not have enough insight into what companies do with their collected data.

But studies have been showing for a long time that even small incentives lead many users to forget their reservations about sharing their data. For example, Acquisti and Grossklags found that in exchange for small benefits (discounts, better service or good recommendations), 29% of participants in the experiment gave away their telephone number and 22% even their otherwise strictly guarded social security number (Acquisti & Grossklags, 2005).

This obvious discrepancy between attitude and action is also called the **Privacy Paradox** (Morlok et al., 2017). Although users are generally concerned about their informational privacy and have a more defensive attitude, they do not show the same degree of willingness to take measures to protect this privacy in their behavior. There are many explanations for this. One variant is that the typical consumer underestimates the risks associated with the disclosure of his data, because they are too abstract and too far in the future. Studies also indicate that security measures with regard to the disclosure of information on the Internet are strongly dependent on the age of the users. The younger the users—and the more intensive and diverse the use of the Internet as an information and communication medium—the more unconcerned the users are with their data on the Internet, and this, although younger people hardly differ from older people in terms of their concerns.

A specific supplement should be added here: from a business point of view, it makes sense to offer the customer concerned with privacy a paid premium version in which the processing and forwarding of personal data is completely dispensed with. As early as 2013, a study by Schreiner and colleagues showed how payment for privacy can work (Schreiner et al., 2013). At least some of the subjects of the experiment were willing to pay just under two euros a month for a premium version of a social network that protects privacy. However, this approach has not yet been established. Also interesting are the currently observable attempts to give the user back the control over his data. The idea is often an Internet service through which the user can specifically control the release of the data concerning him, receives money for the provision and can also revoke a once granted permission.

3.2.4 Procedure for the Development of Digital Products and Services

3.2.4.1 Basic Decision on the Procedure

Project management models can be—albeit somewhat simplistic—divided into traditional and agile concepts. These two approaches can also be found in software development processes (Buxmann et al., 2015).

Traditional project management models can be found in particular in plan-based approaches to software development such as the waterfall model or the spiral model. These project management methods are characterized by systematic and comprehensive preliminary planning of the projects, which result in defined work packages and phase-oriented work steps. The defined work packages are worked on in sequentially nested phases, whereby in each phase extensive project artifacts such as a documentation of the user requirements or a specification for the technical design are created. These artifacts finally form the basis for the downstream work phases. Typical for this approach is that first the functional conception and then the technical implementation are in the focus.

Plan-based methods have the advantage that a clear plan is already available at the beginning of the actual project implementation, how the project is to take place. This makes the project well controllable. In addition, the necessary resources as well as the expected project duration, the corresponding costs and the concrete project output are fixed early on in the project. These aspects lead to a reduction of uncertainties for project teams and the "customers" of the project and thus minimize the risk. Nevertheless, classical methods have significant disadvantages, which are due to their inflexible, rigid character and can lead to excessive costs, long project times and poor quality. Classical methods can hardly keep up with the complexity of a constantly changing business environment, as changes in market or customer requirements can usually only be taken into account at the end of a project and customers are integrated too late into the project process. As a result, in the worst case, a product is developed for which there is finally no demand. In addition, plan-based methods are often criticized for the fact that a high overhead is produced (such as specifications and designs), which does not offer any value-added for the customer and thus only generates costs.

Agile project management also originates from software development and is "lightweight" in response to the process and document-heavy ("heavyweight") traditional methods and their difficulties in dealing with rapidly changing requirements. The agile project management methods pursue a "just enough" approach and aim for the highest possible flexibility in order to be able to react quickly to changes in requirements. In addition to an initial specification of the project output, further, detailed specifications, non-value-added processes—such as exact documentation—or extensive pre-planning of the project are dispensed with in order to minimize the expected adaptation effort. So it only follows that agile project management methods do not aim for the development of a perfect product, but rather for a functional product that can be quickly tested on the market. With the help of this **Minimum Viable Product** (MVP), a company can obtain market and customer feedback and further develop the product in accordance with the declared needs. In addition, agile project management methods promote active involvement of the customer in the development process and early consideration of his wishes and requirements.

The starting point for agile project management methods is the so-called Agile Manifesto (Beck et al., 2013), which was published in 2001 and concretizes the basic values and principles. The authors also defined twelve agile principles, which are to serve as a general basis for agile work. The best known methods based on these values and principles include **Scrum,** which is used in both software development and project management.

Often it is wrongly assumed that agile project management methods run chaotically. The exact opposite is however the case. Agile frameworks like Scrum are extremely structured and include, in addition to a concrete approach, also defined roles. These include the Scrum Master—coach of the project team, who checks the correct application of the framework and protects the team from disruptions during the project implementation; the product owner—representative of the customer side, who negotiates the project output with the team; the agile project team—an interdisciplinary, "empowered" and self-responsible team; as well as the customer, whose requirements are to be fulfilled during the course of the project.

The typical course of the Scrum framework sketched in Fig. 3.5 shows the structured approach within an agile project clearly. It should be noted that the preliminary planning is almost exclusively concerned with the specification of the project output, which is recorded in the product backlog (list of open product requirements). Subsequently, the actual development or implementation of the project starts.

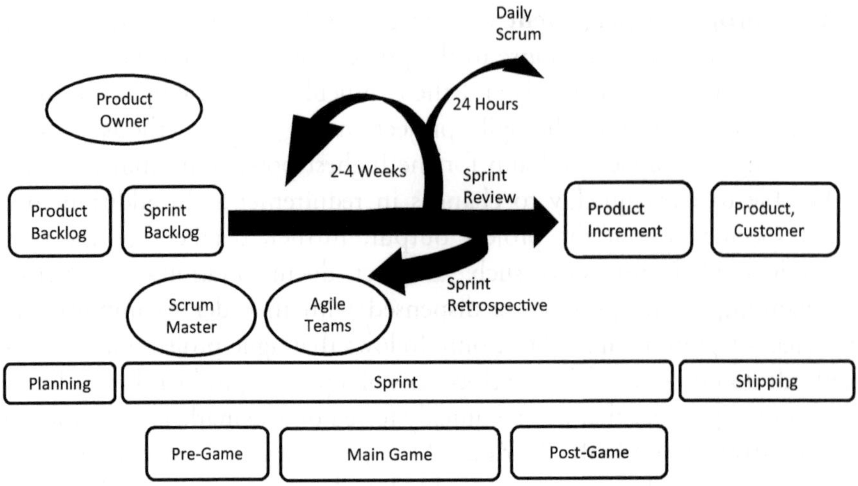

Fig. 3.5 Procedure within the Scrum Framework (based on Sutherland & Schwaber, 2017)

The core of agile methods is an incremental, iterative, and cyclical approach. Within the Scrum framework, these cyclical iterations are called "Sprints". Within a Sprint—which typically lasts between two and four weeks—a defined work package, the so-called Sprint Backlog, is worked on. At the beginning of a Sprint (Pre-Game), the work package for the upcoming Sprint is defined and prioritized in the Sprint Planning based on the higher-level Product Backlog (list of open product requirements). As a result, several Sprints are usually necessary to produce a project output. Individual, smaller projects can also be completed within one Sprint. During the Sprint (Main Game), so-called Daily Scrums (daily Scrums) or Daily Standups (short daily meetings) often take place within the team together with the Scrum Master (moderator/mediator). These are daily ca. 15-minutes meetings in which the project team explains what it has achieved within the last 24 hours, what it will work on within the next 24 hours, and what obstacles exist. At the end of a Sprint, the result of the Sprint is presented to the Product Owner (functional client) and the customer of the project in the Sprint Review, and in the subsequent Sprint Retrospective (Sprint debriefing), the team discusses together with the Scrum Master (moderator/mediator) what worked well during the Sprint and what can be improved. Finally, when all aspects from the Product Backlog (list of open product requirements) have been fulfilled or outstanding ones have been defined as not relevant for a Shippable Product (deliverable product), the project output is brought to market.

As this short description already shows, the resulting project output is regularly shown to the customer in order to obtain feedback and to incorporate potential change requests into the next Sprint.

Agile approaches are particularly suitable when the dynamics are high and the complexity of the project is great (Buxmann et al., 2015). The potential for new technologies is typically not clearly assessable in advance. Also, newer technologies are still changing. Both lead to a high degree of dynamics. At the same time, the inevitable connection between the technical and the expert view of a project for the development of digital products and services automatically makes a project complex. In addition, there is usually a large number of stakeholders to be involved. A product development project in a digital context is therefore typically characterized by a high degree of complexity.

Empirically, this assessment seems to be confirmed. For example, a recent practice study by Lünendonk shows that agile methods are used at least partially in transformation projects in 79% of companies in the insurance industry (Lünendonk, 2018). Similarly, the consulting firm etventure was able to determine in a survey on digital transformation that the mediation of agile methods is one of the most important measures for preparing for digital transformation (etventure, 2018).

3.2.4.2 Design Thinking as a Special Form of the Agile Approach

Design Thinking is a user-centered and systematic approach to complex problems. Originally developed by the company IDEO, which in the early 2000s had to solve increasingly complex problems such as the design of an alternative learning environment for a university, in addition to traditional design tasks. Therefore, IDEO oriented itself to an innovative methodology in order to design consumer experiences instead of consumer products. This new type of design was later called "Design Thinking" by David Kelly, founder of the Hasso-Plattner Institute of Design at Stanford University. Other universities, business schools and companies also adopted this methodology and disseminated it further.

The design thinking approach (Uebernickel et al., 2015) is based on the fact that valuable innovations arise at the interface of technological feasibility (technology), economic viability (economy) and human desirability (human). These have to be identified step by step in a flexible process. Typically, the steps shown in Fig. 3.6 are carried out.

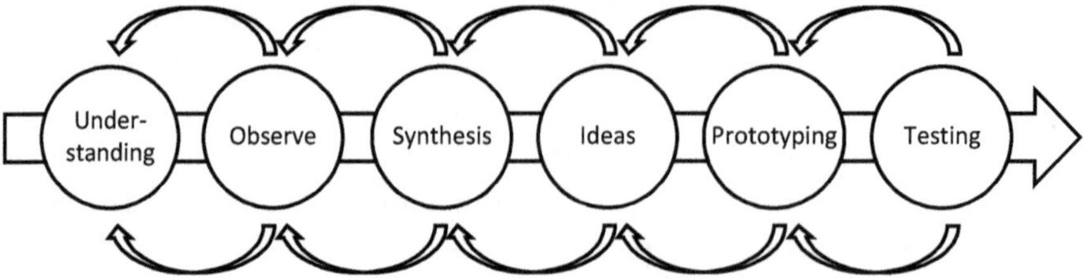

Fig. 3.6 Process of Design Thinking (Grots & Pratschke, 2009)

As Fig. 3.6 shows, the design thinking process is not to be understood as a purely sequential phase model, but rather as an iterative process that always allows for feedback into previous phases. So it is basically an agile approach. Thus, when testing the prototype, new ideas may arise that require further brainstorming sessions or even research. But errors can also be detected. For the individual steps:

- **Understand:** In the first step of the design thinking process, the underlying problem must be recorded and understood. For this purpose, the team first researches in detail and unprejudiced.
- **Observe:** A large part of the research is carried out within the framework of the design thinking process on the basis of qualitative studies and field research. For this purpose, the team observes people using or rejecting a product or service and then enters into a dialogue with these people. In particular, this communication in the direct context of the product or service is important in order to gain a deep understanding of the design problems. In order to build up a common knowledge base within the team, the collected material is documented and visualized in detail using photos, notes or sketches.
- **Synthesis:** The team's common knowledge base is ultimately created in the synthesis phase. Here the team members "brief" each other using stories. In this aggregation of knowledge, connections are revealed and first findings are derived. In addition to building up a common knowledge base, the aim of the synthesis phase is also to develop an abstract framework which can represent the findings in a simple visual form, for example processes such as the customer journey.
- **Ideas:** In the ideas phase, the focus is on generating and deriving specific questions from the framework. Brainstorming is often used as a method for generating ideas. After the brainstorming sessions, the findings are again visualized. This is often done using notes and post-it notes directly

on the framework. Based on the basic principles of innovation—technology, economy and human (with the latter in focus)—the ideas are evaluated and ranked.

- **Prototyping:** Similar to agile project management methods such as Scrum, the design thinking process also relies on quick and iterative prototyping. Prototypes can take different forms. They can be stories, Lego models, or role-playing games, with the level of development determined by the number of iterations.
- **Testing:** After developing a prototype, it is tested and feedback is collected. Often, testing of prototypes is carried out directly with potential users, with reference to the user-centeredness of the design thinking approach. Again, in addition to observation, active dialogue and interaction with testers is emphasized.

The design thinking approach has two additional components in addition to the actual innovation process, which must not be neglected. First, the approach is usually used in inter- or multidisciplinary teams. This means that team members with different professional backgrounds come together. Furthermore, the approach is supported by a suitable spatial environment. For example, there are usually flexible furniture, variable office furniture and materials for dealing with and designing ideas, such as Lego bricks, pictures or certain tools, available.

Of course, design thinking is not a panacea that should always and everywhere be used. After initial analyses, it primarily serves the purpose of generating ideas, especially in situations where creative solutions are required in the event of unclear goal setting. Accordingly, the approach is primarily used in product related areas, such as research and development, marketing, but also in consulting, IT and sales. Design thinking approaches are rather rarely used in operations and production or in accounting. Companies rather attribute an improvement of soft factors, such as corporate culture, innovation processes and user integration, to the approach, while a hard success measurement in the form of cost reduction or increased profits is rather difficult (Schmiedgen et al., 2015).

3.2.5 Product-Oriented Design of an Organization

The idea of a flexible, product-oriented design of the structure of an organization is currently intensively discussed. The core idea is that product development teams with a flexible composition are useful for the continuous further development of the products and services of a company in order to develop a product together in short cycles—just as the Scrum logic prescribes for the development of software. In this sense, a company would consist of two areas: the product-related area and the product-distant area. All employees who could potentially contribute to the further development of the offer on the market would be located in the product-related area. A team would then be assembled from this pool for the improvement of a product. Secondly, the employees would be divided according to areas of knowledge and, thirdly, possibly also according to locations. In product-distant areas, e.g. in human resources, however, little changes; a classical functional organization is typically found there.

One of the best-known companies with an agile organization in the German-speaking world is Xing SE (Vollmöller, 2018). The company operates the leading social network for professional contacts in the German-speaking world with 14 million members. Founded in 2003 and listed on the stock exchange since 2006, the company achieved sales of around EUR 190 million in 2017. Xing employs more than 1200 employees at various locations in Europe, mainly in Hamburg and Munich. Their positions can be found in a functionally organized organizational chart, but in day-to-day business Xing relies heavily on agile teams in 2018, which circumvent the classical reporting lines. Around eight to ten people work together on projects. These teams include, for example, backend and frontend developers, mobile developers, user experience designers and project managers. They complete sprints, at the end of which reviews are due. As part of their agile project work, team members report either to the Chief Product Officer, the Chief Sales Officer or the Chief Technology Officer. In this way, around one third of Xing's employees, organized in 50 teams, ensure that the company can react quickly to market developments and drive technological innovation in product development. Xing also works partly agile outside product development. However, in areas where project work only plays a minor role, such as sales, the company usually relies on a classical functional organization.

3.3 Digital Customer Interfaces

Digital products and services can change a company's offering significantly. But this is not the only possible change through digital technologies on the demand side. Significant changes are also possible in the interaction with the customer before, during and after the purchase. While in the past advertising, customer approach or customer service took place over a limited number of channels, in the first case, for example, through billboards or television spots, in the case of customer service, usually by telephone or post, the possibilities have multiplied today due to digital technologies and in particular through the Internet. Social networks, apps, chats, etc. allow companies to always and everywhere connect with their customers. New possibilities for digital and possibly even mobile interaction between companies and customers are constantly emerging, and the number of digital customer interfaces is growing steadily. An increasingly systematic approach to the options of new technologies is therefore required at the interface to the customer. Under the term "customer journey analysis", a new analysis approach has established itself, which is described below.

3.3.1 Basic Understanding of the Customer Journey

The customer journey (Lemon & Verhoef, 2016) is the process a customer goes through to buy a product or use a service. One or more providers can be involved in this process. The customer journey can therefore also be seen as a **sequence of customer contact points** that influence the image a customer has of a company. Theoretically, the individual customer journey therefore begins with the customer's first contact with the company and ends either with the death of this customer or with the end of the company. However, such a broad view of the customer journey is hardly practical. In practice, therefore, as a rule, the process is analyzed, which begins with the emergence of a certain need in the customer and ends with the time at which the customer feels the need to replace the product.

A **subdivision of the customer journey** has established itself, which is understood as an iterative and dynamic process that represents the customer's entire "journey" with a company over time during a purchase cycle across multiple interfaces. Figure 3.7 gives an overview of the customer journey as defined according to this understanding.

With targeted management and intensive engagement with all customer interfaces, a company can pursue various goals. For example, valuable customer information can be collected at the points of contact, which makes it possible to better recognize and understand expectations and needs. This can have a positive effect on both new customer acquisition and long-term customer retention. In addition, the customer interface can be used as a source of new ideas to strengthen the company's innovation and competitiveness.

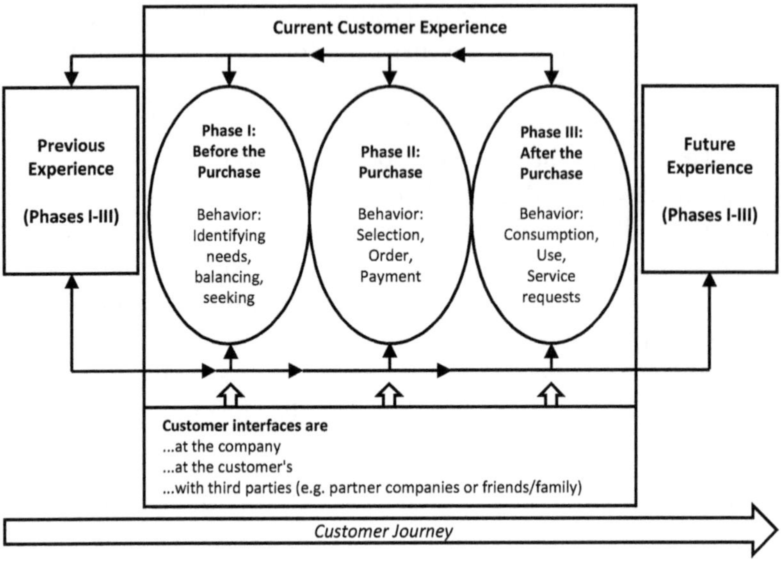

Fig. 3.7 Basic Model of the Customer Journey (based on Lemon & Verhoef, 2016)

The **customer journey in the narrower sense** shown in Fig. 3.7, that is, the current purchasing experience, goes through three essential phases:

- The first phase **(before purchase—"Pre-purchase Stage")** begins with the customer's need and includes all aspects of the customer's interaction with the brand, product or service category and environment before purchase. This includes, for example, the search and evaluation of different offers. Typical customer interfaces in this phase are, for example, advertisements and catalogs, newsletters or the exchange of information with family and friends. In this phase, companies should focus on creating a strong brand awareness in the customer and clearly demonstrating the customer benefit in order to stand out from the competition.
- The second phase **(purchase—"Purchase Stage")** covers all customer interactions with the brand and its environment during the corresponding purchase event. This includes, in particular, the purchase decision, the order and the payment. In order to confirm the customer in his decision to purchase the product or service, companies can, for example, ensure a pleasant atmosphere during the purchase process. It should be noted that the corresponding customer interfaces such as business branches, salespeople or product packaging appear particularly inviting and trustworthy.

- The third phase **(after purchase—"Post-purchase Stage")** includes all interactions that a customer has with the brand or his environment after the purchase has been made. This includes, for example, consumption and use, re-purchase or also the recommendation of the purchased product to family and friends. In this phase, the product or service itself is therefore a critical interface to the customer. The satisfaction of the customers and the extent to which the expectations were exceeded finally decide whether the customer develops brand loyalty and is committed to the company in the long term.

In addition to the division of the customer journey into the three phases described above, the division of the **customer interfaces** can be helpful along the customer journey in four different categories. Their meaning and relevance depend on the type of product or service and the customer-specific customer journey.

- **Direct customer interfaces** ("Brand-owned Touchpoints"): This category includes customer interfaces that are designed and managed by the company itself and are within the company's control and influence. Advertising, websites or the design of products and packaging can be cited as examples.
- **Indirect customer interfaces** ("Partner-owned Touchpoints"): This category includes contact points that are not designed, managed and monitored by the company itself, but by third parties (possibly in cooperation with companies at the same or higher / lower value-added level). Examples here could be parcel services that deliver a purchased product to the customer, but also marketing agencies and multi-channel sales partners.
- **Customer-owned customer interfaces** ("Customer-Owned Touchpoints"): Actions of customers that a company and its partners cannot influence and that are outside their control are assigned to this category of customer interfaces. This could, for example, be the consumption or use of the product after purchase. But also the considerations that a customer makes before a purchase about his needs and wishes or the choice of the payment method are examples for this category.
- **Social/external customer interfaces** ("Social/External Touchpoints"): This category includes all external contact points that surround a customer during his customer journey and influence the purchase process. This can be, for example, the influence of family and friends, but also of

other customers. Evaluation portals and social networks, with which customers can inform themselves and exchange experiences, play a decisive role.

A number of studies indicate that the analysis of the customer journey makes sense for companies (Rawson et al., 2013). Often, companies can achieve higher customer satisfaction, lower attrition rates and higher sales. Through the improved adaptation of customer interfaces to customer needs and the creation of an excellent customer journey from the customer's point of view, customers can also be drawn into so-called "loyalty loops". This refers to the shortened customer journey in terms of information research and the selection process, in which, ideally, no other providers are considered (Edelman & Singer, 2015). For example, in the United States, Apple has introduced an upgrade program for iPhones for this purpose. Under the slogan "getting the latest iPhone has never been easier", customers are offered the opportunity to exchange their old iPhone for the latest model every twelve months for a monthly basic fee.

3.3.2 The Customer Journey Map

In order to fully capture, visualize, and discover the potentials along the entire customer journey of a company, a customer journey map can be created (Lemon & Verhoef, 2016). This is typically used as an entry point in the context of an agile and technically integrated project management approach and supports the analysis of how the individual customers currently interact with the various customer interfaces and how they move along the customer journey from the purchase intention to the purchase to the re-purchase and recommendation. In this way, the behavioral possibilities and decisions of customers can be better understood.

The customer journey map is used to trace how customers behave during the individual phases of the purchase process. A company should therefore put itself in the position of the customers in each of the phases shown above and along the customer journey at each interface. What motivates the customers to this behavior? What do they feel about it? Are there possibly contact points that confuse or even overwhelm the customer? These can easily lead to a customer breaking off the information or purchase process at this point and possibly switching to another provider.

The basic idea of the Customer Journey Map is based on the **Sequential Incident Technique** (Stauss & Weinlich, 1997). In comparison to the

Critical Incident Technique, which only captures particularly extraordinary events ("Moments of Truth"), all customer interfaces are completely captured throughout the process with the Sequential Incident Technique. In the classical structure, the identified customer interfaces are assigned to the phases of purchase intention, purchase and customer loyalty as well as recommendation (Lemon & Verhoef, 2016). Figure 3.8 shows a Customer Journey Map using the example of online purchase of craft beer. In the purchase intention phase, the customer first notices the product through advertising (e.g. through word of mouth, bloggers, social ads), then obtains information about price and product quality, and then visits the online shop of the craft beer manufacturer. When purchasing, the customer pays for the product using an online service. In the following phase of customer loyalty and recommendation, the customer writes his own reviews of the product, recommends it via social media and exchanges information about it in special beer forums.

Customer Journey Maps can not only be used to represent the actual path taken by customers, but also to plan customer journeys. This allows companies to create or alternative designs that appear to be particularly well suited for the customer. The customer interfaces are arranged and designed so that they best meet the individual goals and needs of the customer and flow smoothly into each other.

Customer Journey Maps are usually created in cross-departmental workshops. But also qualitative customer interviews and observing customers during the purchase process can give interesting insights into the individual

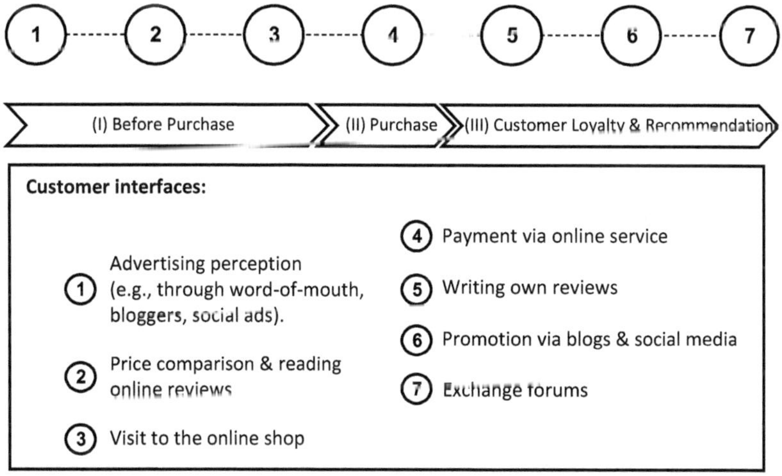

Fig. 3.8 Example of a Customer Journey Map (based on Lemon & Verhoef, 2016)

customer experience. By visualizing and comparing the actual and the planned customer journey, gaps between the expectation of the company and the experience of the customer can be shown. It should be noted that each customer journey is different. Just as customers are different, so are their ways of satisfying their needs. For this reason, it must be determined in advance for which target group the customer journey map is to be created. With these thoughts in mind, a company can, for example, adapt its own landing page or create new channels in the next step, such as apps, to round off the customer experience. However, contact points that are not within the company's own area of control, such as external review or price comparison portals, should not be left out.

3.3.3 The Change of the Customer Journey through Digitalization

Digital technologies offer companies four key points of attack for improvements at the customer interface (Edelman & Singer, 2015):

- Knowing where a customer is in their customer journey at a given moment enables companies to take further steps specifically (**"context-dependent interactions"**). For example, if the behavior of a customer in an online shop suggests that the customer is not looking for a specific product at this moment, but is only browsing, popular products in the lower price range can be displayed more often to tempt him into a purchase.
- Modern CRM systems enable companies to easily identify their customers and understand their customer experience better (**"proactive personalization"**). In this way, marketing and sales measures can be better adapted to the individual customer. Amazon, for example, increases its success in its online shop through intelligent, personalized product recommendations, resulting in higher basket values and conversion rates. Of course, this requires the acquisition of data about the customer see Sect. 3.2.3.
- However, digitalization also offers companies new opportunities to relieve their customers of complex and time-consuming processes through automation (**"automation"**). This makes many activities along the customer journey faster and easier to carry out. Currently, many companies are testing new methods of speech recognition for initial stages of dealing with customer problems.

- To continuously improve or completely reinvent customer journeys, the ongoing analysis of customer needs, technologies and service processes as well as the testing of various variants is required **("Journey Innovation").** With so-called A/B testing, for example, different variants of a user interface design are compared with each other. If a design leads to significantly more customers continuing their customer journey, the other design is discarded. This process can be applied in various areas. For example, different advertising messages in newsletters or different times at which they are sent can be examined for subsequent visits to the website via the link contained therein and adjusted accordingly.

3.3.4 Gatekeeper of the Digital Customer Interface

However, companies today are not only facing the challenge of expanding their interfaces to customers with digital offers. They also have to deal with new market participants who want to displace them from these interfaces or make it more difficult for them to access the customer.

This fight for customer interfaces is often referred to as the **gatekeeper problem of the Internet** (Hess & Matt, 2012). The gatekeeper problem describes in this context a constellation in which (new) market participants position themselves between an established company and the customers and can thus control the access to the end customers. The problem is well known in the classical media sector, and that too in two ways. In the classical media system, i.e. before the introduction of content platforms such as social networks, the journalists were between reality and the public; in the end, they decided what the public was told about reality and in what way. But the term was also used in the media sector to describe the strong position of the operators of closed networks (e.g. cable networks). They decided which channels were fed into the network—and thus also acted as gatekeepers.

Analogously, the gatekeeper problem also arises on the Internet. Gatekeepers on the Internet can also intervene at the level of technical infrastructure, software and data. Points of attack at the technical infrastructure can be the network and the used hardware including the associated system software. For example, a network operator can prevent the calling of selected Internet services or can no longer charge for the calling of selected Internet services. The former "Stream On" feature of T-Online is an example of this, where the use of participating streaming services was not taken into account in the data volume. Hardware manufacturers can only allow very specific application software or data formats for their hardware—as Apple did, for example, when introducing the music download service iTunes, thus effectively forcing the purchase of its hardware if one wanted to use iTunes.

But today the role of so-called navigation hubs is practically most significant, and this is by no means true only for information retrieval. Navigation hubs are services on the Internet that enjoy very high demand and search for follow-up offers from consumers or that allow consumers to offer quick personalization. Currently, this is especially true in Germany, mainly for the search service of Google and, to a lesser extent, for Facebook as a broadly based social network. A not inconsiderable part of consumers searches for new online offers via the search service of Google. Google therefore basically has the possibility to control the flow of users, to position itself well and at the same time to build up extensive data sets on consumers. The high advertising revenues resulting from the high market share in an important market (in the case of search engines) and from the data sets built up reinforce this. In the field of social networks, Facebook has a high market share. Based on the self-description of the users and the relationships between users stored in its social network as well as the records of page views, etc., Facebook also knows a lot about its users and can use this for navigation, again in connection with high advertising revenues. The role of Facebook in shaping political opinion, especially in the run-up to elections, should not be underestimated—because the available data allows for very targeted advertising placements.

In the classical media sector, there is, in particular with regard to the question of feeding into networks, a long tradition of regulating potential gatekeepers in many countries. So network operators are forced in many countries to take up a certain number of channels (the so-called must-carry rule). For the network level and thus for telecommunications companies, similar regulations are now emerging for the Internet. However, the handling of the aforementioned navigation hubs is still largely open. Affected companies are currently active on two levels: On the one hand, they try to improve their own visibility on the hubs, in particular on the search engines, via the so-called search engine optimization. On the other hand, they try to influence politics and thus a corresponding regulation.

3.4 Digital Business Processes

Every company has processes. But for a long time these were given little attention. This only changed in the 1990s of the last century. At that time, new application systems, such as ERP systems, could only develop their actual potential if processes were changed in the context of their introduction. Almost all companies have carried out projects to improve their processes in recent years. However, new technologies, new products, services and customer interfaces, but also creeping inefficiencies over time, always require companies to deal with their processes. The following describes how this is best done.

3.4.1 Delimitation of Processes

Even in a smaller company there are a variety of processes. Many of these processes are certainly improvable. But companies typically focus on the processes that are critical to competition for a company (business processes, core processes) and map them out in a process map even before individual projects are carried out. In Fig. 3.9 the process map of a car rental company is shown as an example.

At first glance, it can be seen in this figure that the organizational structure of a company is irrelevant for the delimitation of business processes. The same applies analogously to the support provided by application systems, i.e. a business process is usually supported by different application systems. In other words, processes usually cross the boundaries between different areas of a company and IT application systems.

The typical distinction between operational, support and management processes is also made in the figure:

- **Operational processes** map the process of creating value from customer demand to service delivery. Examples of this are order processing, product development, production, distribution and service.
- **Support processes** support the operational processes. This usually includes the provision of important resources such as IT systems or personnel.
- **Management or leadership processes** are responsible for the interaction of all parts of a company. Management processes therefore refer to the higher-level control processes of a company, such as strategic and financial planning.

3.4.2 Process Modelling

There are now various approaches for documenting and analyzing a single business process. These methods provide a framework with guidelines

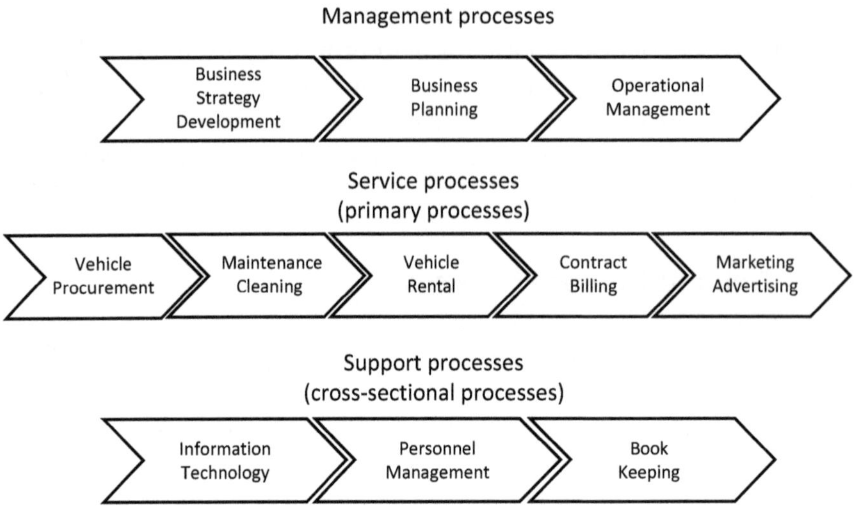

Fig. 3.9 Process Map of a Car Rental Company (Gadatsch, 2012)

to make the models created readable, understandable, uniform and reusable. Business Process Model and Notation (BPMN) belongs to the class of flow-oriented languages, has been managed by the Object Management Group (OMG) since 2005 and has established itself as a standard in many companies.

Figure 3.10 gives an overview of the essential symbols of BPMN. Figure 3.11 illustrates the BPMN modeling using an exemplary process.

There are numerous software packages available for the tool-supported analysis of business processes. The range of functions of these tools extends from mere visualization to modeling and prototypical simulation of processes (Gronau, 2017). Visualization tools make it possible to graphically represent processes that have been identified. Modeling tools can also check the integrity of the model based on the method used. Simulation tools take this one step further and allow for the comparison of modeled actual and desired processes based on predefined parameters, such as event probabilities or resource expenditure (e.g. costs and time). The goal of tool-supported process analysis is to uncover, document, and potentially quantify improvement potential. The improvements that have been identified should then be evaluated based on the relation of potential impact to the estimated effort, and implemented if necessary.

Symbol	Designation	Meaning
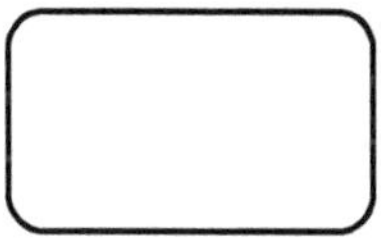	Activity	An activity describes a process that is carried out by the company. It can be atomic (task) or composite, i.e. contain enterprise processes (subprocesses).
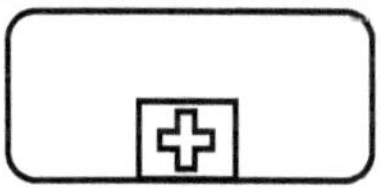	Activity (with Sub-Processes)	
	Start Event Intermediate Event End Event	Events are occurrences that happen during a process. They can be triggering or the result of an activity. There are three basic types (start, intermediate and end) and special cases.
	Decision (Gateway)	Gateways are synchronization points in the process flow. They decide on the further course of the process. There are several gateway types: XOR, OR, AND and event-based decision.
	Control Flow (Sequence Flow)	The control flow describes the timing of activities in the process.
	Message Flow	The message flow describes the exchange of messages between two objects (activities, events or decisions).
	Connection (Association)	The connection indicates that data, text, or other objects are connected to the control flow, for example, input or output of an activity.
	Data Object	The data object indicates which information/data is required as input or output of an activity.

Fig. 3.10 Elements of the BPMN Notation (Gadatsch, 2012; Object Management Group, 2011)

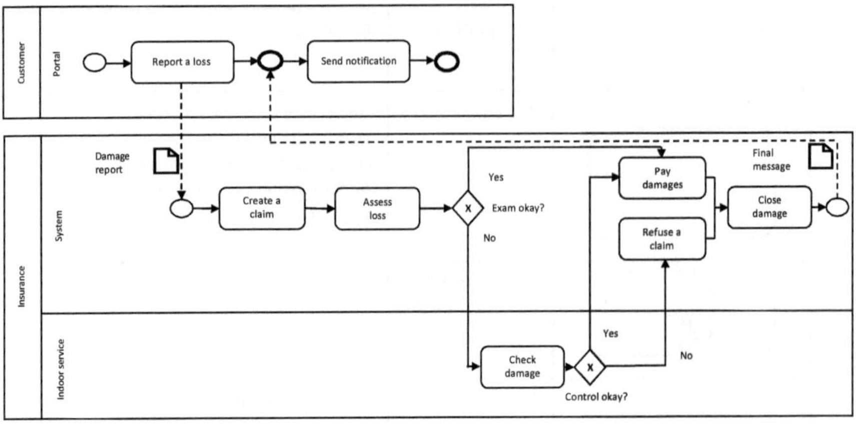

Fig. 3.11 BPMN Modeling Example

3.4.3 Typical Starting Points for Process Improvement

Improvements to processes can be made on the technical and organizational sides. On the technical side, it must first be checked whether new technologies have emerged that make new application solutions and, based on these, new processes possible.

A classic example of a technology-induced process change is Ford's introduction of a company-wide database for purchasing from suppliers (Hammer, 1990). Previously, the accounting department received documents for orders, goods receipts, and invoices, and after reconciling these three documents, finally paid the invoice. The introduction of the database enabled a changed billing process, in which orders and goods receipts are automatically synchronized. Based on this data, the deliveries are immediately credited. This makes a comparison of the supplier invoices superfluous, as prices and quantities are already fixed and stored in the database with the order in the new process. This simplifies the control of the material stock and the processes of the accounting department. The introduction of a new technology thus made it possible to radically change the supplier billing process, by which Ford was able to significantly reduce the administrative costs per order.

Currently, in the context of the discussion of improved possibilities of artificial intelligence, for example, the transfer of tasks previously reserved for humans to the machine is being discussed. But new technologies always allow new forms of division of labor, for example the overburdening of tasks on the customer. Two significant approaches in this regard, which are made

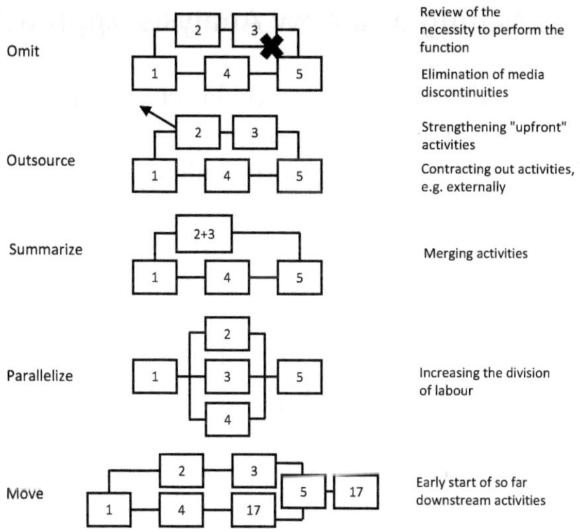

Fig. 3.12 Organizational Approaches for Process Improvement (based on Bleicher, 1981)

possible by digital technologies, are co-creation and user-generated content. With co-creation, the company involves its customers in collaborative product development and innovation processes (see also Sect. 3.2). With user-generated content, on the other hand, the company transfers the concrete design and production of a variety of content to the users of its platform(s) to tap the creative potential of a large mass of individuals.

Also to be assigned to the technical approach points is the improvement of the cooperation of existing systems. Often, process documentation reveals (especially if it also includes the support processes with the corresponding tasks), that the systems supporting one process do not exchange data. This often has the consequence that data that is already available must be captured a second time—certainly an undesirable condition that can be easily remedied once it has been recognized.

Regardless of technology-driven changes, there are numerous generic change potentials on the organizational side. Figure 3.12 provides an overview of a variety of organizational approach points for improving processes.

Decisive for the evaluation of concrete ideas for the improvement of a process—whether they originate from technology or are purely of an organizational nature—are the goals pursued by a process. These are always to be specified specifically. Possible starting points for this are, for example, costs, cycle times or quality. It is particularly important here not to measure the specified goals only once, but to analyze them continuously.

3.4.4 Process Mining as a New Analysis Approach

Business processes today are often based almost entirely on the support of IT systems. Every action of a user is logged in detail in these systems, originally rather for technical reasons. Process mining visualizes process-related relationships and thus also provides insights into complex, less transparent process flows (Tiwari et al., 2008). For this purpose, process mining uses sophisticated algorithms to automatically generate a process model from the log data of the respective system.

Compared to the classical approaches to process surveys, such as questionnaires, interviews or workshops with process participants, which are generally very time-consuming and cost-intensive, process mining techniques can generate and visualize process models in a short time on an objective data basis, as real-lived processes are actually carried out. Not only the effort for the manual creation of a process model is eliminated, the extracted process models are also realistic and reflect the actual process flow, as they are based solely on facts and not on assumptions. Therefore, the application of process mining methods offers significant advantages over traditional approaches to the creation and also to the analysis of process models.

The process-relevant information must first be extracted, cleaned and consolidated from various participating systems. Attention must be paid to the quality and completeness of the recorded data. Lack of completeness and redundant information are two central issues that can affect the results of process mining. A lack of completeness can be caused by hidden activities that are not captured in the log data. This can happen, for example, with manually executed process steps that are not considered by the software system. Duplicate activities are present when different activities occur under the same name. It is therefore necessary to prepare the data in a preliminary step in an appropriate form.

The actual analysis of the process can take place on the basis of the processed log data. Here, three approaches are conceivable:

- The starting point of the analysis is usually the automated detection of process flow models from the given event logs. The representation provides insights into the complexity of the process by displaying both the process activities and their transitions.
- With the help of a variant analysis, it can also be determined which different paths the process actually took and with which frequencies the individual variants occur.

- Afterwards, it can be checked on the basis of the extracted process model whether the actual processes in a company correspond to the desired behavior.

The differences between actual process models and desired process models identify the need for action to achieve the desired state and serve to derive concrete measures. For example, process loops give an indication of redundant steps or show missing or skipped process activities. However, too complex process chains can indicate unnecessary additional work. In the case of highly standardized processes, for which a sequence is prescribed, rare sequences with divergent process executions are in the focus of interest and have to be filtered out. Incorrect or non-conformant behavior can be identified by comparing them. For example, compliance with safety requirements can be checked automatically and cases deviating from the specifications can be pointed out.

3.4.5 Procedure for Business Process Optimization

Traditionally, projects to improve business processes are carried out in a structured approach that is based on the classical, plan-based approach of project management. This also means that an ideal process is developed in a first step which is then handed over to the IT department which is responsible for the implementation.

For the concrete design of such an approach, three important decisions have to be made (Hess, 1996):

- Such projects often begin with detailed **modeling of the current processes.** This is typically associated with considerable effort, but is indispensable if it is about more incremental improvements of the process. If, on the other hand, fundamental changes to the process are in the room, then a detailed capture can not only be superfluous, but even counterproductive. The background is that detailed captures of the status quo often obscure the view for fundamentally new organizational solutions. For this reason, the approach of the "Clean Sheet of Paper" (the start without detailed capture of the status quo) has proven to be the way to major changes.
- A second essential aspect for the design of a process optimization project is the question of how much the solution is already given. Such **specifications** typically come from an standard software, but occasionally also

from regulatory requirements. If such specifications exist, then so-called **reference models** often exist in their context. Reference models describe the processes possible on the basis of the technology or the observed requirements. In particular, the large providers of standard software usually provide such reference models.

- It is also necessary to clarify the question of how detailed the target process is to be described. The decisive factor here is whether the target process is only to serve as a specification for the persons involved or as a template for the implementation of software solutions or the control of processes using the so-called workflow management systems. If the latter is the case, then at least in part, a **detailed** description down to the level of individual work steps as well as a specification of the possibly underlying features of software systems is required.

Agile approaches for the implementation of projects for business process analysis are hardly used so far. On the one hand, the complexity of many projects speaks for this. On the other hand, processes and supporting systems are closely interlinked, so that the previously practiced sequential switching of functional and technical design is basically not necessary. However, the relatively stable requirements in the context of process changes speak against this—at least according to the current assessment. In addition, many standard systems of companies are further developed in the back office according to the classical approach.

It remains to be seen whether in the future methods will also gain a foothold in this field which integrate agile, functional and technical aspects. In this way, modified processes could be developed and tested together with a modified technical support, possibly supported by a workflow control software.

3.4.6 The Idea of a Process-Oriented Organization—and its Reality

At the height of the discussion about IT-driven process re-organization, the idea of a process-oriented structuring of the corporate organization kept coming up. Specifically, this would mean that a company would not be structured according to functions or business fields (or products, see Sect. 3.2.5), but rather according to its processes. In this sense, for example, a car insurer would be divided into the areas of product development, marketing, claims processing, infrastructure provision, resource provision, etc.

However, this idea did not prevail. While this would certainly ensure cross-departmental consideration, the associated loss of economies of scale in the use of resources obviously did not weigh as heavily as this advantage. Nevertheless, a number of companies have moved to set up a process-oriented secondary organization, and this with the continuous monitoring of process indicators. In some companies, process responsible persons (process owners) are even installed.

3.5 Digital Business Models

In recent years, business model analysis has increasingly established itself as an essential management tool. This is characterized by the integrative view of a company. A business model analysis shows, in a highly simplified way, the basic relationships in a company, for example how values are created or which cost-revenue structure underlies the value creation. Similarly, the embedding of a company in the value creation structure becomes clear from the consideration of a business model. The networking with central partners across the boundaries of the organization is thus explicitly taken into account and pays tribute to the influence of digital technologies and their systemic character. Many other questions, such as the organization of a company, are also left out, as are the details.

Many of the aspects discussed in the previous sections, such as the introduction of new products or customer interfaces or the change of processes, flow in a highly aggregated form into a business model. However, an abstract-isolated view of business models is rather rare.

Digital business models are often mentioned in one breath with data-driven business models or platform approaches, which count as prominent expressions of the development. However, the key question of when a business model is digital cannot be answered conclusively. In general, a business model is said to be digital if a company and the way it generates revenue are significantly influenced by digital technologies (Hess & Engert, 2021). Even if the degree of digitalization of a company and thus its business model cannot be determined exactly, this can nevertheless be approached by means of the observation of the degree of digitalization of the processes and the products (Porter & Millar, 1985). Companies can thus be classified into a matrix according to these two dimensions. A cement manufacturer with analog products and processes thus finds itself in one corner, while a cloud provider with a completely digital business model is opposite diagonally (Fig. 3.13).

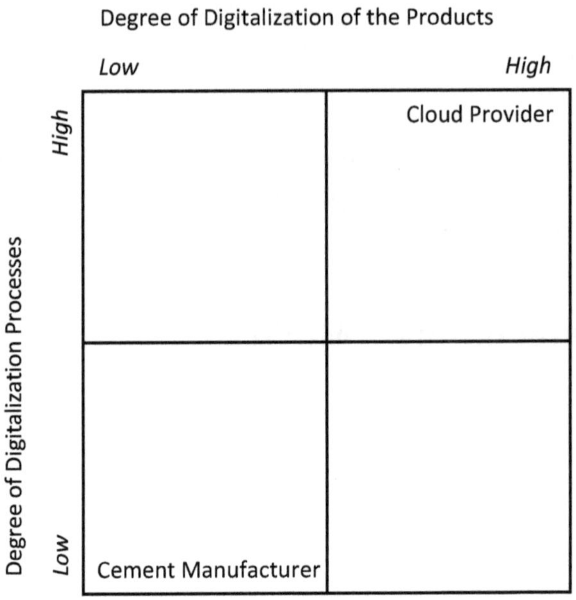

Fig. 3.13 Digital Degree of Business Models (based on Porter & Millar, 1985)

In the context of digital transformation, the consideration of business models has gained particular importance. Thus, the increasing spread of the Internet since the early 2000s has triggered a development that forces companies—against the background of ever-faster technical progress, but also of increasing international competition—to repeatedly question and adapt their business models in order to check and, if necessary, improve the position of their own company.

Business models are to be distinguished in particular from strategies and business plans. A **business model** describes the way a company acts and generates value for its stakeholders, while a **strategy** can be described as an action plan for achieving a specific goal. Thus, the business model reflects the implemented strategy of the company. A **business plan** specifies and details further aspects of the company, such as marketing and sales, customers and competitors.

The following describes the most important topics that should be considered when using the construct of business models.

3.5.1 Description of Business Models

An established concept for the representation of business models is the **Business Model Canvas** (Osterwalder & Pigneur, 2011). The aim of this model is to enable a discussion about business models in a simple and intuitive way. The model acts as a common language to exchange ideas about the abstract basic principle by which an organization creates, communicates and captures value.

Osterwalder and Pigneur distinguish between a performance-oriented and a financial level. At the center of the performance-oriented level is the value offering of a company, that is, its products and services. On the side of the sales markets, customer segments, customer relationships and channels are considered. On the production side, central activities and central resources are listed, supplemented by a description of the key partners. On the financial level, revenue streams and cost structures are considered. Overall, the concept comprises nine elements. Figure 3.14 shows these nine elements at a glance.

- In the **value proposition** element, the products or services are aligned with the defined customer needs and wishes. It represents the benefits for the customer that are created by answering the customer needs on an aggregated basis. This requires a detailed analysis of customer needs. Based on this, existing products or services can be adapted or completely

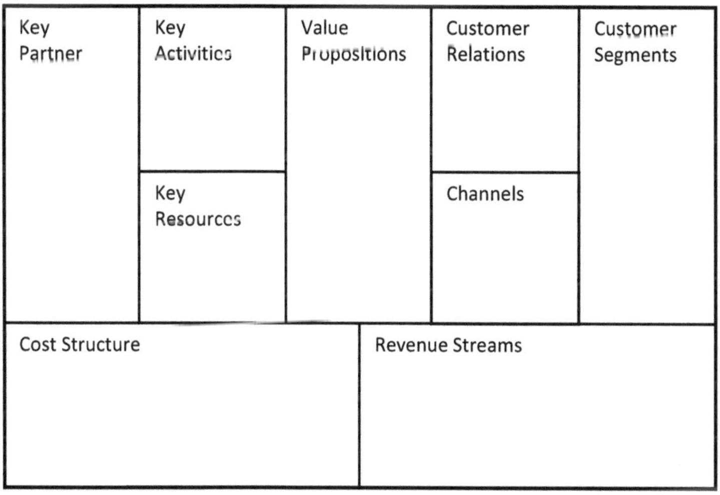

Fig. 3.14 Business Model Canvas (based on Osterwalder & Pigneur, 2011)

new ones introduced. The value offered to the customer manifests itself in different forms. For example, the product or service can offer the consumer advantages through a low price or an extraordinary customer experience.

- The definition of the **customer segment** is central to every company. Many other elements are built around the customer and tailored to them. Thus, one of the nine components deals with the customer segments that are relevant to the company. Here the customer groups to be reached are defined and the characteristics, needs and expectations of the target group(s) are described. Depending on the company and the company's goals, there are different types of customer segments. These can be broad or very specific customer segments or niche markets.
- The element **channels** connects the two elements mentioned above and deals with the question of how the value proposition actually reaches the customer. It thus represents the interface between the company and the customer. A company can use a range of communication and distribution channels—also via partners—to reach all customer segments. The channels enable a variety of actions and contacts with the customer, from creating awareness of the product to customer service after the sale.
- Through the channels mentioned above, the company can build and maintain **customer relationss.** This plays a central role in the entire business model, just like customer segments. This relationship enables (new) customers to be acquired, bound and even to use additional potentials through the sale of additional or complementary products and services. Depending on the product or service and the market situation, the focus may be different. The relationship with the customers can be personal, automated or a combination thereof. In addition, there are special opportunities that can be used to involve the customer in the value creation process (e.g. through co-creation, i.e. close cooperation in product development).
- **Key resources** include not only the most important means of creating the product or service, but also the tools necessary to bring the product or service to market, that is, to offer it to the customer, but also to maintain customer relationships and ultimately to convert the value proposition into sales. The company does not necessarily have to own the necessary resources itself, but can also borrow or receive them from a partner. They can be physical, financial, intangible or personal.
- Analogous to key resources, **key activities** include the most important activities necessary to realize the value proposition. These can differ depending on the business model. For example, the production process

and the activities associated with it are of high importance in the manufacturing industry, while in the consulting industry greater emphasis is placed on personnel and knowledge management.

- Another element closely related to key resources and key activities are **key partners.** These are the partners who are necessary to implement the activities and provide the necessary resources. Partnerships play an important role and offer a variety of benefits. For example, companies enter into cooperation agreements in order not to have to bear the business risk alone, to save costs or to gain access to resources. There are different degrees of binding, from traditional supplier relationships to joint ventures.
- One result of the value offering accessed through the channels are the **revenue streams** that a company generates. These arise then when customer needs and wishes are satisfied. In this element, the potential sales are represented, which are already achieved with the different customer groups now or can be achieved in the future. Important are here in addition to the identified streams (such as. B. Subscription revenues) also their drivers (such. B. the number of customers).
- The last element is the **cost structure** which visualizes and breaks down the costs for implementing the value proposition. Costs can arise through any activities, such as the acquisition of resources, the maintenance of customer relationships or ultimately the creation of a value offering. As in the classical cost accounting, a distinction can be made between fixed and variable costs.

Further development of the established Business Model Canvas offers the **Lean Canvas** by Maurya (2012). The modified concept is primarily aimed at start-ups, but is also increasingly used by classical companies undergoing digital transformation in the context of digital innovation projects. The model replaces the four element of groups customer relationships, key partners, key activities and key resources with four greatly simplified components (Maurya, 2012):

- **Problem:** Start-ups with innovative business models focus on creating new value for their customers by solving central problems for them. However, often start-ups fail because they are not able to correctly understand customer needs and as a result waste resources by setting the wrong product. Successful start-ups therefore work with hypotheses about the problems of their customers, which are validated or rejected by continuous testing. Therefore, in the "problem" element, the (allegedly) biggest problems of the customers are taken up.

- **Solution:** In response to the "problem" element, possible solutions are found and defined in this component. The formulations should be kept short, as companies should not fix themselves too early on a solution and formulate it in detail. Otherwise there is the risk of fixing too early on a path and thus losing (necessary) flexibility.
- **Unfair advantage:** Another element that was introduced in the Lean Canvas is the so-called "unfair advantage". This describes the competitive advantage that a company has. This is a single ability or resource that is very difficult for competitors to copy. The element thus describes the entry barriers for other companies. Start-ups often have no unfair advantage at the beginning of their activities and have to work for it. But since successful business models are often copied, it is important not to lose sight of and defend the acquired unique selling point.
- **Indicators:** Every company has a lot of information about central processes. It is especially important for start-ups and innovation projects to repeatedly substantiate entrepreneurial success with indicators. However, as a rule, only a few indicators are of central importance or significance. In order to focus on the most important indicators, the "indicators" element was introduced in the Lean Canvas, in which the most important indicators for (alleged) business success are outlined.

On the same abstraction level lies the **Application System Architecture** (Krcmar, 2015). It is part of the IT landscape, describes the essential software components and their interaction and should "mirror" the business model on the software side—according to the two sides of a medal, as they were already outlined in the digital innovations. The architecture should support the integration of the functional and technical perspectives required for transformation projects. Figure 3.15 describes a very simple example of an application system architecture.

There are also a variety of description methods for describing application system architectures. However, in the context of business model development, the intuitive description approach is sufficient.

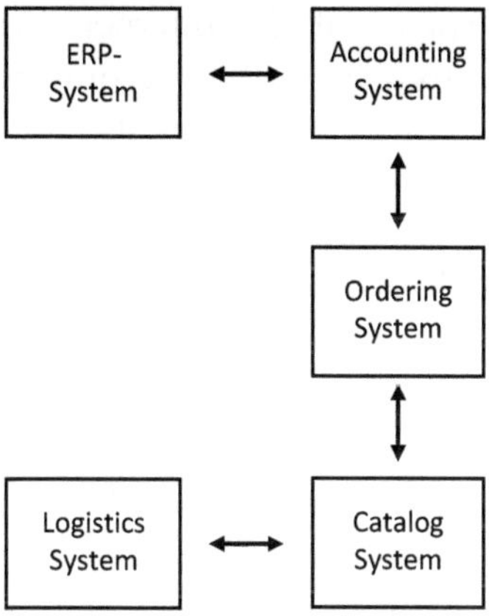

Fig. 3.15 Example of an Application System Architecture

3.5.2 Typical Business Model Innovation in the Context of Digital Transformation

In the age of digital change, the "lifetime" of a business model has shortened considerably. The rapid pace of technological progress and the resulting increased competition mean that business models must be constantly questioned. In order to react to this danger and secure the existence of a company, or even an entire industry, existing business models must be continuously adapted to the dynamic environment. But in addition to the risks, there are also opportunities in the change caused by digitalization. New potential can be exploited by optimizing or completely redesigning existing models.

Examples from Retail Banking For a long time, the business model of banks in the business with private customers was very stable. Offered were account management, simple investment opportunities, buying and selling securities as well as simple loans. The interface to the customer was the branch. All products were, unlike in private banking and wealth management, very standardized. The processes in the background were already automated and digitized in parts. Revenues were generated through interest on loans, through the further exploitation of the capital on the accounts and through transaction fees for capital market transactions. In many cases, the account was free of charge for the customer—at least from a certain amount of payment.

With the increasing spread of the Internet, many customers have the already mentioned desire to manage their account online, first from stationary terminals, later also from mobile terminals. The banks responded to this wish step by step and are now gradually reducing their branch network. By means of a more consistent automation of the processes and the increased use of standard software, but also by more outsourcing as well as cooperation and mergers, the banks are trying to improve their cost position. On the one hand, new banks are emerging in the retail banking sector, which do not have a branch network and have already strongly aligned their online access with today's customers and their needs. In addition, companies are established that, from the customer's point of view, offer very efficient solutions for the processing of payments, the granting of small loans and the mediation of loans. In connection with a low interest margin, high regulatory requirements, emerging start-ups from the FinTech sector and a market split into three camps, the retail business of many banks in Germany is facing great challenges.

Example Cloud Computing and Software Providers Also noteworthy is the fundamental change of software providers due to the technology of cloud computing (see Sect. 4.1.3) A few years ago, standard software had to be completely installed on the user's computer. All data was also stored there. This is no longer necessarily the case. According to the cloud computing model, it is enough if only a small part of the software is installed on the user's computer. Essential parts of the software and also the data can be stored with a service provider. If cloud computing takes hold, the business model of a software company will change fundamentally. On the one hand, the company does not provide a product, but a service with extensive requirements for availability, service, etc. as well as the management of updates. This in turn requires the appropriate expertise on the part of the provider or at least the management of commissioned service providers. The way software companies generate revenue also changes fundamentally. In the classic model, a software company charges a fee for the provision of a license to use its software up-front. For larger software packages that companies use, maintenance fees were and are still due every year of use. After a few years, the total can come back to the level of the up-front payment. In the cloud computing model, the user pays a usage fee.

Examples of Innovations in Sub-Areas Changes are also partly found in individual elements of a business model. An example on the **market side** is the **Freemium model.** Under the term Freemium, one understands a revenue model for online services, in which the operators offer users two different options (Wilson, 2006): on the one hand a free version with the basic functions of the service, on the other hand a paid premium version with additional features, such as ad-free or bonus content. The aim of this segmentation is to continuously acquire a wide mass of users via the free version and then to convert a part of the non-paying users into paying premium customers. Since the conversion rates from free to paid version are usually low, providers of Freemium services mostly use advertising-based models as an additional, indirect source of revenue. The providers make advertising space available to advertisers on their platforms, which they use to advertise their products to users of the free version (see Fig. 3.16).

A much-discussed example of the Freemium model is the music streaming service Spotify. Non-paying users of this service are able to consume an unlimited portfolio of millions of songs, with the content occasionally interrupted by advertising. For the paying users of the premium version, on the other hand, the consumption of music is continuously ad-free, and there are also additional comfort features for them, such as the ability to listen to favorite songs offline. The example of Spotify also makes it possible to illustrate the special trade-off to which Freemium services are exposed. On the one hand, it is necessary to attract as large a user base as possible, so that as many users can be converted to the paid premium version. On the other hand, of course, there are also deployment costs for each user of the free version, e.g. in the form of license and server costs.

A prominent example of innovation on the **production side** and thus also in part of a business model, is the **modular production of media content** (Grau, 2008). Technological innovations for media-neutral content

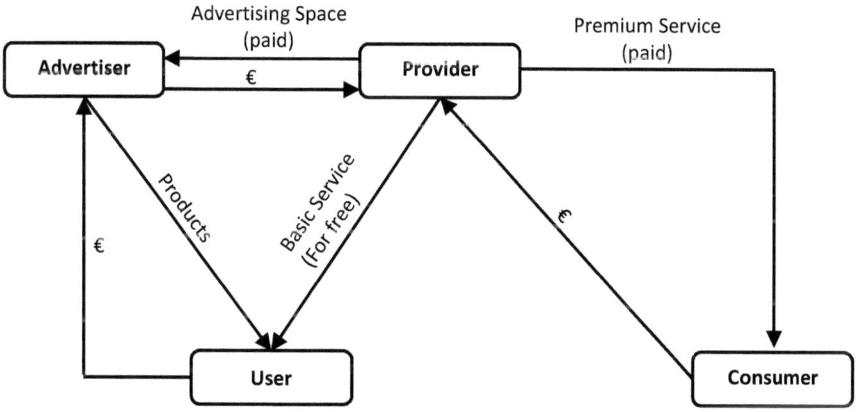

Fig. 3.16 The Freemium Revenue Model (Wagner et al., 2014)

storage (e.g. with the Extensible Markup Language, XML) and content management (in the form of content management systems) led to new possibilities in media production. Analogous to concepts in the automotive industry, it became possible to use individual modules for several products. While products used to be planned as isolated units, they can now be designed modularly, based on a set of media-neutral units.

Production changed to a three-stage model through the modular creation of content (see Fig. 3.17). In the first stage, companies produce modules as the smallest units of value creation that cannot be marketed on their own. In the next step, the individual modules are then combined into marketable bundles, such as magazines. Finally, companies couple the assembled bundles to specific media, after which they reproduce and distribute the finished media products.

The effects of modular production on the business model can be illustrated using the example of a daily newspaper. At its core, each issue of a daily newspaper is made up of text- or graphics-based modules. Only by bundling these modules does one get a product that is marketable. Due to modularization, the individual components of the daily newspaper can be used cross-medially and reused several times. As an example, the multiple uses of articles in print and online versions of the daily newspaper can be mentioned here. In addition, modularization simplifies the offering of personalized products that are bundled on the basis of individual customer wishes.

The genesis of data-based business models is currently also strongly debated. The concept of data-driven business models is not entirely new, one thinks, for example, of the high relevance of data for insurance companies. However, more innovative data-driven business models have only been made

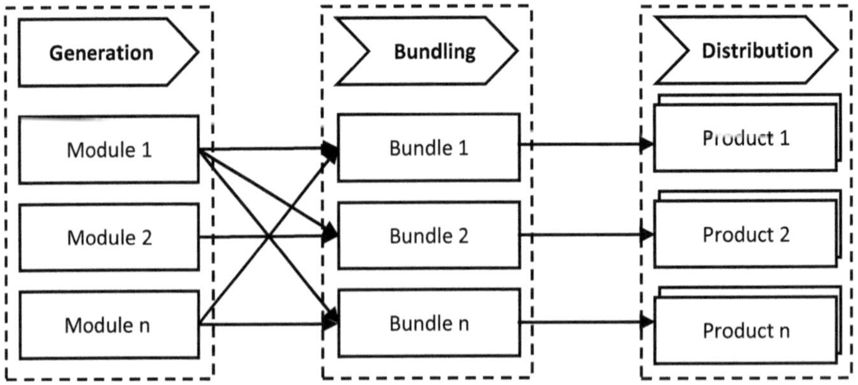

Fig. 3.17 Model of Modular Media Production (based on Grau, 2008)

possible in recent years by new technologies that allow data from various sources (e.g. social media, sensors or mobile devices) to be collected, linked, processed, analyzed and distributed.

The structured use of data through algorithmic analysis makes it possible for companies to redesign value offerings, value creation or revenue models. In doing so, five basic schemes for the **data-driven innovation** of a business model can be identified by combining these three elements (Schüritz & Satzger, 2016):

- **Data-driven value creation**: Data can have a great impact on value creation for companies. The structured analysis and evaluation of large data sets make it possible to optimize products or processes in the company itself or in cooperation with external partners in order to enrich the existing value creation. For example, the use of sensor data can reduce errors or waste products in production and thus save costs. This type of data-driven innovation is widely used in entrepreneurial practice, but is limited to the value creation element of a business model.
- **Data-driven revenue models**: In addition to changed value creation, data can also be used for innovative revenue models by finding additional information on customer buying habits or characteristics of customer segments and using it to adapt pricing categories. A broad data analysis can, for example, lead to the discovery of additional revenue potentials through dynamic pricing mechanisms—based on temporal, geographic, seasonal, or demographic data.
- **Data-driven value offerings in connection with value creation:** Often, data-enriched value creation can be combined with new, innovative value offerings. The data-driven insights allow the company to offer its customers improved or additional services. If sensors monitor the performance of machines and thus optimize processes, the resulting data can also be used to predict future maintenance needs. This allows repairs to be better planned and costly production failures to be prevented.
- **Data-driven value offerings in connection with revenue models**: However, the evaluation of data also offers companies the opportunity to combine their value offerings with data-driven revenue models. Insurance providers can use data from intelligent devices to calculate individualized insurance premiums for policyholders based on the driving and, in particular, braking behavior of each customer and the associated risk. This not only creates additional benefits for customers with proactive driving behavior, but the company also benefits from the possibility of tailor-made pricing.

- **New data-driven business models**: When all dimensions of the business model, that is, value propositions, value creation and revenue models, are affected by the use of data and these fundamentally change, entirely new business models arise. Companies whose entire economic logic is based on data or is dependent on it, offer aggregation or analysis services, trade with data as a product or enable their customers to use personalized services whose value increases steadily with increasing use through the permanent data-based optimization of performance. When data and the information derived from it are brought into the center of the business model, this results in numerous innovation paths for companies.

3.5.3 Procedure for Business Model Analysis

Description approaches for business models, as presented above, are the basis for describing an existing business model, for its analysis and for describing a future business model. Around these description approaches, procedure models have established themselves in practice, which should give companies hints for proceeding. Usually, these suggestions contain three typical steps:

- **Analysis of the existing business model:** Basically, the transformation of a business model begins with an analysis of the existing business model. For this purpose, the existing business model is to be captured with a description approach such as the Business Model Canvas. As a rule, it is worthwhile to identify the strengths and weaknesses of the status quo on this basis in order to address or reduce them effectively. It must be examined which parts of the existing model support the competitiveness and which parts make the company vulnerable. In this context, all stakeholders in the environment of the company must be included and any dependencies identified.
- **Identifying the untapped potential of new technologies:** After analyzing the existing business model, one looks at ways to improve the model in the context of technological potential. Each individual component of the model and the value creation process is examined with the question of whether the company could shape it more efficiently or closer to the customer using digital technologies. The aim is not only to improve weaknesses, but also to rethink well-functioning parts of the existing model. The potential of new technologies and the resulting changes in the behavior of customers and employees or in market constellations are often not at all clear. It therefore makes sense to work with scenarios. These

scenarios should always include the application system architecture outlined above, which should take into account the interfaces to important partners in particular.
- **Implementation:** Before actual implementation, the goals should be formulated in detail. This results in the necessary adjustments and changes to the existing business model and the products and processes required for implementation, as well as technical solutions and possibly structures within the company. In this step, the "user experience" is also designed and optimized. The new transformed business model is played and adjusted repeatedly in a series of tests, possibly in variants, until it meets the management's expectations.

These three steps show that business models often serve as an "integration platform" with the help of which detailed analyses of products, customer interfaces and processes are brought together and (e.g. by looking at revenue models and value creation structures) supplemented.

Classifications of business model innovations have also proved to be practically useful. Nemeth's classification (2011) describes the different areas of change. He differentiates between three cases:

- **Value innovation:** Value innovation refers to the value offering of a business model. Here, customer needs are defined again in detail and the product or service is adapted or even created anew in order to continue to provide the greatest possible benefit to the specific customer segment. This creates new products that, as a result, bring about further changes to the business model in other areas, for example in the value creation architecture.
- **Revenue model innovation:** Revenue model innovation refers to the revenue structure of a business model, because here too new economic potential can be tapped through innovation. It deals with the question of how revenue is generated. For example, existing sources of revenue can be changed by, instead of higher one-time payments, lower but more regular streams of revenue being generated—as in the usage-based revenue model pursued by automobile manufacturers with car sharing.
- **Architectural innovation:** This type of innovation deals directly with the value creation architecture of an existing business model. The focus here is on how production can be optimized or revolutionized. The question arises of how the value chain can be designed efficiently, both internally and externally. This can be, for example, process innovations in production or new sales channels.

In order to facilitate the creation and optimization of business models in business model transformation, companies can rely on software tools. Compared to paper-based methods, software solutions are supposed to help create, adapt and check business models more efficiently. Loos et al. (2018) have examined and compared different tools for business model creation. The majority of the tools examined are based on the Business Model Canvas, as it allows both the company and customer perspectives to be represented interactively and structured. It also shows that most tools focus on the mere representation of the business model and provide little or no support for the creation or optimization. However, some tools also include analysis functions that allow the business model to be not only represented, but also viewed and evaluated in a differentiated manner. In addition, some tools allow for the joint, synchronous editing of the business model. But only a few software solutions offer both analysis and collaboration functions. Software-based solutions for business modeling therefore serve in most cases only as an optional supplement to existing methods. The importance of tools is lower in this area than, for example, in business process analysis.

References

Acquisti, A., & Grossklags, J. (2005). Privacy and rationality in individual decision making. *IEEE Security and Privacy, 3*(1), 26–33.

Anding, M. (2020). *Value creation with digital products and services: Digital value canvas.* https://www.excubate.de/de/insights/value-creation-with-digital-products-and-services-digitalvalue-canvas-3/. Accessed 22 Sept 2020.

Barthel, P., & Hess, T. (2020). Towards a characterization of digitalization projects in the context of organizational transformation. *Pacific Asia Journal of the Association for Information Systems, 12*(3), 31–56.

Barthel, P., Stark, N., & Hess, T. (2020). Exploring new areas for project portfolio management – Evolving practices for digital transformation projects. In *Proceedings of the 28th European Conference on Information Systems (ECIS 2020). A virtual AIS conference* (pp. 1–11).

Barthel, P., Perrot, C. M., Benlian, A., & Hess, T. (2021). Towards a method for evaluating digital innovation projects. In *Proceedings of the 29th European Conference on Information Systems (ECIS 2021). A virtual AIS conference* (pp. 1–16).

Beck, K., Beedle, M., van Bennekum, A., Cockburn, A., Cunningham, W., Fowler, M., et al. (2013). *Manifesto for agile software development.* https://moodle2016-17.ua.es/moodle/pluginfile.php/80324/mod_resource/content/2/agile-manifesto.pdf. Accessed 30 Aug 2018.

Benlian, A., Hilkert, D., & Hess, T. (2015). How open is this platform? The meaning and measurement of platform openness from the complementors' perspective. *Journal of Information Technology, 30*(3), 209–228.

Bleicher, K. (1981). *Organisation – Formen und Modelle*. Gabler.

Buxmann, P. (2018). Der Preis des Kostenlosen – Das Spannungsfeld zwischen dem Wert von Daten und der Privatsphäre von Nutzern. *ifo Schnelldienst, 10*, 18–21.

Buxmann, P., Diefenbach, H., & Hess, T. (2015). *Die Softwareindustrie: Ökonomische Prinzipien, Strategien, Perspektiven* (3rd ed.). Springer.

Châlons, C., & Dufft, N. (2016). Die Rolle der IT als Enabler für Digitalisierung. In F. Abolhassan (Ed.), *Was treibt die Digitalisierung: warum an der Cloud kein Weg vorbeiführt* (pp. 27–37). Springer Gabler.

Edelman, D. C., & Singer, M. (2015). *Competing on customer journeys*. https://hbr.org/2015/11/competing-on-customer-journeys. Accessed 30 Aug 2018.

Etventure. (2018). *Study digital transformation. Hemmnisse, Fortschritte und Alternativen*. https://service.etventure.de/digitale-transformation-2018. Accessed 23 Sept 2018.

Forbes. (2019). *Companies that failed at digital transformation and what we can learn from them*. https://www.forbes.com/sites/blakemorgan/2019/09/30/companies-that-failed-at-digital-transformation-and-what-we-can-learn-from-them/?sh=6a72d35f603c. Accessed 9 Sept 2021.

Gadatsch, A. (2012). *Grundkurs Geschäftsprozess-Management: Methoden und Werkzeuge für die IT-Praxis: eine Einführung für Studenten und Praktiker* (7th ed.). Springer Vieweg.

Gothelf, J., & Seiden, J. (2017). *You need to manage digital projects for outcomes, not outputs*. https://hbr.org/2017/02/you-need-to-manage-digital-projects-for-outcomes-not-outputs. Accessed 1 Sept 2018.

Grau, C. (2008). *Kostendegression in der digitalisierten Medienproduktion: eine Neukonzeption des First-Copy-Cost-Effekts*. Kovač.

Gronau, N. (2017). *Geschäftsprozessmanagement in Wirtschaft und Verwaltung, Analyse, Modellierung und Konzeption* (2nd ed.). Gito-Verlag.

Grots, A., & Pratschke, M. (2009). Design Thinking – Kreativität als Methode. *Marketing Review St. Gallen, 26*(2), 18–23.

Hammer, M. (1990). *Reengineering work: Don't automate, obliterate*. https://hbr.org/1990/07/reengineering-work-dont-automate-obliterate. Accessed 30 Aug 2018.

Hess, T. (1996). *Entwurf betrieblicher Prozesse*. Springer Fachmedien.

Hess, T. (2014). What is a media company? A reconceptualization for the online world. *International Journal on Media Management, 16*(1), 3–8.

Hess, T., & Engert, S. (2021). *Glossar. Digitales Geschäftsmodell*. https://www.bidt.digital/glossar-digitales-geschaeftsmodell/. Accessed 20 Aug 2021.

Hess, T., & Matt, C. (2012). Gatekeeper in der digitalen Medienwelt. *MedienWirtschaft – Zeitschrift für Medienmanagement und Kommunikationsökonomie, 9*(3), 48–51.

Kanter, R. M., Stein, B. A., & Jick, T. D. (1992). *The challenge of organizational change: How companies experience it and leaders guide it*. Free Press.

Krcmar, H. (2015). *Informationsmanagement* (6th ed.). Springer.

Lemon, K. N., & Verhoef, P. C. (2016). Understanding customer experience throughout the customer journey. *Journal of Marketing, 80*(6), 69–96.

Loos, P., Klein, S., & Emrich, A. (2018). Softwaregestützte Modellierung und Optimierung von Geschäftsmodellen. *MedienWirtschaft – Zeitschrift für Medienmanagement und Kommunikationsökonomie, 15*(3), 54–59.

Lünendonk. (2018). *Versicherungen in der Zeitfalle: Wie die digitale Transformation gelingt und das Spannungsfeld aus Innovation und IT-Modernisierung aufgelöst wird*. Lünendonk & Hossenfelder GmbH.

Majchrzak, A., & Meshkati, N. (2007). Aligning technological and organizational change. In G. Salvendy (Ed.), *Handbook of industrial engineering* (3rd ed.). John Wiley & Sons.

Markus, M. L. (2004). Technochange management: Using IT to drive organizational change. *Journal of Information Technology, 19*, 4–20.

Maurya, A. (2012). *Running lean: Iterate from plan A to a plan that works*. O'Reilly Media.

Mertens, P., & Wieczorrek, H. W. (2011). *Management von IT-Projekten: von der Planung zur Realisierung*. Springer.

Meyer, H., & Reher, H.-J. (2015). *Projektmanagement: Von der Definition über die Projektplanung zum erfolgreichen Abschluss*. Springer Fachmedien Wiesbaden.

Morlok, T., Matt, C., & Hess, T. (2017). Privatheit in den Wirtschaftswissenschaften – Individual- und Marktperspektive. *Arbeitsbericht des Instituts für Wirtschaftsinformatik und Neue Medien*, 1.

Nemeth, A. (2011). *Geschäftsmodellinnovation – Theorie und Praxis der erfolgreichen Realisierung von strategischen Innovationen in Großunternehmen*. https://www1.unisg.ch/www/edis.nsf/SysLkpByIdentifier/3921/$FILE/dis3921.pdf. Accessed 1 Sept 2018.

Object Management Group. (2011). *Business Process Model and Notation (BPMN)*. https://www.omg.org/spec/BPMN/2.0/. Accessed 2 Nov 2018.

Osterwalder, A., & Pigneur, Y. (2011). *Business Model Generation: ein Handbuch für Visionäre, Spielveränderer und Herausforderer*. Campus-Verlag.

Porter, M. E., & Millar, V. E. (1985). How information gives you competitive advantage. *Harvard Business Review, 63*(4), 149–160.

Rawson, A., Duncan, E., & Jones, C. (2013). *The truth about customer experience*. https://hbr.org/2013/09/the-truth-about-customer-experience. Accessed 30 Aug 2018.

Schadler, T. (2016). *Digital transformation budgets will top the Billion-Dollar bar*. https://go.forrester.com/blogs/16-11-01-in_2017_digital_transformation_budgets_will_top_the_billion_dollar_bar/. Accessed 30 Aug 2018.

Schmiedgen, J., Rhinow, H., Köppen, E., & Meinel, C. (2015). *Parts without a whole – The current state of design thinking practice in organization*. Technischer

Bericht des Hasso-Plattner-Institut für Softwaresystemtechnik an der Universität Potsdam.

Schreiner, M., Hess, T., & Fathianpour, F. (2013). On the willingness to pay for privacy as a freemium model: First empirical evidence. In *Proceedings of the 21st European Conference on Information Systems (ECIS 2013)* (pp. 1–7).

Schüritz, R., & Satzger, G. (2016). Patterns of data-infused business model innovation. In *IEEE 18th Conference on Business Informatics (CBI), 2016* (pp. 133–142).

Stauss, B., & Weinlich, B. (1997). Process-oriented measurement of service quality: Applying the sequential incident technique. *European Journal of Marketing, 31*(1), 33–55.

Sutherland, J., & Schwaber, K. (2017). *The scrum guide.* https://www.scrumguides.org/docs/scrumguide/v2017/2017-Scrum-Guide-US.pdf#zoom=100. Accessed 2 Sept 2018.

Tiwari, A., Turner, C. J., & Majeed, B. (2008). A review of business process mining: State-of-the-art and future trends. *Business Process Management Journal, 14*(1), 5–22.

Trepte, S., & Masur, P. K. (2015). *Privatheit im Wandel: Eine repräsentative Umfrage zur Wahrnehmung und Beurteilung von Privatheit* (Bericht vom 18. Juni 2015). Universität Hohenheim.

Uebernickel, F., Brenner, W., Naef, T., Pukall, B., & Schindlholzer, B. (2015). *Design Thinking: Das Handbuch* (2nd ed.). Frankfurter Allgemeine Buch.

Vollmöller, T. (2018). Communities sind der Weg, um Inhalte intelligent zu streuen. *MedienWirtschaft – Zeitschrift für Medienmanagement und Kommunikationsökonomie, 15*(3), 8–11.

Wagner, T. M., Benlian, A., & Hess, T. (2014). Converting freemium customers from free to premium – The role of the perceived premium fit in the case of music as a service. *Electronic Markets, 24*(4), 259–268.

Weinreich, U. (2016). *Lean Digitization: Digitale Transformation durch agiles Management.* Springer.

Wilson, F. (2006). *Freemium business model.* http://willoughby.ucsd.edu/files/2017/01/Caliber-Freemia.pdf. Accessed 1 Sept 2018.

4

Creating the Conditions for Digital Transformation

The digitalization of products, processes and business models requires flexible IT landscapes, innovation-promoting organizational structures, a digital corporate culture and comprehensive digital competence. By no means are these requirements always met in full, rather they must be created to a greater or lesser extent. The following section describes how this can be achieved. For example, is bimodal IT the perfect solution for embedding new technical solutions created in the context of digital transformation? What benefits do hackathons bring to competence building? And which instruments can help make a company culture digital?

4.1 Prepare IT Landscape: Make Expandability possible

An innovation always includes a technical element. An online service offering, for example from a bank or an airline, typically consists of a client-server solution including an app and a server. Similarly, more automation of a process often requires a so-called workflow management system.

In the simplest case, this is a stand-alone technical solution, i.e. a technical solution that works autonomously and independently of the other technical systems. But this is only very rarely the case. Typically, a new technical solution has to be integrated into the totality of all technical solutions, the IT landscape. The reason for this may be that data is stored on another computer, for example because customer data (reasonably) is stored on a central

T. Hess, *Managing the Digital Transformation*,
https://doi.org/10.1007/978-3-658-38424-1_4

computer. But the reason can also be that other computers offer specific functions, for example for analyzing purchase behavior overnight—in this case too, the new technical solution must be integrated into the IT landscape. In addition, specific technical skills are required to implement new applications, which are still lacking in many companies today and can only be built up in the short term. The following describes why the integration of a new solution into the IT landscape is often a greater challenge and how to assess the two most important concepts for solving this problem.

4.1.1 Why doesn't everything work immediately? The Changeability of IT Landscapes

The realization of an application required for a new product or a new process comprises two steps:

- First, the application must be designed and implemented.
- Then this has to be integrated into the existing IT landscape.

For IT users, the realization of new applications, typically based on innovative technologies, is often a problem. Often, many IT resources are bound to the operation and further development of existing systems. In addition, the paradigms of classical software development often prevail in a company—but these are based on stable requirements for the system and sufficient time for development. Both are often not given in the context of digital transformation. However, new development teams, which may also use new development methods, can usually not be set up quickly.

In addition, the integration of a new application into an existing IT landscape is often a real challenge. Integration requires the definition of which data is to be exchanged between which computers and in which format. This question arises, for example, when computer A contains the address data that computer B needs for issuing invoices. For this case it must be known that the data is stored on computer A and in which format it is stored. This problem would be easy to solve if there were a small amount of data with simple exchange relationships. But both are not typically the case in companies. Rather, there are usually complex IT landscapes that have grown over decades. These consist of a large number of systems that exchange data in the most diverse formats. Often, the fact that many companies do not have a detailed overview of their system landscape at all makes the situation even more difficult. Over the years, new systems have been integrated and networked with other systems again and again. The clean documentation of these interfaces was often neglected. Projects to simplify the landscape were often avoided.

Below are two approaches to how the topic can be approached if it becomes a real problem in the company.

4.1.2 Bimodal IT as a Solution Approach?

A first possible way to reduce the complexity of an IT landscape and quickly implement new applications is sketched out in the concept of bimodal IT (Haffke et al., 2017). It was developed a few years ago by the analyst house Gartner. The core idea of this concept is to set up a largely separate IT landscape for new solutions and to align the IT organization differently for this and for the existing landscape of legacy systems. This concept thus follows the idea of complexity reduction through separation as well as the improvement of software development through the partial introduction of a new method. In the first (classical) part are the core systems of a company. These should run reliably and cost-effectively. They should be operated and further developed according to the paradigm of "stability and reliability". The systems in the second (new) part often have more experimental, customer-oriented characteristics. Further development takes place here with agile methods. Not infrequently, the projects are risky. Figure 4.1 compares the two approaches.

The traditional approach is appropriate to update an outdated enterprise-wide IT system (e.g., ERP system) or replace it with a modern system, or renew an in-house monolithic application software, such as an invoicing and billing system. Typically, such projects have clear requirements and desired results that are defined and intended for a longer period of time. The agile approach, on the other hand, is more suitable for shorter-lived pilot projects (e.g., IoT projects, Big Data projects) in which a concrete application case only crystallizes during processing and therefore more leeway is required. Also, customer-oriented digital products and services are often developed agilely in order to be able to take customer wishes and feedback from the use of the services (e.g., app) directly into account in the further development of the software.

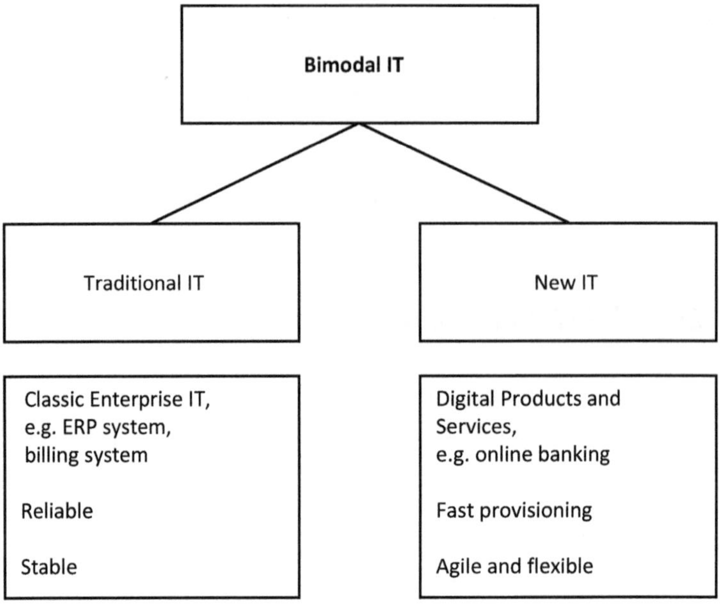

Fig. 4.1 The Two Modes of Bimodal IT

4.1.2.1 Organizational Mapping of Bimodal IT

The two organizational modes of bimodal IT can be differentiated on the basis of their different structures, procedures and risk appetites, as already indicated. Table 4.1 shows clearly that the mode of traditional IT is based on stability and security in the development and operation of IT systems, whereas in agile IT the focus is on agility and speed with regard to new solutions.

- In projects in the traditional mode, the focus is often on the stability of the software and hardware as well as on clean and good data quality. In

Table 4.1 Traditional and Agile IT Comparison (Horlach et al., 2016)

Characteristics	Traditional IT	Agile IT
Goal	Stability and reliability	Innovation and differentiation
Focus	System-centered	User-centered
Planning horizon	Long-term	Short-term
Methods	Plan-driven	Iterative and agile
Development cycles	Long	Short
Development and operation	Strictly separated	Integrated

project management, so-called linear, plan-based development models (such as the waterfall model) are often used, with the advantages of systematic and quality-oriented development, but also with the associated disadvantage of long release cycles.
- The development culture of agile IT, on the other hand, is oriented towards innovation and experimentation. The developers of agile IT solutions often aim for the development of the already mentioned Minimum Viable Product and the rapid testing of their prototypes with the end customer. Agile project management methods, such as the Scrum approach, allow for short release cycles.

The bimodal approach is not without controversy. The following section briefly explains the relevant advantages of the concept and possible risks.

4.1.2.2 Advantages and Disadvantages of the Bimodal Approach

As already indicated, the setup and use of a bimodal IT can be understood as a large lever to create necessary conditions for digital transformation in companies. This allows agile IT in the bimodal concept to provide more effective, active and flexible support for digital business initiatives. In particular, the iterative approach in project management within the agile working mode allows for a high degree of flexibility. This makes it possible to start new projects quickly and develop solutions in short release cycles in order to respond to changing customer requirements. On the other hand, this does not mean that traditional IT properties such as stability, security and efficiency have to be dispensed with. They are still present in the traditional mode.

In contrast to traditional understanding, within the scope of digital transformation, the IT department's goal is only partially to optimize costs and incrementally improve hardware and software. Rather, the goal is to provide the basis for innovative ideas and their implementation. The agile mode makes it possible to create a suitable working environment to promote risk-taking or "trial and error" approaches to creative work and to make faster decisions.

The disadvantage: The establishment of an agile development and operational mode can lead to an internal break in existing processes, and working methods, but also in the task and role distributions. For example, the introduction of a Scrum development approach leads to new roles within a development team, which are in contrast to the traditional understanding of roles and to hierarchy aspects and can therefore lead to tensions within a team. Also, the strong divergent risk-taking of both approaches can lead to a different tolerance level with regard to the quality of IT products and thus make it more difficult to find a common ground for discussion and consensus between both development units.

When introducing a bimodal IT, not only an "alignment" between IT and business units is necessary, but also a great deal of play between the two different modes of IT organization. Because despite the separation into two working modes, there are still points of contact and dependencies between the agile and the traditional approach, both on a technical and on a personnel level. These can lead to problems within the organization if, for example, innovative or even disruptive solutions cannot simply be connected to the existing traditional IT landscape via an interface.

A critical aspect is also the resource and knowledge management between the two approaches. In part, subject matter experts are assigned to a traditional or agile project depending on the project and expertise. The resulting frequent changes of individual IT professionals between both approaches can lead to conflicts of interest and thus potentially to diminishing motivation of individual employees. Similarly, the continuous use of individual employees in the new IT mode can lead to knowledge gaps with regard to tasks and operations in the traditional IT core and vice versa.

In many companies, bimodal concepts were introduced, often less planned than out of operational pressure. Currently, it is necessary in these companies to connect the two parts of these solutions both technically and personnel-wise and also, especially with regard to development processes, to design them ideally. Not infrequently, such projects are run as support projects in the context of digital transformation. A not inconsiderable part of companies, however, sees the bimodal approach rather critically and is increasingly relying on agile development for their IT projects (Capgemini, 2018).

4.1.3 Cloud Computing as a Solution Approach?

Cloud computing also promises, in addition to reducing the costs of operation and maintenance, a significant reduction in the complexity of an IT landscape and a rapid implementation of new applications. In Sect. 2.3 the concept was already outlined. In its core, cloud computing means that parts of one's own IT system are outsourced to specialized providers in "small packages"—it is thus a special (granular) form of the long-known and much-practiced IT outsourcing. Like bimodal IT, cloud computing also relies on complexity reduction by separating parts of the IT system, but in a different form. The claim of a quick availability of IT solutions is solved by the provision of standardized solutions and thus quite different from the concept of bimodal IT.

In cloud computing, a service provider provides IT services for a large number of companies and thus benefits from economies of scale. The connection between the own IT systems and the IT systems of the providers is established via interfaces, as is known within an organization. This special form of outsourcing has become possible through the simplified possibilities of coupling the computers of different companies via the Internet (the "cloud"). Technically, cloud computing is based on the principle of virtualization and distribution of IT-based service offerings. It can be described as a model that allows comfortable, demand-oriented, and network-based access to a shared pool of configurable computing resources that can be quickly deployed and released with little administrative effort.

Cloud computing today comes in three forms:

- Software as a Service,
- Platform as a Service,
- Infrastructure as a Service.

1. **Software as a Service** (SaaS) involves the provision of application software over the internet. Application-related services are provided by the cloud provider, who is also responsible for maintaining and operating the software. The software is not installed on the user's device, but on the provider's servers. The user only receives, according to his request, online access, which results in the representation on his device. The management and continuous improvement of the respective applications are left to the provider side. Modern e-commerce systems (e.g. webshops with payment processing) are increasingly being rented from external SaaS providers for a certain period of time, instead of building a website including a webshop internally. In contrast to software that is bought in the form of license fees and usually installed locally in the company (on-premise software), no license fee is usually charged for SaaS. SaaS services are usually rented and paid on a time basis.
2. **Platform as a Service** (PaaS) is an extension of the SaaS concept. This variant also includes the development and execution of software over the

internet. In PaaS environments, it is possible to supplement existing solutions with their own application software or to develop completely new ones. Platforms such as Google App Engine or Windows Azure make it possible to set up development environments including a selection of operating systems, programming languages, technical frameworks and databases independently of location and quickly.
3. **Infrastructure as a Service** (IaaS) means the virtualization of physical hardware. Depending on the demand, a company can be provided with computing power and storage space for different applications. In contrast to the classical IT infrastructure, the offer can be flexibly adapted to the current demand. For example, the access and retrieval of media content from a media library can be "elastic". The user only pays for the actually used computing power. R&D units of a company often use the enormous computing power of an IaaS provider to, for example, perform complex algorithms and simulations in a shorter time.

4.1.3.1 Use of Cloud Solutions by Companies

IaaS solutions make companies more flexible in critical resources such as storage space and can thus save costs. PaaS solutions can make the software development process more efficient. But SaaS solutions are of immediate importance for digital transformation.

SaaS providers can continuously invest in the further development of their solutions. IT users can only do this occasionally. Companies therefore have access to the latest IT solutions in encapsulated form through the use of SaaS solutions. This means that the solutions run by definition at the service provider and only have to be connected to the company's own IT landscape via a standardized interface—which often leads to an old, complex part of the company's own IT landscape being replaced or no new complex partial landscape having to be built up. In sum, the IT landscape of a company loses complexity through the introduction of SaaS solutions—significantly more than with classical standard software.

In addition, the following arguments are put forward for SaaS applications:

- SaaS solutions have a different cost structure. Instead of high investment costs for development or licenses as well as complex server landscapes, there are now periodic constant costs for operation, maintenance and support. In addition, demand (e.g. for work performance) can be adjusted to the current need at any time.

- In many fields, there is a large number of providers. This increases the competitive and quality pressure on SaaS providers. From the user's point of view, this can be expected to result in a continuous adaptation and improvement of the SaaS services. In addition, the fast and easy implementation of extensions and updates on the SaaS provider's side leads to further quality leaps of the offer and the possibility to design corresponding IT solutions in a user-friendly way.
- Furthermore, the use of SaaS solutions enables location-independent use of IT products. Regardless of the geographical location, employees of a company and their customers can access and use the IT services. This results in increasing flexibility for both companies and employees and customers. The relocation of existing IT solutions and their networking in cloud services also creates new value-added services or leaves room to test them in a separate environment, thus supporting companies in terms of their innovation capability.

4.1.3.2 Disadvantages and Risks of Cloud Solutions

The integration of SaaS solutions into the IT landscape entails some risks in addition to the advantages mentioned. Table 4.2 provides an initial overview.

Outsourcing of certain services and data to an external provider implies a certain **dependence relationship** between companies and SaaS providers. Companies give up part of their company-critical resources and knowledge and at the same time run the risk of losing knowledge about company-specific adaptation options for their software.

In addition, there is the **operational risk** that company-critical processes will be impaired if agreed service levels such as availability, performance and interoperability are not achieved. For example, long waiting times or delays in accessing a SaaS-based billing system would unnecessarily delay the

Table 4.2 Risks of SaaS for Companies in Digital Transformation (Benlian & Hess, 2009)

Risks	Short characterization
Strategic risks	Possible loss of company-critical resources through outsourcing to SaaS providers
Financial risks	Hidden or deferred costs from integration effort and additional services
Operational risks	Risk that agreed service levels are not achieved
Security risks	Entrusting critical company data to third parties
Social risks	Outsourcing of applications can lead to resistance within the workforce

billing process of a company and be counterproductive to the goal of possible resource conservation.

Financial risks can arise from hidden costs, such as those that were not finally assessable at the time of conclusion of the contract and only occur during operation. Hidden costs can occur during the integration of the SaaS solution into the existing IT landscape of a company (e.g. commissioning of specialized system integrators), but also when the SaaS provider increases the subscription price over the course of the contract or charges additional costs for services (e.g. mobile access to data).

Furthermore, when using such IT services, a company incurs a certain **security risk**. When transferring internal company data and analysis to an external service provider, the company must have great trust in the provider that the data will be processed, stored and protected safely by this provider. This is especially true for company-critical data.

Despite the risks mentioned, the advantages of cloud services are often seen as outweighing the disadvantages, especially in the context of digital transformation. The gradual use of cloud services is therefore often introduced as a support project for digital transformation (even if other goals are often achieved, such as the aforementioned reduction in IT costs). For example, 66% of companies say that cloud computing is an important step in quickly introducing new applications in the context of digital transformation (bitkom, 2018). In addition, cost advantages are often seen in the operation and maintenance of the systems. It is therefore to be expected that cloud solutions will gradually become an important part of the IT landscape of many companies. Only for very specific applications that cannot be obtained from the market or that should not be given to the outside world, cloud solutions are not an option.

4.1.3.3 Using Cloud Computing for Applications with Private Customers

The problem of integrating new applications, as they arise in the context of digital transformation, primarily affects the IT landscape of the provider—but not only. Often, new applications also have to be installed on the computers of private customers, whether they are stationary or mobile. Cloud computing is also suitable for this, especially in the form of software as a service. Data storage and processing operations take place exclusively with the provider or its service provider. This has been realized, for example, by the Internet services that support the exchange of images.

For end users, the advantages of a cloud solution lie primarily in the fact that they no longer need their own hardware resources for storing data and running application software. The continuous upgrading of storage media and the renewal of computing power lose importance, because both are provided by cloud service providers. In addition, often a rudimentary software in the form of a web browser or a simple client is sufficient to access a cloud service both stationary and on mobile end devices. The central storage and processing simplifiy the exchange and joint editing of, for example, images, music or videos with friends or family members.

Possible risks in the implementation of cloud computing for end users concern—similar to corporate users—above all the areas of security and data protection. The storage and processing of many customer data in one central place can be an interesting target for possible hackers. Therefore, cloud providers invest enormous financial and technical resources to maintain and secure their services.

4.2 Creating Organizational Structures that Facilitate Transformation: Do's and Dont's for Established Companies

In the context of digital change, there are plenty of examples of established companies being displaced, such as the decline of Brockhaus due to the new offering from Wikipedia. Currently, for example, it is the banks that, although they pursue digital visions and roadmaps, do not seem to be sufficiently able to identify innovative ideas early on and turn them into products, for example in the area of payment systems. A key role is played by the organizational structures of the established companies. These are often still focused on the efficient provision and incremental development of their existing products, rather than on the constant development of entirely new products, the business models required for this, and the processes required for their production. Often the problem has already been recognized. For example, a practice study from KPMG from 2016 shows that around 40% of the media companies surveyed consider the establishment of structures that promote innovation to be a very important task in digital transformation (KPMG, 2016). Nevertheless, the answer to the "how" is often lacking. The following section is intended to help with this. It shows which approaches there are to be successful as an established company in generating innovations.

Reference should also be made at this point to Sects. 3.2 and 3.4. There the product-oriented or process-oriented forms of organization are presented, which occasionally flank the creation of digital products or digital processes.

4.2.1 The Dilemma of the (Product) Innovator

Established companies are primarily concerned with incrementally improving their existing products in order to increase their margin. These evolutionary improvements address the needs of existing customers and thus improve the performance of the product. If customer requirements are largely constant, this is a sensible approach. However, if new technologies offer customers completely new and interesting options that are initially apparently irrelevant compared to established requirements, companies do not perceive the products based on these new technologies, because they apparently address a different segment. But if a customer is very convinced by the new product, his preferences change. After a certain time he prefers the new product, the demand for the old product decreases.

Product innovations that trigger this change in customer needs are—as mentioned briefly in Sect. 2.2—referred to as disruptive. Clayton Christensen coined this term (Christensen, 1997). It focuses strongly on changes in customer needs—and thus clearly differentiates a disruptive innovation from a significantly improved satisfaction of largely stable customer needs. Furthermore, he works out the dilemma of the provider, who tries to increase the profit from existing products and services, while on the other hand he is also aware that the customer's needs are changing. A well-known example is the introduction of smartphones a few years ago. As already mentioned in Sect. 2.2 , the first iPhone from Apple can be classified as a disruptive innovation—with it one could rather worse than better phone than with the mobile phone common on the market before, but one could use it as a portable computer.

Another real-world example may illustrate the phenomenon and also lead to a management perspective. In September 2010, the US video rental chain Blockbuster had to close about 6500 stores and file for bankruptcy. In 2010, the then CEO, John Antioco, was also offered the online streaming portal Netflix for US$ 50 million. But he rejected the offer. Today, Netflix has over 100 million streaming customers worldwide, is worth several billion and is the market leader. How did this come about? At first, the service was not interesting enough for Blockbuster customers to make

Blockbuster competitive. Netflix started in 1997 with a DVD shipping service. The founder, Reed Hastings, initially relied on DVD rental by post. But unlike Blockbuster, Netflix reacted early to forecasts and recognized that internet-based video streaming would eventually overtake DVD rental. The reaction of customers and media was initially not very positive. Since 2013, Netflix has recovered and has been growing rapidly since then. Video streaming has become more and more popular, and DVD rental by post has become less and less used. Netflix has successfully avoided an "Innovator's Dilemma" by recognizing the possibilities of the digital business quickly enough and investing in new technologies (Christensen et al., 2015).

Netflix has mastered the challenge. For many other companies this does not apply, they have focused on their established products and have thus ultimately disappeared from the market. These companies had been successful before, had high financial strength and broad knowledge, also about new technologies. So why didn't they invest in disruptive products? Christensen (1997) lists three reasons that contribute to the fact that companies do not make larger investments in disruptive products:

- Disruptive products are initially simpler, cheaper and often have lower margins.
- Disruptive products initially address less important market segments.
- Disruptive products initially often have no benefit for the profitable core customer base.

Although it is not easy for established companies to master disruptive challenges, companies are not helplessly. The first challenge is to recognize disruptive innovations.

One of the best-known approaches to early detection of disruptive innovations is based on a criteria catalog, which differentiates between the view of the established company and the new competitor. In this method, innovations are examined for their disruptive characteristics by means of interviews. Kaltenecker et al. (2013) have used this approach, for example, to check the disruptive characteristics of a cloud-based CRM solution from Salesforce against the established solution from SAP. Table 4.3 shows the result of the analysis from the perspective of SAP, the "Incumbent".

The criteria catalog shown in Table 4.3 is divided into three periods in order to analyze whether the innovation can reach the individual phases of diffusion. If an innovation can make it through all three phases to the end, a disruption is considered to be very likely. For example, in the first phase, an innovation is brought to the market by a new company. This is referred

Table 4.3 Evaluation of a Potentially Disruptive Innovation from the Perspective of an Established Company (Kaltenecker et al., 2013)

Phase	Criterion	Yes	No	Unknown
"Foothold Market Entry"	There are saturated customers	x		
	The main customers reject the new product	x		
	The market for products based on the potential disruptive innovation seems small and irrelevant		x	
Score:		2	1	0
"Main Market Entry"	Established performance features shift	x		
	Customers are not willing to pay for improvements to established performance features			x
	Switching costs are low		x	
Score:		1	1	1
"Failure of Incumbent"	The new products are not offered by the established company		x	
	Established companies flee to premium segments		x	
	The potential disruptive innovation is not realized in a separate organizational unit		x	
Score:		0	3	0
Total rating:		3	5	1

to as the "Foothold Market Entry Phase" because in this time frame the innovation is only demanded by a small, new customer base. The second phase is referred to as the "Main Market Entry Phase". Here it is analyzed whether the innovation can also address the majority of customers of the established market and be successful there. The third phase called "Failure of Incumbent" examines how the established company behaves. All characteristics of the criteria catalog are formulated in a positive way so that, if they can be considered fulfilled, they point to the disruptive potential of an innovation and thus the danger of a disruption. In the present case, it was already apparent at the time of the investigation that the new, cloud-based product has disruptive potential, but that the established company is dealing with this danger in the right way. This has also been confirmed in the aftermath.

4.2.2 Setting up a Digitalization Unit

Classic corporate structures are not necessarily conducive to innovation, as there are often firmly anchored roles and responsibilities, and often thinking is not done across departmental or even corporate boundaries. In addition, complex and lengthy processes, as well as a cumbersome corporate culture, make it difficult to explore new ways. Innovative employees with digital expertise are difficult to win and retain, often feeling that ideas are nipped in the bud. Changing the core organization fundamentally requires a lot of time, if it succeeds at all. Separating innovative activities is therefore an interesting approach that can support the development and implementation of digital innovations (Ebers, 2016). The idea behind this is that new ideas are not rejected as quickly when there is less internal competition for the existing business due to the independence of the organizational units.

The separation of innovation activities into partially autonomous units can also be seen as a response to the innovation dilemma described above. In established companies, disruptive innovations are often not taken into account because they do not generate quick profits and are often unprofitable at the beginning. As a result, evolutionary innovations are usually promoted in these companies. These companies should establish independent organizational units that are responsible for exploratory tasks, that is, for the development and implementation of innovations. The ability to adapt quickly and flexibly to changing environmental conditions is considered to be particularly pronounced in autonomous units. Independent organizational units should enable a faster detection of potential disruptive innovations, as these units can work with different goals than the existing business; they do not have to prioritize quick and profitable projects at the beginning over disruptive innovations. This concept can also prevent conflicts in terms of resource allocation. This makes it easier for employees to take initiative, go down unfamiliar paths, trigger discovery processes, and use innovative knowledge.

Digitalization units (also referred to as digital innovation units) can be seen as a form of these (partially) autonomous organizational units in which digital innovation activities are separated. in With these units, different objectives can be pursued, each of which requires different design forms (Fuchs et al., 2019; Barthel et al., 2020).

4.2.2.1 Objectives and Types of Digitalization Units

The main objective of digitalization units is basically the development of digital innovations. However, secondary objectives such as driving a culture change or building digital expertise can also be pursued. The innovation activities can have either an internal focus on business processes or an external focus on products, services, and business models. With an external focus, it can be further distinguished whether existing business fields are to be further developed or entirely new fields are to be opened up. The target of a digitalization unit is also defined by which steps it is to take in the innovation process. Is it only about generating and selecting ideas? Should the unit develop and implement the innovations itself? Does the unit also take over the marketing of the innovations? With these central parameters, the target of a digitalization unit can be defined.

Roughly, three types of digitalization units can be distinguished, with which different objectives can be pursued (Barthel et al., 2020).

Type 1, the "internal facilitator", is mainly concerned with innovations that concern the internal organization, such as business process innovations. He therefore has a very strong focus on what is already there and is looking for ways to transform the existing organization. Occasionally, a product or service innovation may also be sought, but only as a secondary result. The main task of these units is to collect or generate project ideas, develop process innovations, and then return them to the departments responsible for the implementation of the innovations. An example of type 1 would be the digitalization unit of a large bank, which, among other things, develops, tests, and implements new concepts for the internal business processes in human resources in order to explore new ways of talent acquisition and employee development.

Type 2, the "external enhancer", is concerned with the development of new digital products, services and business models and therefore has a stronger market orientation. Units of this type focus on innovations in existing business fields, i.e. they usually want to address existing customer groups. As with type 1, these units therefore transform the existing organization, but primarily target products and not internal processes. The tasks of these units include the generation and selection of innovation ideas and the development of prototypes. The marketing of innovations is then usually carried out again in the core organization. For example, the type 2 digitalization unit of a tool retailer and manufacturer develops personalized digital services for its B2B customers so that they can recognize the procurement need at an early stage and thus optimize their tool ordering and storage processes.

Type 3, the "external creator", develops new products, services and business models like units of type 2. However, in contrast to type 2, these units focus on innovations in new business fields, i.e. they want to address new customer groups and create entirely new business opportunities. These units often cover the entire innovation process, i.e. they start with idea finding and selection and then market the developed solutions themselves. The digitalization unit of a chemical company, which brings users together with local car workshops for the provision of repair services, could be mentioned as an example. The associated business model is independent of the core business of the company, but fits into the overall ecosystem (the chemical company also manufactures car paints).

Table 4.4 shows a comparison of the three types at a glance.

Which of the three types is chosen has a huge impact on the concrete design of a digitalization unit, which we will look at in the next section. Units of type 1 are usually conducted as close to the core organization as possible, since their innovation focus is also on the transformation of the core organization. Units of type 3 are usually given a lot of freedom so that they can explore new paths completely unhindered by the core business. With units of type 2, a middle way is taken.

A warning should be issued at this point. In various studies, we see that many digitalization units were founded "because one apparently does this when one wants to digitalize". Companies therefore observe, for example, that corresponding units are founded by competitors and then feel under pressure to follow suit. However, they have usually not thought much about the specific objectives of the newly founded units. This is strongly

Table 4.4 The Three basic Types of Digitalization Units (Barthel et al., 2020)

Type	Orientation	Coverage of the innovation process
Type 1, the "internal facilitator"	Internal, existing organization	• Generating and selecting ideas • Innovation development
Type 2, the "external enhancer"	External, existing business fields	• Generating and selecting ideas • Development of innovations • Partial implementation and marketing of innovations
Type 3, "external creator"	External, new business areas	• Generating and selecting ideas • Developing and implementing innovations • Partially marketing innovations

discouraged. Units that are founded without a clear purpose are often doomed to (expensive) failure. In the worst case, the acceptance of digitalization topics in the entire company then decreases and the opposite of what was intended is achieved. Therefore, before a company founds a digitalization unit, it should define clear goals (which may change over time) as far as possible and then decide on the appropriate design of the unit.

4.2.2.2 Design of Digitalization Units

As already mentioned, the design of a digitalization unit must match its objectives. In principle, different parameters influence how closely or loosely a digitalization unit is coupled to the existing core organization.

The selection of employees (**Staffing**) for the digitalization unit can either take place from the existing core organization or new employees can be recruited from outside the company. For the projects themselves, it must also be decided to what extent employees of the core organization, employees of the digitalization unit or external partners are involved. It is generally assumed that the involvement of existing employees leads to a closer coupling and the recruitment of external employees leads to a looser coupling.

The next central question arises with respect to the **budget**. Who provides the digitalization unit with financial resources and in what amount? Is the budget provided centrally or is there decentralized financing from several departments? Is there internal performance billing and/or does the unit generate its own sales? It is obvious that a digitalization unit that finances itself has, as a rule, more freedom than a unit that is perceived as a pure cost factor.

The question of the **location** should not be underestimated either. Especially during the first emergence of digitalization units, the impression arose that it would be advantageous to sit as far away from the core organization as possible, preferably in places with a strong start-up scene like Berlin. Meanwhile, however, many units seem to be moving more towards being located near the headquarters, but in their own premises.

In addition, numerous other decisions have to be made with regard to the **degree of freedom granted and the embedding** of the units. Is the digitalization unit legally independent, is it run as a staff unit or is it embedded in the line organization? Can the digitalization unit autonomously decide which projects it prioritizes? How often is the core organization reported to and to whom? Do managers of the core organization have direct access to employees of the digitalization unit?

Here it is necessary to weigh up carefully. If a unit is too closely linked to the core organization, this takes away the freedom for innovation from the unit, the basic idea of separating innovation activities is thus ultimately carried to absurdity. Instead of setting up a digitalization unit, the innovation activities could just as well be fully integrated. If a unit is too loosely coupled, the core organization cannot control the unit and cannot ensure that the solutions developed for the core organization also create value, for example by complementing the existing product portfolio in a meaningful way or creating attractive, future-oriented new business areas. The goal of making the core organization itself more innovative in the long term through exchange with the digitalization unit can also hardly be achieved in this case. In this case, a complete spin-off would probably be the more consistent variant. So there can be no general statements that one side (close or loose coupling) is always better than the other. However, the types mentioned above give indications of which side should be given more emphasis depending on the target direction.

Design of the Central Digitalization Unit in a Chemical Company

The digitalization unit of a large German chemical company deals with a variety of externally oriented innovation activities, including the enrichment of existing business fields with digital products and services, but also the development and implementation of digital products and business models for entirely new markets (Fuchs et al., 2019). Accordingly, the digitalization unit can be considered a combination of Type 2 and Type 3. The foundation of the unit took place as part of the digitalization strategy decided by the management. The digitalization unit is headed by the CDO of the core organization, which emphasizes its strategic importance. The unit is legally independent and is run as a limited liability company. Although its budget comes from central funds, it also has its own responsibility for profits and can reinvest the revenues it generates in its own projects. Accordingly, the unit also decides on its own project portfolio. The unit's location is near the corporate headquarters, but in its own premises. The design of the unit reflects its goals very well, both to enrich existing business fields digitally, but also to develop new business fields independently.

4.2.2.3 Add-on: Ambidexterity as an Abstract Ability of a Company

Ambidexterity describes in an abstract form the ability of companies to exploit new business areas (exploration) in parallel to the established business (exploitation). In the context of digital transformation, this ability can mean that companies successfully develop innovative digital business models while simultaneously successfully continuing their existing (non-digital) business. The relevant research has shown that there are different forms of ambidexterity (Holotiuk & Beimborn, 2019; O'Reilly & Tushman, 2011). If a company operates its exploitative existing and exploratory new businesses in separate organizational units, this form of ambidexterity is called **structural ambidexterity**. The company divides innovative businesses into autonomous units. This approach can be found, for example, in the previously described creation of (partially) autonomous digitalization units. In addition, there is the approach of **contextual ambidexterity**. Here, employees are given the opportunity to divide their working time freely between exploration and exploitation on an individual basis. Explorative and exploitative activities take place in the same business units, there is no structural separation. Here, the responsibility for innovation lies with the existing business. As a special form of this, **temporal ambidexterity** can be seen, in which employees are allowed to work full-time in exploratory units for a limited period of time, before returning to the established core business. Finally, **sequential ambidexterity** will be discussed. It is assumed here that the entire company alternately goes through cycles of exploration and exploitation. This form of ambidexterity has a very long-term perspective, as it requires "switching" and restructuring the entire organization each time. Therefore, it is questionable whether this approach is suitable for the dynamic context of digital transformation.

4.2.3 Collaboration with Start-ups as an Opportunity for Innovation in Digital Transformation

Digital transformation requires agility, technical innovation and a new approach to risks. However, many established companies lack the internal expertise and structures to meet these requirements and adapt their business model accordingly. One possible solution to this innovation dilemma (see Sect. 4.2.1) and thus a potential alternative to setting up one's own digitalization unit (see Sect. 4.2.2), at least for larger companies, is collaboration with start-ups. This allows established companies to have faster access to digital innovations and to benefit from the creativity and agility of young companies. In addition, this collaborative approach can reduce the later endangerment of one's own business model, as each start-up can also potentially become a competitor. From the start-up's point of view, collaboration with a large, established company can enable access to complementary and otherwise unavailable resources, such as customers, image or technology. Given this apparent win-win situation, it is not surprising that approximately 70% of all start-ups in the European Union work with an established company (Schleef et al., 2020).

Such collaboration entails a multitude of opportunities and challenges that arise from the asymmetry between the parties involved. Therefore, this section discusses the various possibilities for collaboration, such as corporate venturing, after a short characterization of start-ups. After a comparison of the advantages and disadvantages, a decision model is finally presented that can support companies in their considerations.

4.2.3.1 Characterization of Start-ups

In order to be able to evaluate a possible start-up collaboration, companies should first know the basic characteristics of start-ups. These are defined as "young commercial enterprises that were founded no more than five years ago, whose founders are employed full-time, have a founding team or employees and are innovation-oriented or growth-oriented, i.e. they carry out research and development in order to bring a technological innovation to market maturity, or offer at least one […] market novelty" (Metzger, 2020). The number of these young companies in Germany has stabilized in recent years. After the increases in 2017 and 2018, the number of start-ups remained at 70,000 in 2019 (Metzger, 2020). Among the most successful start-ups of recent years in the German-speaking world are (as of 2021) N26 (direct banking app), Horizn Studios (luggage with technical features), Holidu (search engine for vacation homes) and Celonis (process mining software).

The evolution of a start-up can be divided into different phases, which are often not clearly separated from each other and of different duration. In addition, not every startup necessarily goes through every phase. Ideally, the phases idea, foundation, growth and maturity can be distinguished. In the **idea phase** the so-called "market-fit" of the startup is developed. The focus is on the problem to be solved and the implementability of the idea, which is then transferred into a viable business model. Depending on the founding idea, the first prototype or a minimum viable product (MVP) is often created here. Under certain circumstances, revenues can already be generated by first customers. The **foundation** marks an important milestone in the evolution of a startup, because, among other things, the choice of legal form and the entry in the commercial register take place here. In these early phases, successful (tech) startups sometimes already collect subsidies from business angels or other early-phase investors of up to 0.5 million €. In the **growth phase** the start-up is then further developed and the product or service is established on the market. Especially promising tech startups with highly scalable business models (allow for fast and cost-effective expansion) can hope for investments from venture capital companies in the millions here. The growth is increasingly forced, investments are made and further expertise is obtained in order to gain market share. In the **maturity phase** the business model has finally been established and the company is prepared for a sustainable future, possibly the portfolio is expanded.

The success of a startup is initially largely dependent on the **founder's personality**. Successful founders often have special skills and character traits, such as innovative spirit and risk affinity. In addition, there are various measures for evaluating the success of a startup. The first important milestone is the founding of the company after the idea and planning phase, as well as the duration on the market. The "hard" key figures, which are relevant for an investment participation, include growth figures such as sales and number of customers or employees. Profitability only becomes relevant later. In the case of B2B software startups, for example, it is assumed that the achievement of the first ten paying customers marks a substantial milestone for the raising of investment funds and from here a significantly higher company valuation is possible. Many start-ups therefore try to develop a first MVP with little seed capital or purely with the founders' own resources (so-called bootstrapping) and to win customers before institutional investors are involved.

Established companies have different ways of working with start-ups. In addition to company hackathons (see also Sect. 5.2.3), in which start-ups have to work on innovation challenges in a given time frame, accelerator and incubator programs, as well as corporate venturing are possible forms of cooperation, which should be examined in more detail in the following. Figure 4.2 gives a first rough overview.

Accelerator Program	Incubator Program	Corporate Venturing
▪ Development of innovative products/services by start-ups with the aim of reaching market maturity within a few months. ▪ Company provides capital, infrastructure and mentoring	▪ Accompanying start-ups from an early stage with the aim of having them further develop (often their own) ideas ▪ Company provides office space, technical infrastructure, networks and coaching ▪ Investment horizon is adapted to start-ups	▪ Variant of venture capital ▪ Own corporate venture capital unit invests parent company capital in start-ups ▪ Objective primarily of a strategic nature, Investments therefore rather long-term ▪ If successful, full takeover also conceivable

Intensity of Cooperation →

Fig. 4.2 Possible Forms of Cooperation between Companies and Start-Ups

4.2.3.2 Accelerator and Incubator Programs

In recent years, accelerator and incubator programs have established themselves as popular practices for efficiency gains, access to technology and promotion of innovative work practices in companies. Since the terms are often used synonymously in practice, the programs should be presented and delimited below.

The so-called **Accelerator Programs** are programs with a duration of often three to four months, in which companies make start-ups capital in five-figure range, as well as infrastructure and mentoring available. In the shortest possible time, the start-ups should develop products that can be presented to investors at the end of the program. In return for the support, the companies receive a stake in the start-up. To be able to participate in such programs, founders' teams must apply to the companies and present their idea.

In addition, companies have the opportunity to establish so-called **Incubator Programs**. Incubators are facilities that accompany start-ups on the way to set up a company and support them throughout the entire life cycle. In contrast to accelerator programs, the start-up's business idea is still in its early stages and is refined during the course of the program. Often, the established company also brings its own ideas, which are then further developed by start-ups in a safe environment. In these "start-up incubators", companies offer start-ups rental space as office space, make technical infrastructure available, help to form networks and coach in setting up a company. Start-up financing is also possible, partly in exchange for company shares. Overall, the cooperation between companies and start-ups is more intense in incubator programs than in accelerator programs.

Examples of these programs are the Deutsche Telekom's technology incubator hub:raum, which supports early-stage start-ups in the technology sector; or ProSiebenSat.1's accelerator program, under which TV and digital media budgets are invested in promising, mass-market-ready product ideas (as of 2021). Companies can also join networks in this context, e.g. the Start-up Bootcamp with 140 partners, including Intel, Vodafone and Allianz.

Success factors for such programs include, for example,

- Industry focus
- Strong network of investors, customers, suppliers, mentors and partners
- Management team with experience in founding
- Sufficient capitalization
- Appropriate location (e.g. near universities and research institutions)
- Top-level commitment
- Internal marketing to create acceptance within the established company

However, when deciding on the establishment of such a program, companies should take into account the fact that they are not uncontroversial among founders. Reasons for this include unfulfilled promises of care or, on the other hand, too much influence. Companies also have to expect that start-ups with really innovative business ideas will turn directly to venture capitalists. In order to avoid this "mismatch", companies should make sure that these programs are not only designed along their own needs and also require a certain risk affinity.

4.2.3.3 Corporate Venturing

When it comes to **corporate venturing**, this refers to "an attempt by large companies to replicate the properties of small and young companies that are significant for innovative activities and to combine them with their own strengths such as market power and financial resources" (Gruber & Henkel, 2005, p. 139). A well-known example is the Siri language assistant from Apple, which was not developed by the technology giant itself, but by a start-up called Siri Inc., from which Apple bought all rights to the product. For the realization of such investments, established companies have the opportunity to set up their own corporate venture capital unit (**CVC unit**) (Klamar & Prawetz, 2018). These CVC units are often implemented as independent units within the companies, exclusively provided with capital and have the necessary flexibility and speed to compete in the venture capital market. These arms operate similarly to traditional venture capital firms (e.g. Project A Ventures, Unternehmertum, Global Founders Capital; as of 2021), but do not invest the money of various investors, but only that of the parent company. Measured by the number of registered patents, these CVC units are up to four times more successful than the "competing" internal research and development departments of established companies (Klamar & Prawetz, 2018). Of course, the start-up's contribution to increasing corporate value is also counted. In the case of successful investments, a complete takeover or merger is also possible. In addition to the variant of participating in existing ventures, corporate venturing is often also understood as an "inside-out" variant, whereby companies themselves set up start-ups (with up to 100% equity in their own hands), which are then sold, for example, at a later stage.

In contrast to this **external corporate venturing**, venture activities can also be carried out within one's own company. **Internal corporate venturing** focuses on the development of new products/business models within the company's boundaries. Venture capital is thus only made available to the employees of the respective company with the aim of increasing the company's innovation power and motivation and accelerating the founding of new business areas. Although this approach often provides a short-term boost to innovation activities, it cannot keep up with the external variant in the long term due to corporate structures and is therefore not further considered here.

Since the opening of the first corporate venture fund in the 1960s, companies in the fields of technology, pharmaceuticals and telecommunications have been active in this market. However, in the age of digital transformation, companies from other sectors are also well advised to at least evaluate the advantages of corporate venturing for themselves. Established companies thus gain innovation power, technology competence and agility, while the start-up gains financial performance and market access. These opportunities are offset by challenges resulting from the symbiosis of two different market participants, which will be examined in more detail below.

4.2.3.4 Cooperation with a Start-up—Yes or No?

The success of a corporate venture collaboration arises from the combination of the advantages of the established company and the start-up (Schleef et al., 2020). The companies can provide financial resources and have efficient production capacities as well as general know-how, credibility and market access. In contrast, start-ups bring agility, innovation and expertise in new digital technologies (Rothaermel, 2001). The opportunities and challenges for the established company in such a cooperation are shown in Table 4.5.

If you take a look at successful CVC units, they show the following practices (Basu et al., 2016):

- Minimizing contract complexity and protecting the interests of founders increases the reputation of the CVC unit as an attractive and integrated partner, which leads to a higher number of investment opportunities and thus to higher search efficiency
- An investment in the early stages allows for the realization of competitive advantages, as access to future-oriented technologies takes place before the competition
- The development of a collaboration plan before the transaction with the start-up creates a mutual sense of duty and drives integration forward
- By avoiding competition with existing departments, resistance to the CVC unit and to the start-ups is reduced

In view of the advantages and disadvantages as well as success factors mentioned, the question arises as to whether and when an established company

Table 4.5 Opportunities and Challenges of Corporate Venturing for Companies

Opportunities	Challenges
• "Window on Technology" (access to start-ups and the scene in general) • Generating knowledge about new markets and business areas and the resulting growth opportunities • Saving own R&D costs • Faster reaction to new developments • Marketing effect/reputation • Chance of cultural change through contact with start-up culture • Access to new customer groups or knowledge about own end customers (e.g. Flaschenpost acquisition by Dr. Oetker)	• Identification of the right start-up • Complex acquisition processes (can take as long as setting up one's own start-up in doubt) • Integration of the start-up (different cultures and working methods) • Keeping the founders/start-up employees within the established corporate culture • High premiums/multiples for equity investments

should enter into a venture with a start-up. While this question of course depends on the individual case, answering the questions posed in Fig. 4.3 can help companies make the decision.

In **exploratory projects**, established companies typically look for digital know-how and creativity, which young companies usually bring with them. Business competence and absolute customer orientation are also often required here. In targeted projects, a careful assessment is required as to which other competencies and partners are needed. If there is no final business case yet and the project is in the **conceptual phase**, young companies can also be useful in this phase through innovative problem-solving skills. For projects that require greater **implementation capacity** (e.g. for system integration, but also for production and delivery), start-ups may fit less into the profile and cooperation with other established companies could be more advantageous. If the company intends to outsource the **project management responsibility**, start-ups in later phases (so-called scale-ups) are more experienced and therefore better suited than early-stage start-ups.

It becomes clear that cooperation with start-ups should be initiated at the beginning of the innovation process. Once the digital transformation project has left the conceptual phase, start-ups can no longer play their strengths to the same extent. Companies therefore have to carefully consider whether and when to enter into a cooperation with a start-up. These considerations should take into account the project status and the skills required to advance the project. In addition to the digital competence, which is obviously at the heart of the digitalisation, in particular the aspects of solution and project

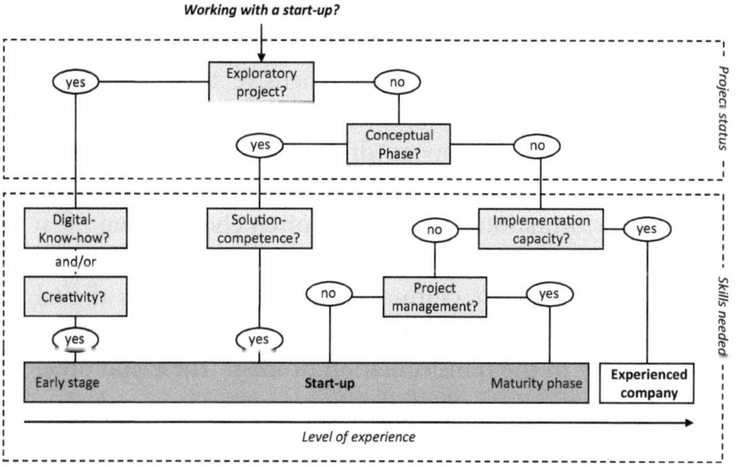

Fig. 4.3 Decision Model (based on Hogenhuis et al., 2016)

management competence must not be neglected. The basic attitude of the management of the company towards start-ups and its risk appetite are also not to be underestimated. Investment decisions are often made quickly and under incomplete information, so that it is more a matter of managing the start-up well than of making a watertight decision on the basis of fixed criteria. In order to "test" the potential of such a cooperation in advance, there is also the possibility of entering into a supply partnership with the start-up. This partnering can be more attractive than a direct investment, as sales are generated. In the event of a positive outcome, the company may possibly participate in the start-up later.

Finally, it should be noted that cooperation with a start-up in order to strengthen digital competence requires a rethink in established companies. Such projects often fail due to insufficient conception and an unclear mandate from management. The CVC unit should be integrated into the company in a sound manner and it should be ensured that existing employees do not feel threatened by their activities and have an appropriate open attitude. In addition, a sufficiently strong strategic fit between the company and the start-up is central in order for cooperation with start-ups to really offer an innovation opportunity in digital transformation.

4.3 Transforming Corporate Culture: A Tough Challenge

Corporate culture reflects the "personality" of a company, so to speak the DNA of the company, which makes it unique and thus represents a competitive advantage. However, the ambivalence of this competitive advantage becomes particularly apparent in comprehensive transformation processes: In the best case, corporate culture acts unnoticed as a catalyst, i.e. as a lubricant, which allows the company to drive and support the transformation. More often, however, corporate culture makes itself felt as a rigid structure that impedes transformation processes and often chokes them off at the root.

But what is corporate culture at all? What role does it play in digital transformation? Which corporate culture is adequate to master digital transformation, and with which approaches and which procedure can culture be changed specifically in the transformation process? These and other resulting questions will be answered in the following section.

4.3.1 What is Corporate Culture?

Edgar H. Schein's three-level model (2010) provides a simple and understandable model to make culture tangible (see Fig. 4.4). The model is often represented graphically as an iceberg to emphasize the distinction between visible and invisible culture elements.

At the top of the iceberg are the so-called **artifacts**—visible elements that allow a first conclusion to be drawn about the culture underlying them. Such artifacts are diverse and range from formal cultural manifestos such as the communicated corporate philosophy, annual reports or products of a company to the "look & feel" of the offices, the dress code, the address of colleagues to organizational symbols or internal company myths and legends. Here one of the problems of an artifact-centered understanding of culture becomes apparent: Although artifacts are easily accessible because they are visible; however, an understanding of the underlying assumptions is necessary for their correct interpretation. So the morality of internal company myths may be obvious to the members of the company, but externals will have a harder time interpreting it without knowledge of the context and the understanding of values, and may even come to quite different conclusions.

Beneath the surface lies the second level of culture of a company (and generally of any organization), which is no longer directly visible, but can still be guessed. This level consists of **collective values** (norms and philosophies) which are considered ideal by the members of the organization and thus influence their behavior. This understanding reveals another property

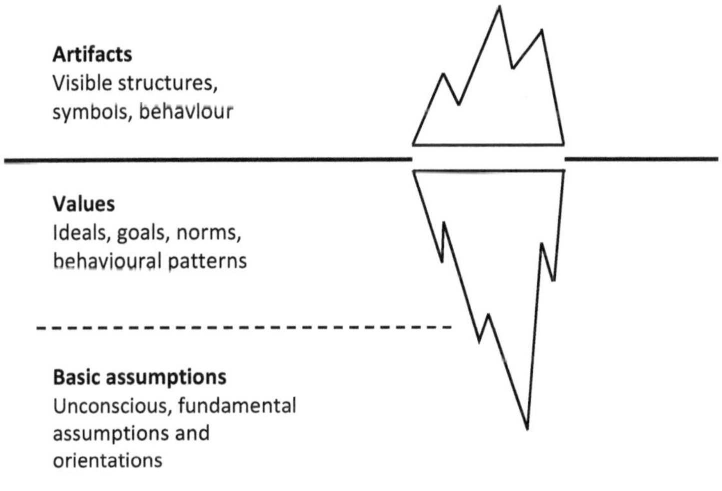

Fig. 4.4 Schein's Culture Model (2010)

of culture: Culture is always a shared, common understanding of what is considered important and desirable by several individuals. However, this understanding does not necessarily have to be shared by the whole company. Within an organization, there can certainly be different, sometimes contradictory value systems of individual subcultures. However, these usually overlap at least in the basic assumptions, the third level of culture.

Basic assumptions are deeply rooted assumptions that have become self-evident over time and are no longer questioned. These implicit, subconscious assumptions about values and ideal procedures, similar to the majority of an iceberg, can hardly be guessed. However, they decisively influence the actions of organization members, their perception and thinking, and form the very context in which artifacts must be interpreted. Historically, basic assumptions arise from values that have proven themselves over time and have become increasingly self-evident.

This reflects a significant point: culture is not a static structure, but a growing, evolving system. In the early stages of an organization, its culture is strongly influenced by the founders. The personalities, values, ideals and visions of the founders shape the cooperation and culture in the just-emerging organization. Newcomers find in the organization an increasingly solidified set of rules of accepted and expected behavior to which they must adapt. Over time, experience and learning effects play an increasingly shaping role. Therefore, culture is often defined as an expected pattern of behavior expected of a group, consisting of action strategies that have proven to be successful problem-solving patterns in the past. These learned patterns of behavior now set the expectations for future behavior and thus serve as a rulebook with regard to what is considered correct behavior and approach to problems.

The justification for past success explains in principle why it is so difficult to the change culture. Statements like "we've always done it that way" are only the manifestation of a much deeper problem: the internalization of behavior. While successful action strategies initially served only as orientation for future behavior, they solidify with continued success to "normal" and self-evident behavior—that is, they develop increasingly into expected, idealized behavior that manifests itself as a value of a group. Since these are implicit cultural elements, the members of an organization are not necessarily aware of their value-determined expectations, which is why their influence on behavior is much more difficult to grasp and change than just the pattern of a "we've always done it that way". In summary, it can be said that the culture of an organization is shaped by its founders or other role models and consists of internalized patterns of behavior of the members of the organization.

How strongly corporate culture influences the actions of its members or how uniformly values are represented within an organization depends, on the one hand, on the strength and clarity of the values and visions lived by the leaders. On the other hand, the strength of culture has a temporal dimension: its influence is all the stronger, the more stable a group is in itself, the longer it has already existed and the closer the group members work together, that is, exchange common experiences. Culture does not have to be uniform across the entire organization. As already mentioned above, subcultures with divergent value systems can exist within an organization, which have developed, for example, due to different task requirements or professional backgrounds. It is quite conceivable that the subculture in a controlling department focuses much more on a guideline-oriented and minutely documented way of working than the subculture in the graphics department of the same company, which is likely to support creativity and deviation from the norm. But both subcultures can have common values and basic assumptions that are shared throughout the organization—so to speak, the intersection of subcultures, which makes up the core of corporate culture, the DNA of the company.

4.3.2 Adequate Culture for Digital Transformation

Corporate culture plays a key role in the digital transformation of companies, culture significantly affects the success of digitalization measures and thus ultimately the success of transformation into a digital company. According to a survey by Capgemini (Schaefer et al., 2017), in 2017 more than half of the companies surveyed cited culture as the biggest obstacle to successful digital transformation. It is therefore not surprising that both in various practice studies and in the press as well as within the companies themselves, the call for a necessary cultural change is loud. And quite rightly: Comprehensive transformation measures, such as those necessary in the course of the digital transformation of companies, are doomed to failure without a supportive corporate culture as a basis. In order to fully exploit the potential of new technologies, it is not enough to implement them in the company through new products, processes and business models—even the best technologies only work if the employees know how to deal with them, what they are for and how the resulting possibilities can be perceived. The introduction of a new communication system to promote cross-departmental cooperation in a siloed work supporting culture without corresponding accompanying change measures is wasted money. Innovation competitions will remain unused as long as the respective corporate culture does not promote innovation as a desirable ideal.

4.3.2.1 Resilient Organizations as Cultural Role Models

In connection with the call for a cultural change, the ideal image of a digital culture is often evoked, but mostly without defining it more precisely. So what does this digital culture look like, which represents an adequate corporate culture for the successful digital transformation of companies? In order to answer this question, the short- and long-term tasks and challenges that need to be mastered with the support of a suitable corporate culture in the digital transformation have to be considered first.

On a **first level**, digital culture should support the transformation from an analog to a digital company, which fully exploits the potential of digital technologies in its products and processes and for its business models. On a **second level**, digital technologies present companies with much more comprehensive challenges. Due to the ever faster emergence of new digital technologies, companies are finding themselves in an increasingly uncertain business environment. The existence of companies whose value creation can be easily digitalized is threatened. Through new business models that are based on digital technologies and can be scaled quickly, entry barriers are falling away. Intruders can disrupt entire industries, and established companies are increasingly confronted with a change in customer needs driven by new technologies. In order to continue to be successful in this uncertain and constantly changing environment, companies must adapt to this, act flexibly and anticipate future digital-driven innovations. A strongly hierarchical, process-focused corporate culture would be fatal here. The digital culture appropriate for this environment is similar to the concept of a resilient organization.

The term **resilience** (Lengnick-Hall et al., 2011) primarily describes the ability to anticipate fundamental changes at every relevant level, to respond accordingly, and to recover from them if necessary. When comparing successfully resilient companies in the past, it becomes apparent that they share commonalities: a company-wide commitment to improved resilience, active and situation-oriented monitoring of opportunities and risks for the company—and above all a culture that promotes adaptability, agility and innovation.

These are, according to initial results, also the cornerstones of a digital culture adequate for digital transformation. A corporate culture that supports companies in their digital transformation and promotes long-term resilience is based on market- and employee-oriented values that, in combination, promote the agility of the company. This digital culture and its values, which have been identified here, are described in detail below (Duerr et al., 2018; Hartl & Hess, 2017). An overview can be found in Fig. 4.5.

4.3.2.2 Market Orientation as a Value in the Context of Digital Transformation

As described in the introduction, companies undergoing digital transformation are initially confronted with the development of new products, processes and business models based on digital technologies. They must react in order to remain relevant in the digital age. The foundation for this is a **market orientation** of the company, including the culture, which enables digital innovation. Innovation also serves as a countermeasure and protection measure to anticipate market developments and disruptions in an increasingly uncertain environment, to react as quickly as possible, and to ideally use them for themselves.

A central and essential value for a market-oriented and innovative corporate culture is a strong **customer focus.** This means an attitude of the

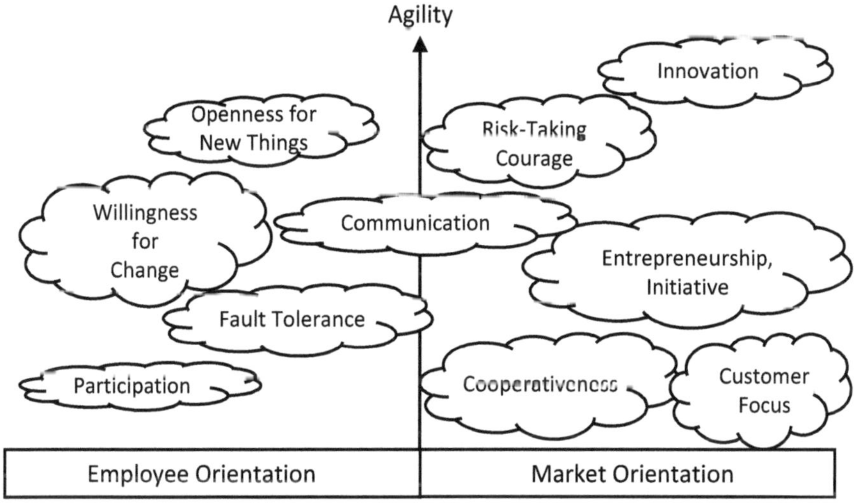

Fig. 4.5 Central Values of a Digital Culture (Hartl & Hess, 2017)

company that is customer-centered, that is, the orientation of all processes and products to the needs of the customer and the desire to serve them in the best possible way. This value is often praised as an ideal, regardless of the digital transformation, but it gains enormous importance against the background of the rapidly changing customer needs or expectations and requirements for products and services resulting from the progressing digitalization. An understanding of the customer needs changing through digital technologies is essential in order to be able to serve them and to take up corresponding market developments.

In order to be able to use the potential of new technologies, not only the resulting market developments have to be recognized, but these have to be subsequently implemented in innovations. Therefore, an **innovation-promoting culture** should primarily promote the development and further development of ideas. Values that promote the development of new ideas are **entrepreneurship** and **initiative.** This refers to the mindset of employees to develop and pursue ideas independently. A corporate culture that gives its employees the mantra of continuous improvement and further development implicitly requires them to develop ideas continuously. The basis for this is the empowerment of employees: If employees are given space and support for independent experimentation and the further development of ideas into more mature concepts, these quickly mature into testable prototypes—which can be tested and either discarded or developed into real innovations and ultimately drive the digital transformation of the company.

Further development, as well as early testing and experimentation of ideas, are of course mostly associated with uncertainty. The courage to take risks is therefore a central and not to be underestimated value of innovative corporate cultures. This means the willingness to take risks and not to shy away from decisions under uncertainty. In the course of digital transformation, new and unknown approaches are necessary, the success of which is often not predictable in advance. The courage to explore and radicalize them anyway and to accept them must be clearly promoted within a corporate culture so that employees can "conscientiously" take such risks. For this, a climate of tolerance and mutual respect is necessary in which employees can dare to suggest also unconventional ideas. In a digital corporate culture, the development of new, unconventional ideas is not only tolerated, but actively supported and promoted. The following therefore considers the second pillar of digital cultures: employee-oriented values.

4.3.2.3 Employee Orientation as a Value in the Context of Digital Transformation

In a corporate culture that punishes mistakes and puts the blame on someone, it is unlikely that an employee will leave his or her comfort zone to drive digital, risky initiatives. Keywords such as error culture, trial & error, "try often—fail fast" therefore reflect an important aspect of a digital culture. This refers to the values of **fault tolerance**—and contrary to what the name suggests, this is not just about tolerating errors, but even about actively promoting them. Tolerating errors creates an environment on the one hand that takes away the fear of employees to pursue radical and also unusual ideas, to make risky decisions and thus to promote the innovation of the company. On the other hand, actively promoting failure can also have a positive effect on the organization and accelerate the digital learning curve. If employees are encouraged to try out radical ideas, the failure of some projects is actually programmed. The awareness within the organization that this is not only okay, but that a fast failure is even desired, as this can generate useful insights, creates a fertile environment for far-reaching innovations.

Another value that companies should urgently give their employees is **openness to new things.** Digital technologies not only pose risks for companies, but also hold new potential and opportunities. In order to be able to seize these, however, companies and their employees must be willing to leave their comfort zone and adapt to new conditions in order to make use of the resulting opportunities. There needs to be an openness to new things within the company, a sort of basic curiosity, in order to discover and try out the unknown. Closely linked to this is the **willingness to change.** Not only a new, constantly changing environment created by new technologies requires adaptation by companies, but also the digital transformation of the company itself—or rather its measures—require a willingness to change. For a successful transformation of a company, it is crucial that the employees are open to new technologies, working methods and general changes and show the willingness to accept new things. The opposite of this would be a company culture oriented towards stability, which gives its employees security in known processes and thus leads to a certain resistance to change and everything new. This would be fatal for the success of any measure designed to promote digitalization, and thus deadly for a successful digital transformation of the company. An organizational value that promotes the willingness to accept changes and invest in the success of change measures is **participated** within the company. If employees of all levels are involved in change processes from the beginning, if their opinion and feedback is obtained and reacted to accordingly, change measures achieve demonstrably greater success because change is better accepted.

4.3.2.4 Agility as a Value in the Context of Digital Transformation

The two pillars of the above-mentioned values oriented towards the market and employees aim at a more resilient organization which is able to act and react agile. Agility, i.e.—in this context—the ability to act and react quickly and flexibly as well as make decisions, is crucial for the success of transformation measures and the existence of digitally transformed companies and thus an overarching value of a digital corporate culture. In order to be able to work customer-centered in an increasingly uncertain environment, product development cycles need to be shortened. Hierarchical, strictly predefined waterfall models have become obsolete. In their place, more agile approaches are emerging, in which development teams work closely with the customer side to include customer needs in product development to the best possible extent. Departments that have previously operated largely independently of each other now need to work closely together.

However, the cultural soil must first be prepared. The values of **communication** and **willingness to cooperate** are therefore important basic requirements for a digital corporate culture that makes agility possible. A hermit-like culture à la "us against them" could destroy all cooperation. In a digital culture, silo thinking is broken down and values such as teamwork and open communication support both internal collaboration and external cooperation with partners. An open, collaboration- and communication-oriented culture can support the new requirements for cooperation and thus contribute to faster production cycles, decision-making and ultimately a more agile company.

The values mentioned so far do not stand alone, but rather depend on each other and only then enable further values. For example, many of the values mentioned above for employee-oriented companies only enable an environment in which new ideas can be generated and developed into innovations. On the other hand, employees of a customer-oriented company would be striving to meet the changing customer requirements on their own and therefore be more willing to accept and implement the necessary changes. A customer-oriented corporate culture can thus promote the willingness to change and adaptability of a company, as it is able to provide employees with the justification and meaning behind these measures and thus involve them in the transformation of the company.

4.3.2.5 Conclusion

If you put all these values and aspects of digital culture together, you can simply describe it as **both family and business culture**—a corporate culture that is also common in digital start-ups. Therefore, established companies often use them as role models and target images for their digital transformation and digital culture. Now, a 20-person start-up is often participatory by virtue of its small size alone, and the employees naturally bring more initiative and openness to new things than is common in a medium-sized company or corporation that has been established for decades. A start-up culture, as it is found in start-ups, will therefore be difficult to transfer to established companies—and the question of whether this is even desirable remains open. However, the general direction is quite right.

The conclusion that this proclaimed ideal digital culture helps companies to meet the requirements of digital transformation seems to be confirmed in practice. A study conducted in cooperation with Deloitte at MIT shows that digitally advanced companies have an agile, risk-taking, collaborative culture with decentralized power structures than companies that are still at the beginning of their digital transformation (Kane et al., 2015). 80% of digitally advanced companies said they were actively taking measures to support and develop a digital culture. In German companies, culture is often still seen as the biggest obstacle to the success of transformation measures and a change in culture is considered urgently necessary. By acquiring digital start-ups or recruiting "digital natives", it is hoped that their culture can be adapted and a change "bottom-up" can be promoted. However, culture management remains the task of executives who actively promote and live the culture change.

But how to proceed and where to start? This will be explained in the following paragraph.

4.3.3 Selected Tools for Managing Cultural Change

There are a large number of ways in which the culture of a company can be analyzed and changed. Three important approaches are described below.

4.3.3.1 Culture Analysis

The **"Organizational Culture Assessment Instrument"** (Cameron & Quinn, 2011), abbreviated OCAI, developed by Cameron and Quinn, is a very simple and easy to use tool for capturing the status quo of a company's culture and tracking its change. The basis for the OCAI is the "Competing Values Framework" which has been validated multiple times through studies. This framework distinguishes between two basic value dimensions: flexibility versus stability and internal versus external focus. If you cross both axes with each other (see Fig. 4.6), you get a typology of four ideal-typical company cultures: clan, adhocracy, hierarchy, and market cultures. The digital culture desired for the digital transformation would correspond to a mixture of clan and adhocracy culture in this field—that is, the combination of collaborative and entrepreneurial culture described above.

The OCAI captures the prevailing culture of a company based on six dimensions:

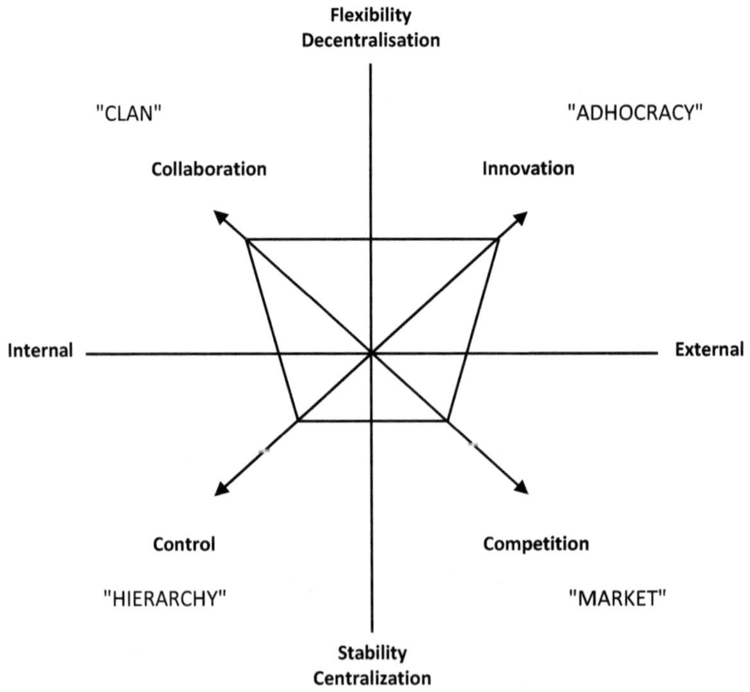

Fig. 4.6 Application of the "Competing Values Framework" (Cameron & Quinn, 2011)

- dominant characteristics,
- leadership style,
- employee relations,
- organizational cohesion,
- strategic orientation,
- success criteria.

For each of the cultural dimensions, four possible answers are given, each representing one of the cultural types. The respondent must first distribute 100 points over each of the four possible answers in order to capture the current manifestation of the company culture. If desired, another 100 points can be divided up afterwards—this time to capture the desired ideal culture of the respondent. Based on the results of the status quo analysis, the direction and necessary measures for a change towards a digital corporate culture can be derived. During the change process, the OCAI can also be used to show changes in the perception of employees and to make a cultural change measurable. For example, a company could conduct a company-wide employee survey using the OCAI questionnaire. Possible areas of focus:

- How far is the current corporate culture from the digital culture described above? This could give an indication of the extent of the necessary cultural change.
- Are there any differences in the perception of culture between employees and managers? If so, it would be necessary to create a common, realistic picture of the prevailing corporate culture in the first step. If the managers have a false image of the culture, this can prevent their support for change measures in the worst case—in the sense of: "Why should my team participate in the workshop? We've been working together openly and participatively for a long time now …".
- Are there any cultural differences between the departments? A departmental evaluation could show how much support the respective departments need in their cultural change.
- How successful have the previous change measures been? A re-survey three, six, or twelve months later could show, in comparison with the results of the first survey, whether and in which areas the corporate culture has changed.

4.3.3.2 IT Systems as Tools for Cultural Change

The question of whether the digitalization of the company, i.e. the implementation of certain IT systems, can itself be a tool for changing culture has not yet been finally clarified. It is clear that the introduction of IT systems and their use by employees strongly influences an organization and can contribute to changing habits and behavior (Volkoff et al., 2007). It would also be naive to believe that IT systems are value-neutral and that their introduction has no impact on the culture of a company. In the literature, several studies have indeed shown a change in corporate culture after the introduction of ERP, database or project management systems. In particular, the latter, together with communication or so-called enterprise social network systems, is said to have a great potential for changing corporate culture in relation to digital transformation.

As an example, the introduction of a classical chat tool is considered. Before the introduction of the tool, employees of the company only had the possibility to communicate via classical channels such as e-mail and telephone and to obtain feedback from their colleagues on urgent questions. However, colleagues may often be in meetings, so they cannot be reached by telephone, and in the flood of e-mails, short requests quickly disappear, so the answer is delayed. From a purely functional point of view, the new tool now enables employees to chat with their colleagues for a short time—but this opens up completely new possibilities for action: faster, informal communication, which makes it possible to obtain quick feedback on short questions and thus enables a more efficient, flexible and informal way of working—all values that are carried into the company through the introduction of the chat tool and can change existing work processes and -procedures. However, it is and remains essential for such an IT-induced organizational change that the systems introduced for change are also accepted and used by members of the organization—because without contact with the user, the potential for change of IT will remain unused.

Cultural Change Through IT Systems at Klöckner & Co

An example of how the introduction of IT tools can successfully support digital cultural change is provided by Klöckner & Co. The company deliberately used Yammer, an internal corporate social network, to support its far-reaching transformation strategy with a profound culture change.

Klöckner & Co is one of the largest international metal traders and digital pioneers in the steel industry. The supply and value chain in the steel industry was previously highly inefficiently organized: Many transactions were still carried out by telephone, fax or e-mail, and there was no consistent digital order and production management. As part of the company strategy "Klöckner & Co 2020", Klöckner therefore aimed for the complete digitalization of the supply and value chain in order to build an internet-based industry platform for the steel and metal industry, which would eliminate the prevailing information asymmetries through the digital networking of all market participants and thus significantly increase efficiency for all parties involved. In order to implement this vision, the business model of Klöckner & Co had to be completely modernized and digitized—in short: the company had to be digitally transformed. One of the most important drivers of the associated culture change was the introduction and use of a company-wide social network. A social network supports employees in the development and implementation of new ideas and promotes hierarchy-free communication with colleagues across departmental boundaries. This made it possible for Klöckner & Co to break down communication silos and create fast, hierarchy-free communication channels and thus the best conditions for innovative work (Klöckner & Co, 2018).

4.3.3.3 The Role of Leaders

The role of leaders in change processes, especially in cultural change, should not be underestimated in any way. Their contribution to the success of change can hardly be emphasized enough. Culture is something shared within a company, but ultimately it is in the hands of leaders which values are lived or can be lived—by promoting or prohibiting corresponding behavior. This makes it the leaders who largely shape the culture of a company and who must necessarily contribute to a cultural change (Alvesson & Sveningsson, 2015).

In the first step, this primarily means involving leaders in the change. A promising step would be, for example, to tune the entire leadership team into the change in a digital bootcamp in order to awaken commitment and above all enthusiasm in the participants, which they can then pass on to their employees in the next step. That leaders not only communicate the new values to their employees, but live them themselves and actively demand them, is essential in order to trigger a cultural change at all. Whether leaders live the new values themselves or not makes the difference and decides whether the values are only perceived as pretty letters on the office wall or as new guidelines of action and thus determine the behavior and work of employees. As simple as the instrument "leading by example through leaders" may sound, it is a very decisive factor for the success of the digital cultural change.

4.3.4 Specific Procedure in a Cultural Change Project

There is not much disagreement about how to approach cultural change concretely. Alvesson and Sveningsson (2015) bring together two different approaches to cultural change in their approach: the "Reframing of Everyday Life" and the "Grand Technocratic Project". While the former is based on rather local, limited initiatives by individual managers, the "Grand Technocratic Project" is an approach to change culture comprehensively and across the company.

Since a company-wide cultural change in the course of digital transformation is the goal, the focus is subsequently on the **"Grand Technocratic Project"**. Here, a comprehensive change process is carried out, which typically takes place "top-down" and offers itself as an approach for a support project for digital transformation. Typically, two phases are gone through: an analysis phase and an implementation phase.

Both phases, their most important steps and exemplary tools are described in detail below. In Table 4.6 you will find a first overview.

4.3.4.1 Analysis Phase

In order to manage a corporate culture sensibly and make it fit for digital transformation, the status quo, i.e. the current corporate culture, must first be recorded. It is essential for a manager not to rely on his gut feeling and his own perception of the corporate culture. Because, as the results of a survey conducted by Capgemini show, managers and employees often have widely divergent ideas about how digital the culture of the company already is (Schaefer et al., 2017). While 20% of the managers surveyed in German companies said that their corporate culture was already digital, not a single one of the employees surveyed was of the same opinion.

Table 4.6 Procedure in a Grand Technocratic Project (Alvesson & Sveningsson, 2015)

Analysis	Step 1: Evaluation of the company situation and determination of goals and strategic direction
	Step 2: Analysis of the status quo culture and target culture
	Step 3: Show gaps between status quo and target
	Step 4: Development of a change plan
Implementation	Step 5: Implementation of the plan: Unfreeze, Change, Refreeze
	Step 6: Evaluating the change, monitoring changes and adapting the plan

A very simple and easy to use tool to get a first impression of the prevailing corporate culture is the "Organizational Culture Assessment Instrument" (OCAI) developed by Cameron and Quinn, which was introduced in Sect. 4.3.3.1. The results of the OCAI provide a good first impression of the culture prevailing in the company. However, a more detailed insight is necessary for a more detailed analysis, for example, a depth interview-based analysis. Here it is recommended that both interviews and analyses be carried out by external partners, because which manager would like to hear that he or she practices a hierarchical leadership style or which employee would make such a statement in a hierarchical culture? After determining the prevailing culture, the desired target culture is to be defined in order to derive appropriate measures and strategies from the gap between the status quo and the target image. At this point, it is important to mention that although the digital culture described above is considered ideal for a successful digital transformation, the "perfect corporate culture" does not exist. Which culture is ideal for a company depends on its products, processes and natural environment. So every company has to decide for itself which facets of the digital culture would be ideal and should be adopted by the company to what extent.

4.3.4.2 Implementation Phase

The implementation phase is the critical part of a culture change project, as it definitely decides the success of the culture change. Essentially, the implementation phase corresponds to a classical change project. The best-known change model comes from Lewin, and its three stages essentially correspond to the structure of all other process-focused change management models (Lewin, 1951).

At this point it makes sense to briefly join the discussion of whether a model that is just under 70 years old is still relevant today. Indeed, organizational change is now seen as an open, continuous, and unpredictable process without a clear beginning or end. Planned organizational change faces a more chaotic reality: Unpredictable consequences of the planned change approach, resistance, political processes, and misunderstandings are part of this and mean that change management cannot be limited to the execution of sequential steps. Lewin's model of a planned process is therefore subject to some criticism, but this is often based on a misinterpretation of his work. In fact, Lewin took this complexity into account and already proclaimed in his research that both the planning and the control of change should include an iterative component and be adapted accordingly over the course of the project. From this point of view, his model is still relevant—provided that it is not a 1:1 instruction manual with strictly sequential steps, but rather a rough, general orientation regarding the most important phases of a change process.

The key to the approach lies in step five (see Fig. 4.7). There, in the steps **"Unfreeze", "Change"** and **"Refreeze"**, the implementation is to be carried out. The following describes these three sub-steps in more detail.

Unfreeze

Often, transformation efforts fail in the initial phase because the necessary conditions were not created. A suitable corporate culture is undoubtedly one of the most important requirements for digital transformation, so preparing for the necessary cultural change is one of the most important tasks of the transformation manager. In the first step of the cultural change, the "Unfreeze", it is exactly about preparing the corporate culture for change, "defrosting" it literally.

The biggest challenges that culture managers face in this phase are:

- lack of awareness of the urgency of change,
- resistance to change,
- lack of willingness to implement it.

A digital corporate culture that declares openness to new values supports the willingness to change. What is needed above all is an "organizational commitment", that is, the self-commitment of the entire organization to accept the change.

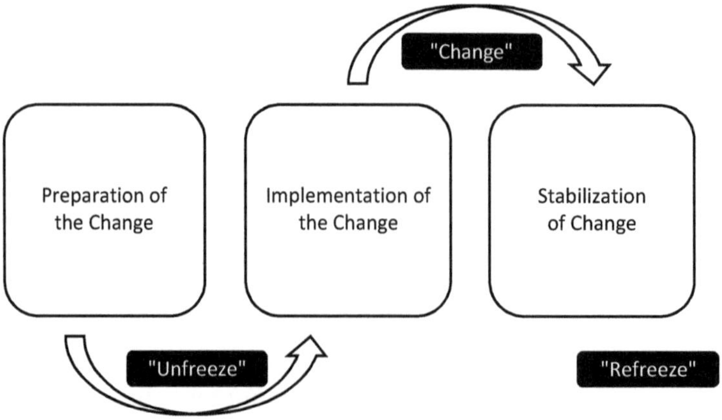

Fig. 4.7 Change Model According to Lewin (1951)

> **Cultural Change Through "Digital Lighthouses"**
>
> The Bremen-based logistics company Hansa Meyer Global (HMG) provides a prime example of how a company in the Mittelstand can drive digital development forward with limited resources and prepare employees for digital transformation. One successful measure is the "digital lighthouses": The focus here is on making new technologies and digital working methods known and visible within the company. The goal of digital lighthouses is to spread interest and enthusiasm for digital topics and to signal to employees above all: Something is happening, now it's starting. Coaching programs form the basis for a sustainable build-up of digital competence, and IT forums give employees the opportunity to exchange ideas, bring in questions and suggestions, and actively participate in the transformation. The HMG employees who are coached thus act as multipliers, spreading the knowledge they have acquired about new technologies throughout the organization and thus creating a digital affinity "bottom-up".

The realization that a change in culture is necessary can promote the willingness to change or reduce resistance to it. However, conveying the urgent need for a change in culture to employees can prove to be a difficult undertaking. As described at the beginning of the chapter, culture and its values usually arise from the success of certain behavioral strategies that are subsequently considered ideal and become the norm. However, it is essential to go against the legitimation of the existing culture. Both formulating a clear vision for the company and its culture and their constant and transparent communication—both central elements of project marketing—are effective measures to gradually dissolve resistance to change. Through targeted project marketing, the formulated vision can be conveyed to employees in order to generate a shared understanding of the company's goal and the urgency of change in the first step and to create the necessary support and willingness for subsequent measures in the second step as part of this vision. Whitewashing the situation would be fatal and completely miss the mark here—because if employees only realize the urgency of a change in their working methods and culture when their job is at risk, it is already too late for a successful change.

Change

As soon as the necessary willingness for a transformation is available, the change itself, the change process, can begin. As already mentioned several times, the digital transformation of a company must go hand in hand with a change in culture towards a digital culture. What initially sounds like an unsolvable task can, however, be divided into smaller, manageable tasks when looked at more closely. It is not necessarily necessary to turn the entire corporate culture upside down in the change process. Often it is enough to interpret the existing core values of the company in a new and digital way. This way, the company's core personality and its core values are retained.

So every transformation manager has to do conceptual work first and foremost for the change phase: Which values and routines will continue to give me advantages as a company? Which ones might have to be reinterpreted, supplemented or changed in order to take my corporate culture into the digital age?

In digitalization projects, various departments work together. This is where subcultures shaped by different professional profiles meet, and misunderstandings are practically pre-programmed. Therefore, it is also the task of a transformation manager to improve communication and collaboration between the subcultures and to align or at least create a better understanding of each other's culture. The best means of approaching the subcultures in the past has been the interaction between key individuals and groups. Possible tools for promoting collaboration are, for example, hackathons (see also Sect. 5.2.3.2) or interdisciplinary rotation systems in training and further education, in order to bring employees closer to the thinking and working methods of other departments and thus promote a successful collaboration at a later stage.

Cultural Change at Telstra

An example of a successfully managed cultural change and the introduction of digital values is Telstra, Australia's leading telecommunications provider. Telstra's digital strategy aimed to digitalize all customer-oriented processes, such as billing, payment processes and customer inquiries. That Telstra was able to increase the percentage of digital customer transactions from less than 20 to 56% between 2011 and 2016 is mainly due to the close cooperation between product teams and digital units, as well as to the overall approach "Focus on culture first" of all transformation activities. Because without a corporate culture that supports organizational collaboration, millions can be invested in technology without anything changing. In order to digitalize the corporate culture, Telstra therefore carried out a number of initiatives, such as agile development methods and a switch to rapid prototyping, in order to create a more agile and collaborative culture. The most far-reaching cultural change took place with regard to the attitude towards the customer: In order to align the company with the customer and to anchor customer satisfaction as a fundamental value, teams received the Net Promoter Score for the customer channel they were responsible for every morning to motivate them to orient all their decisions on the needs of the customers.

During all change measures, employees should be involved and involved as far as possible in order to make them successful. A culture of open communication and transparency is essential for this. If these values do not yet exist in the company, it is not only important for the transformation manager to exemplify them through transparent communication, but also to actively seek the feedback of the employees.

Involving organization members in the change process from the beginning has proven to be a successful measure. Setting up idea platforms or so-called idea jams, in which employees can bring their ideas and feedback to change measures, is also of great importance and gives all organization members the feeling of not only being receivers, but also part of the change. In addition, this represents the first step in anchoring the value of participation within the company.

Refreeze

In the last phase according to Lewin's model, the changes that have been worked out in the company and in its culture should now be anchored. In order to anchor changed behavior firmly in a digital culture through individual initiatives, pilot projects and measures, early successes are important. Culture and its values are legitimized by the success of past action strategies. If the new behavior promoted by change measures is successful, this legitimizes its continuation, so that it increasingly becomes self-evident and is thus expected and seen as ideal behavior in the company—that is, as a new value of corporate culture. Transformation managers can support this cultural anchoring through the communication of successes and by promoting the changed behavior.

However, what is decisive for the long-term success of cultural change is above all the credibility of the cultural change. The new digital culture must be actively lived by the leaders, otherwise all cultural initiatives will lose credibility and quickly be labeled as one-day flies of a political agenda, but not as a new corporate identity, which is accepted as a guideline.

4.4 Building Competence for Digital Transformation

The ability to act in an organization is fundamentally determined by its competencies. Outstanding competencies in certain areas enable companies to secure a dominant position in their markets in the long term, especially if they are difficult to imitate—the resource-based approach to corporate theory has long been worked out (Barney, 1991). For years, Apple's technology and innovation competence allowed it to dominate the market for mobile devices, Amazon's technology and logistics competence allowed it to become a leading online retailer in many countries. Google (Alphabet) was able to use its technology competence to establish itself as the embodiment of an Internet search engine and is today one of the world's leading Internet companies. However, missing competencies often impede entrepreneurial progress. In times of turbulent markets and constantly changing requirements, they can often lead to massive problems and even endanger the existence of a company. Nokia, for example, lacked the innovation competence to exploit the emerging market for smartphones, not only costing them their position as the world's largest mobile phone manufacturer, but also leading to their (temporary) complete withdrawal. AOL, one of the pioneers in the field of online access services, was unable to further develop its competencies in a rapidly progressing market, which ultimately led to a massive loss of importance. The German mail-order company Quelle lacked the necessary competenices to adapt its business model to the new rules of the online mail order business, which is why the company had to file for insolvency as a result of this development.

Digital innovations, as they are at the center of this book, require specific competences. But which competences are decisive for the success and failure in dealing with digital technologies? Which company areas should develop which competences? And how can the development of such competences be concretely approached? These and related questions will be addressed in the following sections.

4.4.1 The Need for Digitalization and Transformation Competence

In the past, many companies got by with relatively little IT expertise. Essentially, it was enough if the IT department knew how to develop IT systems and operate the IT infrastructure, possibly supplemented by skills in reorganizing processes. The specialist departments, the users of the IT systems, were only involved in the early stages of developing technical solutions, sometimes also in prioritizing IT budgets or formulating an IT strategy.

However, due to the increasing importance of IT-based solutions in all areas of the company, this "minimalist" view of technology competence is often no longer sufficient. Rather, building IT competence as part of digital transformation is a key success factor. However, many companies and industries are still well behind (their own) expectations—there is a concrete need to catch up. In addition, building IT competence—which usually takes place mainly in the IT departments of companies—is the first important step in generating digital innovations, but these often require much more than just building technology competence in the narrower sense. In particular, a company needs the competence to recognize innovative digital technologies and possibly digital solutions based on them (e.g. social media marketing) at an early stage and the ability to actually develop digital products or services by mobilizing its digital resources (Wiesböck et al., 2020). This is often only possible to a very limited extent for an IT department, as its distance to products and business models is often simply too great. In addition, new digital solutions must be systematically implemented in an organization—just as technical solutions must be integrated into a system landscape.

Consequently, in the context of digital transformation, competencies are required that go beyond mere IT skills. Building on our definition at the beginning of Chap. 2 these may be referred to as **digitalization competencies**. In addition, competencies must be built for the conception, implementation and organizational introduction of new professional concepts—beyond any existing knowledge of business process optimization. These may be referred to as **transformation competence**.

The following section provides a closer description of these two competencies required in the context of digital innovation—digitalization competence and digital transformation competence (Wiesböck & Hess, 2018). For the sake of simplicity and ideally, a distinction is made here between IT units, specialist departments (such as marketing, controlling or development) and units specialized in digital transformation (digitalization units, see Sect. 4.2.2).

4.4.1.1 Need for Digitalization Competence

The digitalization competence of an organization describes its ability to develop and operate new solutions based on digital technologies. First of all, it is crucial for companies to identify and select the relevant digital technologies. This can pose a great challenge, especially for companies that are inexperienced in digitalization. Not every technology that is currently being hyped up in the media or by management consultants is relevant for every company. The benefits and added value of each technology must be carefully evaluated and aligned with the strategic orientation of the innovation goals. Once the right technologies have been selected, they usually have to be adapted to the specific situation. A "plug and play" approach is not possible in most cases. The thus adapted technology must then be embedded in a new or existing system in order to be usable. From this point on, the operation and maintenance of the resulting digital solution must be efficiently ensured and a process for further development started.

In addition, companies must not only be able to develop new digital solutions, but also to use digital tools, to combine digital and physical resources and to manage the general IT functions (e.g. IT planning, IT design, IT budgeting, IT project management, etc.). Furthermore, it is necessary to further develop and adapt the existing IT infrastructure, otherwise the integration of new digital solutions will be limited. Last but not least, the use of IT also requires a strategy. This typically includes a target image for the future IT landscape, decisions on IT management and statements on the financial framework of IT.

The specialist departments that use the systems should be involved in the identification and selection of important technologies and should also be involved to some extent in the implementation of the systems and their further development. The digitalization units can support this process, which can contribute significantly to the coordination with the transformation efforts. Table 4.7 shows this division in an overview. The more points are listed, the more important the respective organizational unit is for the topic.

Table 4.7 Need for Digitalization Competence

Topics	Specialized department	Digitalization unit	IT unit
Identification and selection of relevant digital technologies	•	••	••
Realization of digital solutions	•	•	•••
Embedding digital solutions in the existing system landscape			•••
Use of digital solutions	•••		
Maintenance and further development of digital solutions	•		•••
Providing IT infrastructure			•••
Developing IT strategy	•	•	•••

4.4.1.2 Need for Transformation Competence

The **Digital Transformation Competency** of an organization describes its ability to develop, integrate and operate digital business concepts. Such digital business concepts (e.g. in the form of new products) complement the digital solutions developed on the basis of digital technologies. These tasks should be equally assumed by the specialist department and the digitalization unit, with the digitalization unit providing the methodological support, supporting the process of strategy development and organizing the creation of the conditions beyond the flexibility of the IT landscape. The role of the IT unit is rather small in the context of digital transformation; it should support the identification of new business approaches, the already mentioned flexibility of the IT landscape and the coordination of the IT strategy with the transformation strategy. Table 4.8 shows the proposed roles in overview. The same notation as in Table 4.7 applies.

4.4.1.3 Differentiation in Practice

Tables 4.7 and 4.8 are, on closer inspection, still very abstract. In operational reality, further differentiation is required, especially when it comes to determining the specific competence requirements.

For digital competence, another differentiation according to technology classes is possible. For example, companies that rely on social media channels must be able to implement social media technologies, embed the resulting solutions, etc. Companies must therefore describe their competence needs in detail, also because many employees in the technology sector are strongly attached to technology.

The same applies analogously to competence in the field of digital transformation. Here, a distinction can be made between products, interfaces,

Table 4.8 Need for Digital Transformation Competence

	Department	Digitalization unit	IT unit
Discover digital business opportunities	•••	••	•
Realize digital business concepts	••	••	
Embed digital business concepts in existing structures	••	••	
Use, maintenance and further development of digital business concepts	••	•	
Creating the conditions for digital transformation	•	•••	•
Developing the DT strategy	••	•••	•

processes and business models. While, for example, the competence of a company in product design and product testing plays a decisive role in digital product innovation, digital process innovation typically requires expertise in process modeling and process mining. Business model innovation (such as tapping into a new revenue stream) also requires specific expertise, often also a different perspective. Analogous to the construction of digital competence, a company must therefore also focus on transformation competence. In media companies, for example, the focus will be on product- and business model-related competence, while insurers currently focus more on competence in relation to business processes and possibly products.

4.4.2 Two Ways of Meeting Needs

After the previous considerations regarding the type of required competence, the question now arises to what extent a specific company should build up this competence itself or buy them from outside.

The question of a company's competence in the field of digitalization, i.e. the realization and maintenance of application systems as well as the operation of the required hardware and network infrastructure, has been intensively described and investigated for years under the keyword of "IT outsourcing" (Haas, 2018; Rickmann, 2013). In the early years of the application of digital technologies in companies, the companies themselves created the software used, and the hardware was purchased. Relatively quickly, a large number of standard software solutions developed for both smaller application areas such as word processing as well as for complex business applications. In this way, existing in-house developments were gradually replaced. The in-house development of software was typically only limited to a few applications and was often realized with the help of development partners near or far abroad. Solutions from outside were also used for the networking of computers that was now necessary; often only the operation of networks within a building remained in the company. With the development of cloud computing (see Sect. 4.1), which is based on the infrastructure of the Internet, the operation and maintenance of the used standard software is also gradually being outsourced to service providers. This should reduce IT costs, facilitate access to the latest technologies and ultimately solve the difficult problem of recruiting IT specialists. The operational focus of the IT departments of companies is now increasingly on the configuration of externally sourced and possibly also externally operated software solutions, supplemented by the development of a few selected applications in places.

The question now arises as to whether this trend towards less manufacturing depth in IT can be maintained in the course of increasing digitalization. In essence, this is confirmed—low differentiation potential, high costs, rapid technological change and often also problems in procuring suitable employees speak against high manufacturing depth in IT. Even in the course of increasing digitalization, companies should usually procure the hardware from outside, give the networks to specialists and limit themselves to the integration and configuration of existing software solutions, possibly supplemented by point-specific extensions. However, the ability to observe and test new technologies at an early stage should be maintained. An exception is if a company places digital offers in its center alone, as is the case, for example, with operators of information services (such as search engines) and marketplaces (such as auction platforms). In these cases, possibly also with some of the hybrid online-offline products, the competence for the creation of these systems should be built up in-house.

A clearly different picture results with regard to transformation competence. Although there are no wide-ranging studies yet, a certain trend can already be seen. The history here is quite different from the technological level. In many companies, competence for the development of digital offers and the establishment of digital business models has so far been largely lacking. These have to be set up at the moment, both in the line departments and in supporting digitalization units. Of course, consultants can be used to create the entry into digital transformation, to set up the appropriate structures and to accompany first concrete projects. Ultimately, however, digital transformation is a permanent task that can only really be solved internally. In addition, in most cases many good initiatives for new products and processes come from the company itself. This also speaks in favor of further developing one's own team or setting up new departments.

4.4.3 Approaches for Building Transformation Competence

Many companies lack the essential and as described above—not sustainable from the outside competencies for the management of digital transformation. Typically, companies have to expand their transformation competencies specifically through internal or external measures. Table 4.9 gives an overview of possible measures.

Internal measures taken by companies aim to create structures and processes that will further qualify the existing staff accordingly. An established way to build technological or digital innovation competence is the targeted training of individual employees, managers or entire project teams. Trainings can be carried out either by internal competence providers, such as the CDO, or by external specialists. The latter has the advantage that new knowledge can thus enter the organization from the outside. Many companies also rely on regular training sessions or training facilities that are firmly established within the company, such as so-called IT dojos, which employees can visit at any time to find out about new technological trends or to receive specific training.

Another way in which innovation and creativity can be promoted within the organization is the creation of so-called innovation labs or creativity labs. These are physical or virtual workspaces and environments that are specially designed for collaboration and in which employees and teams can work on their creative thinking processes and innovative ideas. In addition to building competence, innovation and creativity labs are intended to increase the creativity of employees and promote new developments by enabling employees to exchange information, knowledge and ideas across the board. The rooms are therefore designed to support creative collaboration as best as possible. For example, employees could be provided with labs with a workshop character in which they have the opportunity to try out their ideas with little effort and to create and test first, simple prototypes.

Another common way to build internal competence is through cross-functional teams. By bringing together staff from different parts of

Table 4.9 Approaches to Building Transformation Competencies

Internal measures	Innovation & Creativity Labs
	Targeted training
	Cross-functional teams
	Hackathons
	Enterprise-wide training
	Excursions
	Job rotation
External measures	Recruitment of qualified employees
	Recruitment of competence teams
	Acquisition of start-ups/companies
	Outsourcing to service providers
Hybrid measures	Strategic university cooperation
	Cooperation with start-ups
	Trainee programs
	Dual degree programs

the company, in particular by linking technological know-how and business knowledge, innovative solutions and products can emerge. In addition, these teams also contribute to reducing the digital divide within the company.

Hackathons can be used to generate ideas (see also Sect. 5.2.3.2). However, a number of companies are now using hackathons to position themselves as potential employers and to find and win new employees.

In addition to targeted training, companies can also contribute to competence development with wide-ranging, company-wide training measures (lectures, seminars, online courses). These are usually less expensive than individual training and help to build basic skills (for example in the use of digital technologies) in the workforce. Measures such as job rotation can also contribute to a broader competence base in the company. If employees not only know their own, narrowly defined workflows, but also the tasks of their colleagues, and if they are regularly in contact with new digital tools in the process, this can promote a more holistic and innovative way of thinking among employees. For individual employees with corresponding task areas, a stay in "digital epicenters" such as Silicon Valley can also be beneficial.

Alternatively, companies can acquire the required competencies externally, for example by recruiting new employees, taking over start-ups or corresponding business areas from competitors. In extreme cases, it is also conceivable to outsource to an external service provider.

Through the external acquisition of employees, teams or even entire companies, a company can quickly and effectively acquire highly qualified talents with the necessary skills and know-how, without having to pay "expensive tuition fees" for internal competence building. For the company, the new employees' professional and technological knowledge opens up new development and business opportunities. However, companies are particularly challenged in the digital transformation unit in terms of competition for competent talents, as only partially qualified personnel is available on the market. In addition, the company should be aware of the challenges that can arise from the clash of different working methods and cultures. In order to realize synergy effects that arise from the linking of already existing internal competence with complementary new competence, the onboarding and integration of new employees should be planned in advance. Cultural aspects can often become an essential hurdle. This is especially true for the integration of acquired teams or even parts of companies. Here too, different working methods, corporate cultures and objectives can lead to conflicts. If a company leaves the newly acquired units a lot of freedom and lets them run largely independently, the question arises as to how the newly acquired competence and know-how can be transferred to the existing company. If the connection is too tight and too much adaptation pressure is exerted on the new units, there is a risk that the competent employees will resign and only a relatively worthless shell will remain for the company. Therefore, an appropriate balance between integration and freedom is particularly important in the early phases after the acquisition. A similar situation arises with the takeover of entire start-ups.

Outsourcing to external service providers also carries the usual risks of outsourcing. Companies may become dependent on individual providers and lose control over their know-how. This is particularly dangerous at times when the value-added structures in companies and markets are shifting as a result of digital transformation, as companies may know less about their newly developed core business processes than external service providers. Furthermore, the costs of digitalization and digital transformation projects are often difficult to estimate in advance, as there are few comparable projects that could serve as benchmarks. To overcome these challenges, companies should install strategic provider management, establish a systematic and continuous transfer of knowledge between external service providers and internal employees, and also consider mechanisms for risk sharing in contract design.

Hybrid measures that use both external expertise and internal expertise can be a sensible alternative, for example in the form of long-term strategic university cooperation. Through strategic cooperation between public and private organizations and through participation in university courses specifically oriented towards the digital economy, new expertise can be built up.

Example of a Successful Cooperation Between Companies and Universities

An example of the close and long-term cooperation between science and practice is the Internet Business Cluster (IBC) in the Munich area. The IBC is a non-profit organization in which universities and companies from strongly digitalizing industries in the Munich region have joined forces to jointly tackle the challenges of digital transformation. The members of the association not only receive scientific findings on the subject of digitalization, but also benefit from networking opportunities and access to young talents from the universities.

Cooperations with start-ups are also a popular measure to connect external competencies with internal competence development. In contrast to a complete takeover, and integration into the company is not necessary here, and the degree of exchange or cooperation can be agreed upon in advance. The company thus benefits from the innovation competence of the partner, while the start-up, for example, can use the positive signal effect (to investors, potential employees, partners) of a cooperation with a larger company. This is particularly evident in the financial sector, where the increasing spread of technology-driven companies has put traditional banks under increasing pressure to modernize their core business activities and services. Many banks are responding to this challenge by entering into partnerships with fintech start-ups that offer technology-based financial services (Hornuf et al., 2020).

Corporate trainee programs can also be a suitable way to build the required competencies. In the ideal case, companies gain young graduates who have already acquired valuable competencies during their studies and bring with them a "digital mindset". During the trainee program (usually one to two years), these employees are then specifically trained for the respective application context of the company and can effectively apply external and internal knowledge after completion of the program. A similar approach is represented by dual degree programs, which, however, start a little earlier. Here, companies accompany young talents during their parallel studies and take over the practical training of the students as practice partners.

Other innovative instruments for personnel acquisition are targeted recruiting events, workshops, cooperation with specialized personnel consultants or the use of recruiting apps. New incentive systems that are not only based on monetary incentives, but also, for example, specifically oriented towards the digital world, such as further education and travel, can also be considered. It should also be noted here that the workplace should be designed to meet the needs of potential digital employees, for example by the flexible design of working hours, possibilities for home office or remote working, and freely available time for further education and training.

Example of Successful Digital Competence Building

The exemplary case of a company from the metal processing industry shows how the building of digital competence can succeed. At the beginning of the digital transformation process, the required competence was hardly or not at all available in the company. Training to build these skills was also not possible because there was no one in the company to design and implement them. For this reason, a digitalization unit was set up, a larger number of external specialists were recruited for the areas of digital product development and personnel development, and experts for processes and projects were brought on board. For the targeted building of competence, the company now relies on workshops and training on various topics. Another important building block is also cross-functional projects in which a continuous transfer of knowledge takes place between the employees involved from different company areas and functions. In addition, the company operates long-term university partnerships in order to use knowledge from research for itself and to gain contacts with "digital talents". For this purpose, it also prepares and implements small projects for student groups.

The practice study by etventure (2018) shows that companies so far mainly rely on training programs for employees to convey digital basic knowledge and special agile methods (79%), internal idea competitions (46%) as well as the targeted promotion of employees' entrepreneurial engagement (44%). In addition, employees are given the opportunity to work in other company areas that are responsible for digital transformation (26%) or even to participate in digitalization projects outside the company (22%). In addition, more than one third of companies said they use start-up partnerships. In order to be attractive to potential new employees who bring the required digital skills, strategic employer branding is also a decisive instrument. The positioning of the company as an innovative digitalizer is one of the decisive factors in winning rare and correspondingly desired digital specialists in the labor market (etventure, 2018).

4.4.4 Add-on: Dynamic Skills for Digital Transformation

In the context of digital transformation, it is of enormous importance that companies build up skills to identify trends early on in a rapidly changing environment and exploit them. This is especially important because digital transformation proceeds differently in every organization and therefore requires a separate approach. In addition, companies that have taken a certain path in digital transformation must continuously adjust the required skills due to the dynamic nature of digital change. Due to these properties of digital transformation, it makes sense to examine the development of skills based on dynamic capabilities ("dynamic capabilities"), as they explain how companies can react to the rapid change of technologies and markets (Teece, 2007). Dynamic capabilities describe the ability of a company to a) identify and shape opportunities and threats ("sensing"), b) seize opportunities ("seizing"), and c) maintain competitiveness by adapting the business model and the broader resource base of the company ("transforming").

Warner and Wäger (2019) have conceptualized digital transformation as a process of building dynamic capabilities for ongoing strategic renewal (see Fig. 4.8). The starting point of the model is external impulses, including digital competitors, changed consumer behavior, and disruptive digital technologies, which trigger the building of dynamic capabilities for digital transformation. In addition, the model specifies three internal enablers (cross-functional teams, fast decision-making, and management support) and three internal barriers (rigid strategic planning, resistance to change, and a high level of hierarchy), which influence the formation of dynamic capabilities.

First, companies must develop "digital sensing" capabilities. This includes building competencies in digital scenario planning and digital scouting to identify the new technological, customer, and competitive trends. Specifically, this means using informal and formal networks, big data analytics and artificial intelligence to identify customer-oriented trends that are otherwise difficult to predict. These capabilities are based on developing a digital mindset, i.e. creating a digitally oriented culture and long-term digital vision. With the "digital seizing" capabilities, companies must incorporate strategic agility into their business model to quickly exploit technological opportunities and market opportunities, seize the latest trends, and avoid potential existential threats. Rapid prototyping is essential for increasing strategic agility, as it allows customers to collect and use feedback almost in real-time to respond to trends. In addition, business model innovations should be aligned with existing product-based business models to create a balanced digital portfolio. Finally, companies must develop "digital transforming" capabilities. This includes traditional companies building

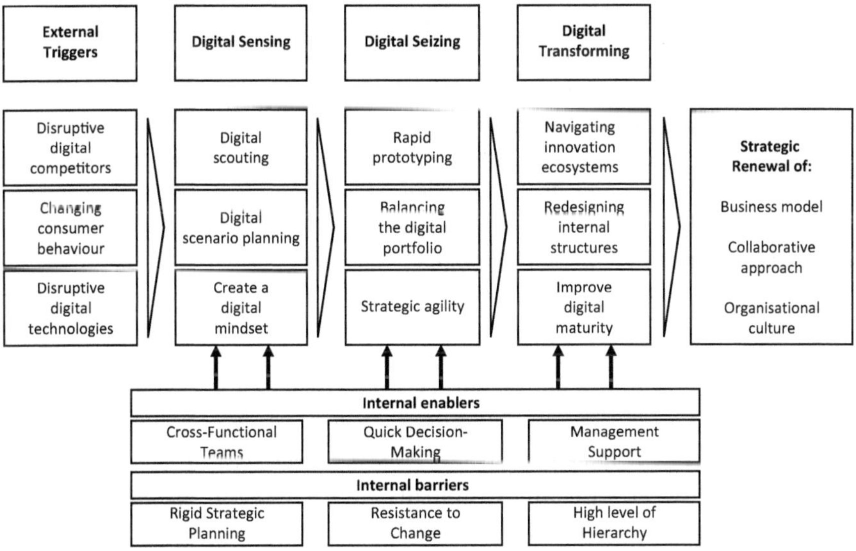

Fig. 4.8 Process Model for Building Dynamic Capabilities for Digital Transformation (Warner & Wäger, 2019)

or joining a digital innovation ecosystem to work with new partners. Companies should also work towards a redesign of internal structures, which can be achieved, for example, by decentralizing business units and setting up independent subsidiaries. Finally, improving the digital maturity of the workforce is a key capability for the digital transformation of companies.

Building dynamic capabilities can ultimately lead to a strategic renewal of the business model, the collaborative approach (the way people work across departments and divisions) and the organizational culture. It should be noted that building dynamic capabilities is specific to each digital transformation, requiring a continuous review and renewal of business models, collaborative approaches, and organizational cultures. In addition, new external impulses can arise at any time, which may re-weight the need to identify and seize opportunities.

References

Alvesson, M., & Sveningsson, S. (2015). *Changing organizational culture.* Routledge.

Barney, J. (1991). Firm resources and sustained competitive advantage. *Journal of Management, 17*(1), 99–120.

Barthel, P., Fuchs, C., Birner, B., & Hess, T. (2020). Embedding digital innovations in organizations: A typology for digital innovation units. In *Proceedings of the 15th Internationale Tagung Wirtschaftsinformatik.*

Basu, S., Phelps, C., & Kotha, S. (2016). Search and integration in external venturing: An inductive examination of corporate venture capital units. *Strategic Entrepreneurship Journal, 1002*(10), 129–152.

Benlian, A., & Hess, T. (2009). Welche Treiber lassen SaaS auch in Großunternehmen zum Erfolg werden? Eine empirische Analyse der SaaS-Adoption auf Basis der Transaktionskostentheorie. In *Proceedings of the 9th international conference Wirtschaftsinformatik* (Vol. 1, pp. 567–576).

bitkom. (2018). *Zwei von drei Unternehmen nutzen Cloud Computing.* https://www.bitkom.org/Presse/Presseinformation/Zwei-von-drei-Unternehmen-nutzen-Cloud-Computing.html. Accessed 23 Sept 2018.

Cameron, K. S., & Quinn, R. S. (2011). *Diagnosing and changing organizational culture: Based on the competing values framework.* Jossey-Bass.

Capgemini. (2018). *Agilität überall: Das Ende der bimodalen IT.* https://www.capgemini.com/de-de/wp-content/uploads/sites/5/2018/07/Capgemini_WP1-bimodaleIT.pdf. Accessed 23 Sept 2018.

Christensen, C. M. (1997). *The innovator's dilemma: When new technologies cause great firms to fail.* Harvard Business School Press.

Christensen, C. M., Raynor, M., & McDonald, R. (2015). What is disruptive innovation? *Harvard Business Review, 93*(12), 44–53.

Duerr, S., Holotiuk, F., Wagner, H.-T., Beimborn, D., & Weitzel, T. (2018). What is digital organizational culture? Insights from exploratory case studies. In *Proceedings of the Hawaii international conference on system sciences 2018* (pp. 5126–5135).

Ebers, M. (2016). Organisationsmodelle für Innovation. *Schmalenbachs Zeitschrift für betriebswirtschaftliche Forschung, 69*(1), 81–109.

etventure. (2018). *Studie Digitale Transformation 2018: Hemmnisse, Fortschritte und Alternativen.* https://service.etventure.de/digitale-transformation-2018. Accessed 23 Sept 2018.

Fuchs, C., Barthel, P., Herberg, I., Berger, M., & Hess, T. (2019). Characterizing approaches to digital transformation: Development of a taxonomy of digital units. In *Proceedings of the 14th Internationale Tagung Wirtschaftsinformatik* (pp. 632–646).

Gruber, M., & Henkel, J. (2005). Corporate venturing. In S. Albers & O. Gassmann (Hrsg.), *Handbuch Technologie- und Innovationsmanagement.* Gabler.

Haas, L. (2018). *Align client and provider perspectives: Best practices in IT outsourcing.* Springer.

Haffke, I., Kalgovas, B., & Benlian, A. (2017). A bimodal IT function resolves the conflicting goals of stability and experimentation. *MIS Quarterly Executive, 16*(2), 101–120.

Hartl, E., & Hess, T. (2017). The role of cultural values for digital transformation: Insights from a Delphi study. In *Proceedings of the 23rd Americas Conference on Information Systems (AMCIS 2017).*

Hogenhuis, B. N., van den Hende, E. A., & Hultink, E. J. (2016). When should large firms collaborate with young ventures? *Research-Technology Management, 59*(1), 39–47.

Holotiuk, F., & Beimborn, D. (2019). Temporal ambidexterity: How digital innovation labs connect exploration and exploitation for digital innovation. In *Proceedings of the 19th International Conference on Information Systems (ICIS).*

Horlach, B., Schirmer, I., & Drews, P. (2016). Bimodal IT: Business-IT alignment in the age of digital transformation. In *Paper präsentiert auf Multikonferenz Wirtschaftsinformatik (MKWI),* Ilmenau.

Hornuf, L., Klus, M., Lohwasser, T., & Schwienbacher, A. (2020). How do banks interact with fintech startups? *Small Business Economics,* 1–22.

Kaltenecker, N., Huesig, S., Hess, T., & Dowling, M. (2013). The disruptive potential of software as a service: Validation and application of an ex-ante methodology. In *Paper präsentiert auf thirty fourth international conference on information systems,* Milan.

Kane, G. C., Palmer, D., Phillips, A. N., Kiron, D., & Buckley, N. (2015). Strategy, not technology, drives digital transformation. *MIT Sloan Management Review, 14*, 1–25.

Klamar, N., & Prawetz, B. (2018). *Corporate Venture Capital Markt in Deutschland.* FAS.

Klöckner & Co. (2018). „Klöckner & Co 2022" – Unsere Strategie. http://www.kloeckner.com/de/strategie.html. Accessed 27 Aug 2018.

KPMG. (2016). *Der Chief Digital Officer – Phantom oder Wegbereiter? Studie zur Steuerung der digitalen Transformation in der Medienbranche.* Managementstudie der KPMG AG.

Lengnick-Hall, C. A., Beck, T. E., & Lengnick-Hall, M. L. (2011). Developing a capacity for organizational resilience through strategic human resource management. *Human Resource Management Review, 21*(3), 243–255.

Lewin, K. (1951). *Field theory in social science: Selected theoretical papers.* Harper.

Metzger, G. (2020). *KfW-start-up-report 2020.* KfW Bankengruppe.

O'Reilly, C. A., & Tushman, M. L. (2011). Organizational ambidexterity in action: How managers explore and exploit. *California Management Review, 53*(4), 5–22.

Rickmann, H. (2013). *IT-Outsourcing: Neue Herausforderungen im Zeitalter von Cloud Computing.* Springer Gabler.

Rothaermel, F. T. (2001). Incumbent's advantage through exploiting complementary assets via interfirm cooperation. *Strategic Management Journal, 22*(6–7), 687–699.

Schaefer, D., Bohn, U., & Crummenerl, C. (2017). *Culture First!: Von den Vorreitern des digitalen Wandels lernen Change Management Studie 2017.* https://www.capgemini.com/consulting-de/wp-content/uploads/sites/32/2017/10/change-management-studie-2017-capgemini-consulting.pdf. Accessed 1 Sept 2018.

Schein, E. (2010). *Organizational culture and leadership.* Jossey-Bass.

Schleef, M., Bilstein, N., & Stummer, C. (2020). „Shh! … I got help to become smart": Should incumbent firms disclose their cooperation with a startup?. In *Proceedings of the 13th international conference on information systems (ICIS 2020). A virtual AIS conference.*

Teece, D. J. (2007). Explicating dynamic capabilities: The nature and microfoundations of (sustainable) enterprise performance. *Strategic Management Journal, 28*(13), 1319–1350.

Volkoff, O., Strong, D. M., & Elmes, M. B. (2007). Technological embeddedness and organizational change. *Organization Science, 18*(5), 832–848.

Warner, K., & Wäger, M. (2019). Building dynamic capabilities for digital transformation: An ongoing process of strategic renewal. *Long Range Planning, 52*(3), 326–349.

Wiesböck, F., & Hess, T. (2018). Understanding the capabilities for digital innovations from a digital technology perspective. In *Management Reports des Instituts für Wirtschaftsinformatik und Neue Medien der LMU München*, Nr. 1.

Wiesböck, F., Hess, T., & Spanjol, J. (2020). The dual role of IT capabilities in the development of digital products and services. *Information & Management, 57*(8), 1–17.

5

Defining Transformation Governance

Digitalization initiatives have been started in almost every company by now. Quickly, the question arises as to whether these are running in the right direction strategically, whether they are not overlapping and whether these should not be supplemented by centrally developed approaches. Should the initiative for a transformation strategy come more from the top-management, or should this only set the framework? Also, the question must be answered as to who actually controls the digital transformation of a company—is this the task of the IT department or perhaps that of a newly appointed Chief Digital Officer? When do digital business areas make sense? This chapter wants to provide first answers to these questions. In particular, two fields of transformation governance will be addressed: the configuration and emergence of transformation strategies as well as the management-roles in the context of digital transformation. In addition, procedures for determining the digital maturity of a company will be presented—they often serve as an entry into the systematic handling of digital transformation, despite some methodological question marks.

5.1 Elements of a Transformation Strategy

Due to the far-reaching consequences of digital change, an increasing number of companies are recognizing the need to approach the phenomenon systematically and to develop a transformation strategy that defines the framework for the digital transformation of a company and provides a direction. Below is an approach to this.

T. Hess, *Managing the Digital Transformation*,
https://doi.org/10.1007/978-3-658-38424-1_5

5.1.1 Function and Delimitation of a Transformation Strategy

A transformation strategy has three functions:

- It describes the required changes in the value creation and management structure,
- it prescribes the use of digital technologies, and
- it takes into account the financial scope and pressure.

It therefore aims to define the direction of all ongoing digital activities within a company or business area, and is thus a central tool for aligning digital transformation efforts with a target image. A transformation strategy is therefore a holistic approach that can be used to coordinate and prioritize digital transformation efforts across all areas of a company. It thus sets the "rails" for the digital transformation of a company.

Due to the cross-sectional character of the transformation strategy, there are numerous **interfaces to other strategies** (see Fig. 5.1).

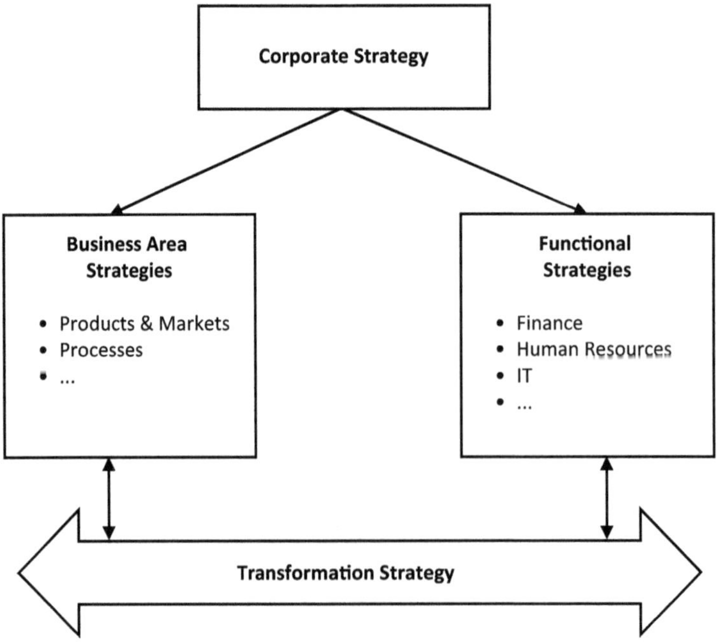

Fig. 5.1 Delimitation of a Transformation Strategy (Matt et al., 2015)

At first glance, one might assume that a transformation strategy is nothing more than an IT strategy with a new name. An IT strategy defines the future IT landscape, i.e. the applications used and the technical infrastructure required for them in the form of hardware and networks. It also describes the organizational and financial framework for IT management. The scope of IT management ranges from the operation and maintenance of individual systems or their interaction to the outsourcing of entire areas to service providers. In the course of the steadily increasing importance of IT, security issues have gained significantly in importance in recent years, partly also demanded by regulatory authorities. In addition, the cost pressure on IT has increased. Of course, the operation and further development of IT are challenging management issues, but they are clearly distinct from the management of digital transformation.

In comparison to IT strategies, transformation strategies focus on the technology-induced changes in the course of an organization-wide digital transformation. Digital transformation has implications for products, processes and business models and therefore usually goes beyond process optimization, which is often still located in the IT department. Its scope is therefore more holistic than that of IT or other functional strategies and explicitly includes digital activities at the interface to the customer. This combines the ideas of an IT strategy with those of a business or corporate strategy, for example by describing which factors can have a positive effect on a company's revenue model.

5.1.2 The Digital Transformation Strategy Framework

The concept of a transformation strategy presented here is designed as an abstract target image that outlines the path chosen by a company to cope with digital transformation. In doing so, four dimensions have crystallized that a company should include in its transformation strategy (Matt et al., 2015):

- Use of technologies,
- structural changes in value creation,
- structural changes in the organization as well as
- financial aspects.

These four dimensions are combined in the Digital Transformation Strategy Framework (DTS-Framework) (Matt et al., 2015). Figure 5.2 also shows

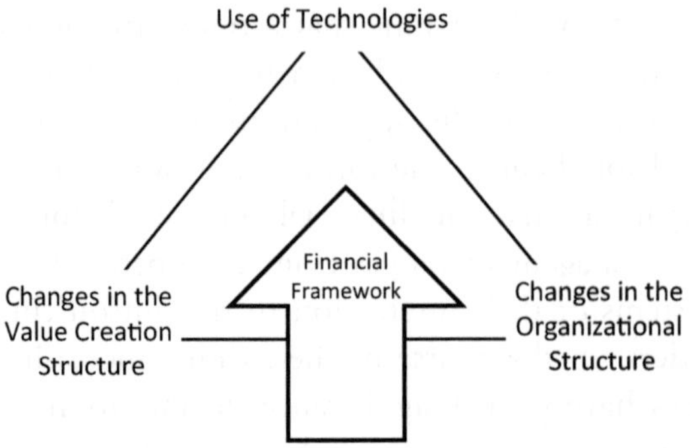

Fig. 5.2 The Digital Transformation Strategy Framework (Matt et al., 2015)

that changes in technology, value creation and structure are interdependent and driven by financial aspects or result from them.

Strategies can and can only ever specify points. Of course, this also applies to transformation strategies. The following section outlines the key points of the four mentioned areas.

5.1.2.1 Use of Technologies

The digital transformation is driven by the emergence of digital technologies. Therefore, the first dimension "use of technologies" deals with the use of digital technologies and the openness of the company to new technologies. The fact that new technologies are gaining ground more and more quickly and that disruptive technologies are turning entire industries upside down shows how important it is for companies to take this dimension into account in their cross-departmental transformation strategy and to use technologies to the best of their ability. At the same time, companies must also ensure that they can integrate new technologies into their IT landscape.

First of all, a company should define which technological developments it really considers to be central and therefore needs to keep an eye on. Such developments can lie on the level of infrastructure (e.g. the availability of networks or end devices), on technologies in the narrower sense (e.g. database systems) or on specific applications (such as customer relationship systems or payment systems on the Internet).

Companies should become aware of their handling of digital technologies. Therefore, the dimension "use of technologies" also questions a company's attitude towards new digital technologies as well as the ability to use technologies to the company's advantage. It describes the strategic role of IT and the future technological ambition of the company.

As part of developing the transformation strategy, companies must also ask themselves whether they are aiming for technology leadership or prefer to build on established solutions. Although technology leadership often comes with the opportunity to gain competitive advantages because other companies find themselves in a sort of dependency situation on their own technological standards, standardization on the other hand also carries the risk that the own technological standard will not prevail or even be displaced on the market. Many companies outside the IT sector have therefore not been ambitious in terms of leadership in fundamental technologies and have also been hesitant in terms of leadership in applications. They are rather concentrating on configuring applications, often in close cooperation with a technology company.

5.1.2.2 Change in the Value Creation Structure

Changes in the area of value creation typically go hand in hand with the use of new technologies as part of digital transformation. This also has an impact on the value chains of companies, because the new digital activities usually deviate from the classical—often still analog—core business. Technology-induced changes offer opportunities to expand the current product and service portfolio, but often these changes are also accompanied by increased requirements for different technological and product-related competencies and by higher risks due to less experience in the new area. If other markets or new customer segments are addressed, digital transformation of products or services can also enable or require different forms of monetization or even the expansion of business areas.

5.1.2.3 Change in Organizational Structure

The use of new technologies and forms of value creation also requires structural and possibly even cultural adjustments in companies in order to create an appropriate basis for new business areas. Structural changes relate to the company's decisions regarding who is responsible for digital transformation, where new (digital) activities are located within the company structure, which structures are affected by the transformation, and how the necessary digital competencies can be bundled and expanded. For example, companies rely on organizational forms such as project houses, the acquisition of start-ups, or spin-offs for their digital initiatives, depending on which changes in value creation are to be achieved. If the extent of the changes is small, it may make sense for companies to integrate new activities and processes into existing company structures, while more far-reaching changes would be better served by creating a separate, autonomous subsidiary or a digital unit within the company that is decoupled from the core business.

5.1.2.4 Financial Framework

However, the aforementioned changes in corporate structure and value creation as well as the use of technologies can only be successfully implemented by taking into account the financial scope for action. In the context of digital transformation, financial aspects can be both drivers and brakes of digitalization efforts. On the one hand, companies feel a need for digital transformation due to declining core business, and on the other hand, sufficient financial resources enable digital transformation to be carried out quickly and comprehensively throughout the company and thus remain actionable. While a lower financial pressure on the core business can reduce the perceived urgency, companies that are already under financial pressure are limited in financing digitalization projects. Therefore, companies should also and especially prepare for digital transformation and, if necessary, support projects during growth phases and explore and discuss their possibilities as impartially as possible and in good time.

5.1.3 Guiding Questions in Formulating a Transformation Strategy

From these considerations, four guiding questions arise for formulating a transformation strategy.

1. **Use of Technologies:** Which technologies are of central importance to the company? What ambition is associated with the use of new digital technologies? What adjustments are required to the company's IT landscape?
2. **Changes in the Value Creation Structure:** With which digital offers and processes will revenues be generated in the future?
3. **Changes in the Organizational Structure:** How is the digital business structured and managed and what structural adjustments are still required in the company?

4. **Financial Framework:** What implications does digital transformation have on results? What investment resources are available to finance the digital transformation project?

The strategy is implemented through the adaptation of products, processes and business models as well as, if necessary, by adjusting the IT landscape, the organizational structure, the culture and the skills available in the company. Budgets are to be defined for all these projects. There is typically an over-demand. For **solving the budgeting question** there are two approaches conceivable: a central and a decentralized one.

In the **central** budgeting approach, the corporate management provides a central budget for digitalization projects. This budget can be made available to a central digitalization unit, for example, or it will be directly allocated by the corporate management or a staff unit to the individual projects. The advantage is that the different corporate areas do not perceive the digital transformation as a burden that they have to bear with their own budget. In addition, the corporate management can directly control and prioritize how many resources are available for which project. However, it should be noted that a central allocation and planning of financial resources is not always the most efficient way and managers of the middle management level may be able to better assess where and to what extent financing needs exist. However, this problem depends heavily on the respective company structure.

Alternatively, digitalization projects can also be financed **decentralized** by the individual departments. As already mentioned, the allocation of resources can be more efficient and demand-oriented in this case. However, there is the danger that projects whose added value unfolds only in the long term are insufficiently financed, since the incentive setting in middle management often does not promote the long-term increase in competitiveness. In addition, there may be conflicts between the participating corporate units, for example on the question of who benefits from a project and should therefore contribute to the budget. In the worst case, the participants only see the project in the (financial) responsibility of the IT department and are not at all willing to contribute.

Even though there is no universally accepted answer to this problem, it is probably unavoidable that management at least to some extent influence the allocation of budgets because of the often far-reaching effects of digitalization projects on the entire organization. However, it should also be noted that a higher budget does not automatically lead to greater success of digitalization projects, because too many financial resources can also make sluggish and reduce the innovative power (Weinreich, 2016).

In addition, it should be mentioned that of course not only companies are facing the task of formulating a transformation strategy. Non-profit organizations should also deal with the formulation of a transformation strategy, which is already happening in parts. The use of technologies, the change of value creation and the corresponding change of structures should also be central themes there. The fourth dimension is more complex than in companies, because in addition to the financial framework, the specific goals of a non-profit organization have to be mapped.

5.1.4 The Strategies of Three Industries in Comparison

The digital transformation poses considerable challenges for companies from traditional industries—this has been pointed out several times. Of course, the extent and speed of the changes that increasingly put companies under pressure to act vary. Due to industry-specific trends and different priorities of the companies, this also results in a variety of approaches to digital transformation. For the transformation strategy, this means in concrete terms that it must be designed accordingly differently.

The following three different industries with an (increasing) focus on end customers are compared as examples, which are currently in the midst of a digital transformation, the business of which is partially changed massively by the digital change and which have different digital maturity levels (Chanias & Hess, 2016c; Hess et al., 2016; Wiesböck et al., 2017): the media industry, the automotive industry and the primary insurers.

5.1.4.1 Starting Situation in the Three Industries

The **media industry** is particularly interesting in the context of digital transformation, as it has long been exposed to changed consumer behavior (just think of the already mentioned Napster shock at the beginning of the 2000s, cf. Sect. 2.1). As one of the first industries, it was forced to deal intensively with the opportunities and risks of new digital technologies with the advent of the Internet as a new medium. The visible effects of digital change within the media industry are manifold: Digital media are increasingly replacing analog media (just think of the print business); distribution via the Internet is replacing offline distribution channels, while online distribution channels and social media are in turn dominated by new competitors from the technology sector (e.g. Apple, Google, Netflix); in addition, new interfaces are emerging with other industries—usually driven by the (mobile) Internet and the resulting technical solutions. As a result, the media industry has also developed management structures for coping with change much earlier than other industries and thus takes on a kind of pioneer position. The business activities of media companies traditionally focus on the creation, aggregation and distribution of content. Web 2.0 and the associated possibilities for collaboration and interaction lead to the increased emergence of new media companies specializing in the exchange of content via online media. These providers operate according to the platform approach by operating IT-based platforms and making them available to users.

Confronted with new advances by digital players such as Tesla, Uber or Alphabet/Google in the field of mobility, the **automotive industry** has now also recognized the need to systematically address the trend of digital change and actively shape the digital transformation with targeted strategies. Four central trends can be identified that are being picked up by almost all manufacturers in their transformation strategies. These four central trends are summarized with the acronym C.A.S.E.: "Connectivity", "Autonomous", "Sharing/Subscription/Smart" and "Electrification". In the foreground is the *connected vehicle* ("Connectivity"), which constantly communicates with its environment, as well as associated digital services ("Connected Car"). This trend makes the centralization of the vehicle architecture mentioned in Sect. 2.1.2 necessary. The connected vehicle in turn forms the basis for *autonomous driving* ("Autonomous"), which depending on the level gets along with more or less active intervention of the driver. In addition, there are new, "smart" mobility concepts such as car sharing and carpooling. Last but not least, the trend of increasing *electrification* ("Electrification") is central, although here other sustainability aspects are now playing a greater role than "just" electromobility (supply chains, recycling of materials, etc.). All companies are now aware that these four trends will fundamentally change the automotive industry and its business models in the medium to long term. As a processing industry with mostly global value chains and a comprehensive distribution structure that includes both B2B and B2C elements, the automotive industry also has to deal with other digitalization trends that do not directly affect the original core product. This ranges from digitally controlled supply chains to networked and automated production to integrated omnichannel sales approaches.

In the course of digital transformation, not only processes but also business models are changing in the **insurance industry**. The latter are characterized by intangible, explicable products and strict regulation, which is why personal contact with a representative has traditionally played a special role in the sale of insurance products. This has contributed to the fact that the digital transformation in the insurance industry has been driven more cautiously than in other industries. In recent times, however, the insurance industry has also begun to regard the transition to the digital world as a central management issue. This puts digital channels for sales and service, but also new insurance products that are only made possible by digital technologies (for example, usage-based car insurance based on telematics), in the spotlight. However, the further automation of processes through the gradual use of new technologies remains an issue.

5.1.4.2 Use of Technologies

Innovative digital technologies (or advanced IT) can create new business opportunities for companies and be crucial for securing competitive advantages. However, the importance of IT and its strategic role differ considerably across industries.

The media industry is now increasingly relying on digital technologies as "enablers" of new products, processes and business models. Of central importance are currently for many media companies—in addition to the expansion of fast Internet as an infrastructure for multi-page and broadband communication—the social computing (ie the involvement of the user in the creation of content), media-neutral databases and personalization systems as well as new solutions for the marketing of advertising.

For manufacturers of vehicles, the expansion of infrastructure is also of central importance, but more in terms of the integration of vehicles into the network. The applications focus on the additional services in the vehicle, assistance systems and the control of car-sharing fleets. In addition, there is a switch to the electrical and electronic architecture in the vehicle. However, these technologies are often seen more as a means to an end ("supporter") than as an "enabler" of new products and business models.

The latter also applies to insurers. There, online portals and various technologies for further automation of core processes continue to play a central role.

Regardless of the (previous) strategic role of IT, companies can follow different approaches in the use of new digital technologies. More conservative companies may use established and widely used technology solutions *("followers")*, while others, more progressive companies, use *"early adopters"* technologies in the early stages of their development.

A riskier approach is to act as an *"Innovator"* and develop new technological solutions independently, rather than sourcing them from the market. In the three industries just described, it has been shown that almost all companies in the field of digital technology have been "Followers" so far. Although few examples of the Innovator approach can be found in the media and insurance industries due to lack of technological expertise, almost all companies in these industries are increasingly striving to recognize and test new digital technologies as early adopters. Only the automotive industry, due to its engineering-oriented culture, still has the ambition to act as an Innovator in digital, vehicle-related areas (such as connected or autonomous driving). In the media sector, Burda Group tested the role of an Innovator with the company "Cliqz". The company wanted to provide a search engine that does not collect and share user data. However, this project has now been discontinued because Burda saw no chance of competing with Google in the long term.

5.1.4.3 Changes in the Value Creation Structure

In all industries, it can be seen that previously analog products and services are either completely digitized (e.g. music streaming/media industry) or expanded or enriched with digital elements (e.g. digital services for cars/automotive industry). Often, the intention is also to create new revenue and distribution models using a digital or digitized customer interface, which at the same time also improves the company's cost position (e.g. in service). However, the insurance industry also sees in the digital transformation the chance to create entirely new insurance products, such as the hedging of risks from cyber attacks.

The media industry also shows that the exploitation of new business areas can be a central part of a transformation strategy. Here, the changes in value creation can be seen above all in the fact that many media companies have already diversified their value chain into the digital world. The low willingness of customers to pay for digital content requires a rethink in the media industry. Therefore, some media companies are trying to move their commercial activities into other business areas where the willingness to pay is higher (e.g. e-commerce).

In total, there can be great differences between the industries considered in terms of the configuration of transformation strategies—both in terms of the extent of digital product diversification and in future revenue generation and possible main business areas.

5.1.4.4 Change in Organizational Structure

It has been shown that structural changes in the course of digital transformation are associated with several sub-aspects. The question arises as to which C-level position should be responsible for digital transformation. The result across all industries is clear and relatively homogeneous here: Ideally, the CEO should take responsibility for the transformation strategy. The operational execution of such a strategy is often delegated to a senior manager who is responsible for large parts of the digital business or for a digital unit or the business unit that is most affected by digital transformation.

Structurally, management clarifies responsibilities as part of a transformation strategy not only in terms of responsibilities, but also decides whether new digital business activities are integrated into existing structures or outsourced to separate units that are decoupled from the core business and the prevailing corporate culture. Across industries, it has been shown that integration into the existing corporate structure can be advantageous if close coordination between traditional and new digital businesses is required. In contrast, the explicit separation of existing business and new digital activities can facilitate disruptive approaches, which can also be observed across all industries.

In the industries considered here, companies usually use several of the digital organizational forms mentioned at the same time.

5.1.4.5 Financial Framework

The increasing financial pressure on the current core business triggers digital transformation in many companies in the first place. But anyone who wants to take on digital transformation needs financial resources at the same time, whether internal or external. Those who first wait and observe developments in the market therefore quickly run the risk of being left behind in the competition. However, if the core business is still profitable, responsible managers or entrepreneurs often do not see the need to trigger a digital change and support it with greater investment.

It can be said of the media industry that companies are under a comparatively high financial pressure, but at least the larger companies in the industry have so far been able to finance the multitude of digital activities from the existing cash flow, possibly accompanied by concentration tendencies.

The situation is different in both the insurance and automotive industries, which have so far experienced only a low to very low financial pressure from digital change. Although various threat scenarios are presented in the (specialist) media, the revenue streams in both industries have so far been relatively stable. Of course, numerous new players are already trying to address the core business of these industries with digital approaches (for example, online direct insurers or internet car dealers), but the financial effects have so far been limited, unlike in the media industry. It is all the more gratifying that both industries are using their comparatively comfortable financial situation to make targeted investments in digital activities on a large scale.

5.1.5 Typical Elements of a Transformation Strategy

Based on this industry comparison, the four dimensions of the DTS framework outlined above can now be further broken down to describe typical elements or content of a transformation strategy for each dimension. These elements provide initial guidance on the content of transformation strategies, but must always be adapted to the specific company and industry context.

Typical Elements of a Transformation Strategy

Use of Technologies

- Adaptation of own IT landscape
- Relevant technological trends
- Role of digital technologies
- Technological ambition

Changes in the Value Creation Structure

- Repositioning in terms of value chains
- Future core business areas
- Revenue sources and cost reduction approaches

Changes in Organizational Structure

- Responsibility for the transformation strategy
- Organizational location of digital activities
- Changes in the IT landscape
- Changes in structure, culture and competence

Financial Framework

- Financial pressure on the current core business
- Financing of digital initiatives

In the three examples explained above, the changes in structures and systems required for digital transformation were hardly emphasized. However, they now play an extremely important role. The implementation of digital transformation also requires changes in the IT landscape, structure and culture as well as the existing competencies in many companies. Such changes must also be specified in a transformation strategy—often they take a long time and require considerable investment.

5.2 The Way to the Transformation Strategy

While the content-related building blocks of a transformation strategy were already explained in Sect. 5.1, there are still no concrete guidelines for entrepreneurs and managers on how a dedicated transformation strategy should be formulated. Therefore, the process of developing transformation strategies is examined in more detail below (Chanias & Hess, 2016b; Chanias et al., 2019).

5.2.1 Two Basic Ways of Development

It turns out that the central determinant for the introduction and implementation of transformation strategies is the interaction between the digital transformation efforts of top management (**"top-down"**) and the employees of the organization (**"bottom-up"**). From this perspective, two variants of the strategy process can be distinguished. Both variants are illustrated below using a real example.

5.2.1.1 Bottom-up Strategy Development at an Automobile Manufacturer

Although it is tempting to assume that the development of transformation strategies is initiated by top management in large organizations, this can only be confirmed to a limited extent from first experiences. Instead, it turns out that the strategy process is initiated in this environment rather bottom-up—that is, from the middle of the organization.

The example of an internationally operating automobile manufacturer makes this clear. In 2015, the company's top management decided, under the direct responsibility of the CEO, to develop a company-wide transformation strategy with the help of the central strategy department. The trigger for the top management was the dynamic development of the company's external environment, which was caused by the emergence of new competitors from the consumer electronics and Internet economies. With the aim of defending the leading competitive position also in the digital age, a new strategy was to be developed. In the meantime, however, the individual company divisions had already started to create facts in the digital transformation. It became clear, for example, that in important company divisions—from research and development via production to sales and marketing—numerous digitalization initiatives had already been launched. Obviously, the center of the organization had already recognized digitalization needs much earlier than the top management due to its proximity to the market and technology knowledge and, with the support of the middle management, had already launched strategic initiatives. For example, a comprehensive Connected-Car initiative had its origin in the After-Sales division's desire to increase the utilization of contract workshops by means of (connected) vehicle data. However, what was lacking in the already running digital activities was a unified target image and systematic control by the top management. Because in the meantime a growth of decentralized digitalization initiatives had taken place and some stakeholders had deliberately avoided cross-departmental coordination in order not to lose speed. This led to a situation in which—from a corporate perspective—the overview of the ongoing activities was increasingly lost and synergy potentials were not used.

This uncoordinated emergence as well as the described developments in the external environment finally moved the top management and the responsible strategy department in this example to give the digital activities a uniform direction after all by means of a transformation strategy, to prioritize activities and, if necessary, to eliminate existing conflicting ideas. Thus, the transformation strategy created in this way aimed at creating a unified target image for all ongoing digital activities within the organization and measuring the multitude of separate and much earlier created digitization initiatives against this target image. In terms of content, the transformation strategy largely picked up the existing strategy content of the individual business areas and embedded it in a formalized framework.

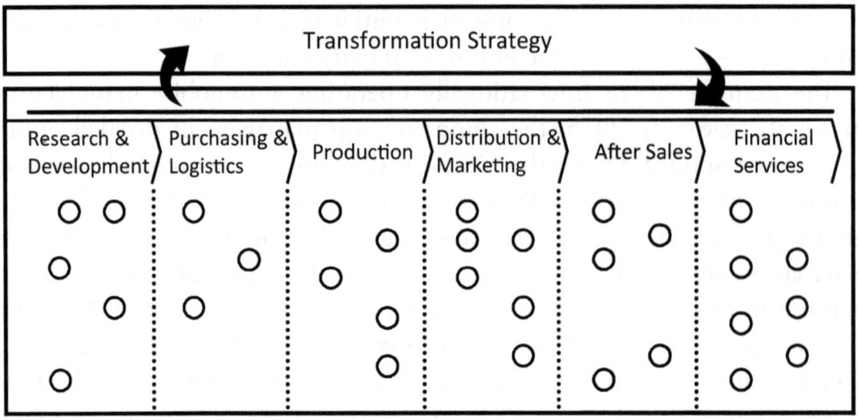

Fig. 5.3 Example of a Bottom-Up Strategy Process

From a processual point of view, the transformation strategy was thus initiated by bottom-up activities, which were finally responded to top-down (Fig. 5.3). In other words, the contents of the transformation strategy were already largely in place before it was even developed by the top management. Contrary to the widely held assumption that strategies arise on a blank sheet of paper, this bottom-up strategy process thus ran completely differently than expected.

5.2.1.2 Top-Down Strategy Development at a Financial Service Provider

The counterpart to this is the initiation of strategy development by a top-down approach. But even in this case, a combination with the second direction, in this case the development of ideas from the organization, is required. The example of a medium-sized financial service provider illustrates this.

In 2016, in response to a preliminary project in the field of direct sales, the CEO of this company decided to make the company one of the first in the industry to be consciously digital. For this purpose, a digitalization responsible person was appointed under his responsibility, who in turn was given the task of heading up a newly set up digital unit. The central task of the digital unit was to formulate a company-wide transformation strategy and to implement it quickly. Up to this point, the company had hardly any experience with digitalization initiatives—not least because the

IT department—as is typical for the financial sector—was subject to strong regulation and control and therefore always placed the safe operation of the infrastructure in the foreground. To drive digital innovation, it was therefore not only lacking in the necessary resources and know-how, but also in the required claim.

The company now pursued two approaches in the formulation of the strategy. The first approach provided for the gradual derivation of digitalization requirements in the form of a roadmap by the top management for core areas of the company in order to achieve a fundamental digital transformation of the business model. The second building block should help to raise digital innovation potential within the organization. Individual departments or employees were therefore asked to participate in a company-wide ideas competition and to bring their own ideas from their field of work. On the basis of these two building blocks, the contents of the transformation strategy were to be created within a given framework.

Interestingly, it turned out that the bottom-up building block bore fruit much faster than the top-down building block. While the former led to concrete digitalization initiatives and at the same time drove the cultural transformation after a relatively short time, the latter was hardly effective due to indecision and disagreement within the top management. This made the bottom-up activities initiated for the top-down strategy process a central success element. At the same time, however, it also became clear that the bottom-up ideas won were of a more incremental nature.

5.2.1.3 Conclusion

Already from these two cases, the first interesting observations can be made about the process of developing strategy. On the one hand, it can be said that digitalization strategies are difficult to plan centrally, but on the other hand, a pure bottom-up approach is also not enough. Rather, a combination of bottom-up and top-down elements is required. Ideas for incremental development can be generated from the organization. However, fundamentally new approaches that, for example, lead to entirely new business areas, should be initiated centrally. An empirical study from the media industry confirms this latter finding (KPMG, 2016).

5.2.1.4 Add-on: Transformation Strategy as an Emergent Phenomenon

As early as the 1980s, Mintzberg (Mintzberg & Waters, 1985) described that realized strategies arise in a planned manner and thus follow the intentions of top management, or else they can "emerge" through continuous and unplanned patterns of behavior—with both variants of strategy formation usually being observed in reality. The reasons for this can be manifold: On the one hand, analytical processes for formulating a strategy—which are still widespread and may be driven by an internal strategy department or even with external support from strategy consultants—are not able to take into account all eventualities and uncertainties in future implementation; on the other hand, dynamics in the internal or external context of a company can change the course of the strategy process, for example through personnel changes in top management, through unforeseeable activities of important competitors or through new developments in the field of technology.

The uncoordinated mode of formation shown in the context of the discussion of the bottom-up strategy process points to a primarily emergent nature. This is not entirely surprising, since almost all areas of the company are affected by IT-induced changes as part of the digital transformation. The proliferation of digitalization initiatives shown indicates that many stakeholders within the organization have recognized the need for action early on and wanted to address it as quickly as possible. Top management therefore faces the challenge of keeping an overview and not being overtaken by already ongoing decentralized digitalization efforts. Accordingly, transformation strategies are to be designed in such a way that emergent strategy content can subsequently be reconciled or aligned with the intentions of top management; it should also be ensured that strategy content is created for the future that follows the intentions of top management (for example, cross-platform IT platforms that offer synergies for the entire company). In a bottom-up strategy process, a formalized framework is thus created by means of the transformation strategy, which is accompanied by a specific steering function.

Although top-down strategy processes initially often create the appearance of a planning nature, here too a specific function of the transformation strategy can be seen, which rather points to an emergent process. Because in the case of the financial service provider examined above, the top management only set a rough framework within which specific digitization initiatives and thus strategy content should arise over time. Mintzberg (Mintzberg

& Waters, 1985) describes such strategies as "intended emergent", because they aim to ensure that strategy content only arises "on the way", but within a consciously managed framework. As with bottom-up strategy processes, the intention of the top management should ultimately be brought into line with the intentions of the organization's employees in the top-down strategy process—which, in addition to the emergent character, is another similarity of both strategy processes.

However, the fact that the formation of transformation strategies is conditionally or even completely emergent also implies that there can be no large "toolbox" with many differentiated instruments for the development of transformation strategies—this would only be necessary if a transformation strategy were to be planned to a large extent centrally, but this is obviously not the case. Rather, mechanisms are required that allow the entire organization to be involved in the development of the strategy.

5.2.2 Further Peculiarities in the Formation of a Transformation Strategy

The following describes two further specifics of the process of formation of transformation strategies.

5.2.2.1 Interplay of Planning and Implementation

It has been shown that transformation strategies do not follow the planning conventions of strategy formulation. On the contrary: The formulation and implementation of a transformation strategy should be approached completely differently. It is recommended to understand the realization of such a strategy as a **learning, dynamic and open-ended process** in which formulation activities go hand in hand with implementation activities. The transformation strategy is a moving target, with formulation and implementation having no foreseeable end, as the strategy is continuously developed through a "trial and error" approach. A metaphor for this is the image of a feedback loop in the iterative development of product increments (minimum viable products) using agile methods, which are increasingly used in the implementation of IT projects (see also Sect. 3.2.4.1). For example, new developments in the field of digital technologies, but also changes in the market environment, can be picked up in a further "strategy loop" at any time.

It has also been shown that a large number of **novel and unconventional approaches** are used in the formulation and implementation of transformation strategies. These are approaches that are developed and used by digitalization responsible persons and made available to affected stakeholders in the form of concrete recommendations or specifications to a certain extent. Examples of these practices are:

- Cross-functional, cross-hierarchical, and interactive formats for developing and discussing strategic content (e.g., cross-functional strategy off-site meetings involving upper and middle management or company-wide innovation competitions),
- the conscious use of a variety of digital media and channels for internal communication of strategic goals and approaches throughout the company (e.g., using videos distributed via the intranet), and
- the conscious promotion of knowledge exchange on digital topics with experts, service providers, start-ups, competitors, or companies from more digitally mature industries.

Some of the listed procedures are emblematic of an opening of the strategy process to the entire organization—with the goal of achieving the best possible result. This approach, which is also referred to as **"Open Strategy"** and has established itself in digital contexts (Tavakoli et al., 2017), represents a departure from the convention that strategies are exclusively "closed" by top management—that is, a small group—and formulated in secret. Open Strategy, in contrast, refers to an inclusive and transparent approach to formulating a strategy that involves various actors both within and outside the organization. Most often, these open approaches are IT-supported, i.e. companies use collaborative and social tools and platforms to carry out the strategy process. Examples of possible IT solutions are blogs, wikis, survey tools, crowdsourcing platforms or enterprise social networks. For example, as early as 2008, IBM integrated more than 150,000 internal and external participants into the company-wide strategy process on the basis of an innovation jam using a social IT platform, resulting in the generation and discussion of some 32,000 ideas. The main advantages of this open approach are the full exploitation of the creative potential of an organization, but also better and faster (strategic) decisions that also find more support or acceptance within the organization. Although such an approach inevitably entails a high degree of coordination, Open Strategy thus offers the possibility of allowing a transformation strategy to emerge intentionally emergent.

5.2.2.2 Dialogue-Oriented Approach

In addition to choosing contemporary approaches, sensitivity to the internal political tensions that usually surround digitalization efforts is also of central importance for the success of strategy implementation from a management perspective. In particular, in the context of digitalization, some initiatives are started by stakeholders with the (individual) intention of advancing their own careers or expanding the competencies of their own area in order to cement their own existence. Not a few digitalization initiatives have already failed because the participating areas and managers could not agree on the distribution of competencies, responsibilities or budgets. Employees from other industries who are increasingly being recruited in many companies for knowledge transfer in the context of digital change often encounter resistance and rejection within organizations due to their unconventional thinking and approach. Political developments can thus quickly become an obstacle to digital transformation. It is clear that there is no panacea for resolving such tensions or conflicts of interest in strategy implementation. However, it has been shown that a dialogue-oriented approach involving higher management levels and the clear definition or written fixation of responsibilities is a first, essential step—which should ideally take place before the first tensions arise.

5.2.3 Two Instruments for Generating Ideas Bottom-up

The bottom-up approach, i.e. the picking up of existing ideas, is—in the outlined nuances—an important approach for generating ideas from the organization. In addition to development work in R&D departments and project work in middle management, idea competitions and "hackathons" are important instruments for this. Both are introduced below.

5.2.3.1 Idea Competitions

An ideas competition is a competition of innovators who use their skills, experiences and creativity to generate ideas or provide a solution to a specific task (Walcher, 2010). Ideas competitions are also known under terms such as innovation competitions or design competitions, although they focus on generating ideas. At its core, an ideas competition is an idea of classical proposal management that many companies are familiar with.

In the context of an ideas competition, a target group is given a task on an IT-based platform that must be completed within a specified period of time. Often, the selection of the submitted ideas takes place in a multi-stage process, with the ideas being roughly filtered the a first stage and the remaining ideas being gradually further concretized. The results are usually evaluated by a jury, which awards the winner of the competition with a monetary or material prize. Under the aspect of competition, the aim is to improve the quality and quantity of submissions. The award should be transparent and motivating. It can be beneficial to make resources available to the winners for further implementation of their idea.

By involving the innovators, the company gains access to the participants' implicit knowledge regarding their needs (need information) and their expertise in solving problems (solution information).

An ideas competition can be held online and/or offline. Internal innovators (e.g. employees) or external innovators (e.g. customers, consumers or partners) can be invited to the competition as organizers of the competition in the sense of the open innovation approach. An overview of the most important design features for competition ideas are given in Table 5.1.

Innovation competitions can also be carried out with external partners. If a company deliberately opens its innovation process in the early stages and involves the outside world in this process, it realizes the **Open-Innovation-Approach** (von Hippel, 2001). The existing research and development departments of companies are not to be dissolved or replaced by open innovation. Rather, it is about supplementing, additional input from customers, suppliers and other external actors in order to be able to react more quickly to changed environmental conditions and trends.

An example of a successful open innovation approach is Lego's Ideas Platform, where customers can submit creative product suggestions for building blocks, increasingly also for ideas with a digital focus (Lego Ideas, 2018). But Deutsche Bahn is also open to external idea generators and awards a "Supplier Innovation Award" to promote new ideas from suppliers. The submitted solutions are evaluated by a jury and are intended to enable Deutsche Bahn to offer its products or services with significantly better performance characteristics (e.g. in terms of quality, punctuality, flexibility, efficiency, costs, comfort, experience) (Deutsche Bahn, 2018).

A characteristic of the company's opening is that users of the product and thus external knowledge are involved in the innovation process (see also Fig. 5.4). The opening of idea generation also makes it possible for companies with a small budget to generate a large number of ideas. These ideas are often developed with simple and pragmatic means. Open innovation

Table 5.1 Design Variants of an Ideas Competition (Walcher, 2010)

Parameter	Expression
Medium	Online Mixed Offline
Organizer	Company Public organization Nonprofit Individual
Task specificity	Low (open task) Defined High (specific task)
Degree of elaboration	Idea Sketch Concept Prototype Solution Developing
Target group	Specific Unspecific
Participation as	Individual Team Both
Evaluation	Jury evaluation Peer assessment Self-assessment Mixed
Community functionality	Available Not available
Incentive system	Monetary Non-monetary Mixed
Runtime	Very short Short Long Very long

processes therefore have a flexible "trial & error" mentality and thus also allow for unforeseen developments. The idea generators are aware that they are making their knowledge and ideas available to a self-organized community. In this type of idea generation, companies may therefore have to find solutions for the protection of the intellectual property of the idea generators. One possibility for this could possibly be open source licenses.

In this sense, the IBM Industry Solution Lab in Zurich analyses external innovation impulses from customers. Customer workshops are held annually and research projects, product offerings or new technologies are presented. In addition, the IBM Industry Solution Lab hosts the so-called "Innovation

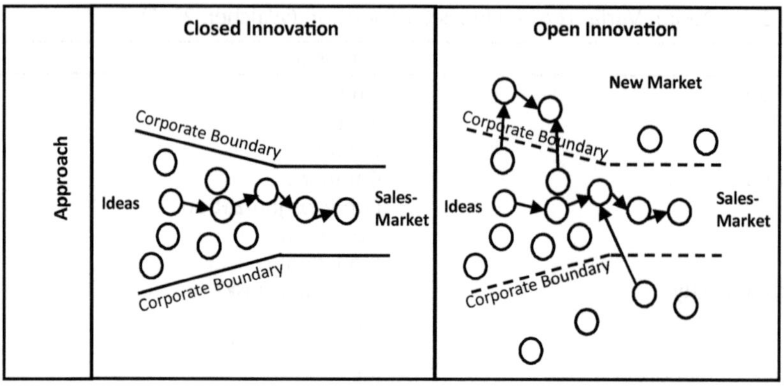

Fig. 5.4 Open Innovation versus Closed Innovation

Days" once a year, where leading scientists, customers, suppliers or potential partners meet to give impulses. This exchange enables IBM to become aware of new business areas at an early stage and thus to react faster than the competition. The success of IBM in this case is clearly based on the opening of the innovation process, which makes the company more flexible in responding to new market requirements (IBM, 2018).

The possibilities of internet-based communication tools (e.g. innovation platforms) accelerate and support the open innovation approach in a very decisive way. Web platforms act as drivers here, as they make the easy integration of users into different phases of the innovation process possible in the first place. The intelligence of the masses can be tapped via crowdsourcing platforms. This makes crowdsourcing platforms an extreme form of open innovation that only works IT-based.

5.2.3.2 Hackathons

A hackathon is a collaborative problem-solving event that aims to produce concrete solutions within a very short period of time (Schroll, 2007). This type of event is offered by a variety of companies, not just IT start-ups. The term hackathon, which is made up of the words "hack" and "marathon", first appeared in 1999 when OpenBSD and Sun Microsystems developers met independently to work on solutions to existing problems and challenges. Alternative terms are "hack day", "hackfestival" and "codefestival". The hackathon gained greater importance in the 2000s when some companies recognised the potential to develop new software technologies within a few hours and thus promote innovative ideas for digital innovation with the help of fewer resources.

Programmers and software architects, but also graphic designers and project managers from different companies and industries are invited to a hackathon competition to develop new software or work on related, IT-centred issues in teams. Often, ideas are proposed and solutions developed, codes programmed and results checked and improved within just 24 h. So the participants should not only have excellent programming skills, but also the ability to work under time pressure with previously unknown team members. It is not unusual for a prize to be awarded for successful completion.

Basically, two types of hackathons can be distinguished. The focus of the **"tech-centric" hackathons** lies in the development of software using a specific technology or application, for example programming an app using a specific programming language for a specific interface. **"Focus-centric" hackathons** on the other hand pursue specific corporate or social goals with their software innovations. For example, Facebook and Google regularly invite external developers to hackathon events, in addition to hackathons involving only internal company employees. A hackathon with a social goal is, for example, a call for improving the urban public transport system.

An example of the successful integration of hackathon events into the innovation culture can be observed at Facebook (Meta) (2012). Facebook organizes hackathons several times a year to generate ideas and promote the company's innovation capability. In doing so, programmers develop new innovations in the context of existing operational platforms that are solution- and future-oriented. Hackathons offer a great advantage for Facebook because they promote the personal encounter of different programmer communities that are often geographically separated from each other, and give employees the space to realize new concepts. The idea for the "like button", for example, is said to have originated in the context of such a hackathon. Incremental product innovations are a typical result of hackathons.

5.3 Management Roles in Digital Transformation

Digital transformation is a task for top management—this sentence would probably be signed by everyone today. But: can a CEO delegate the topic or does he have to drive it forward himself? Furthermore, the question arises as to whether the known role models are sufficient at all. Is the Chief

Information Officer (CIO) really the driver of digital transformation—or does he "only" ensure an efficient and fast technical implementation? All these are questions that deal with management roles in digital transformation. The following chapter provides the first answers.

5.3.1 Digital Transformation is a Top Priority

Table 5.2 shows the result of a practical analysis of German media companies as early as 2016 (KPMG, 2016). The decision on the transformation strategy, the alignment with the corporate strategy and the change in corporate culture are the responsibility of the CEO for more than 80% of the participants. But even in the other tasks he bears the main responsibility in most cases, even in areas that are traditionally the responsibility of the CFO or CHRO. Only the modernization of the IT infrastructure (which here also includes the development of new applications) is primarily the responsibility of the CIO and not the CEO in the majority of companies. Surprisingly, the CIO, who actually has proximity to technological issues and in the past has also been seen as a driver of innovation and further development of the business or at least the processes, has little responsibility that goes beyond IT.

Table 5.2 Distribution of the Main Responsibility for the Management of Digital Transformation in the Media Industry (KPMG, 2016)

	CEO (%)	CDO (%)	CIO (%)	CFO (%)	CHRO (%)
Give ideas and impulses for digitization	68	16	3	0	0
Decide on digitalization strategy	84	12	0	0	0
Alignment with corporate strategy	88	7	0	0	0
Project portfolio management	52	14	3	3	0
Allocate financial resources	65	3	1	27	0
IT infrastructure modernization	28	7	46	3	1
Building structures that promote innovation	65	7	3	1	6
Transformation openly and intensively communicate	70	10	1	0	3
Change mentality and company structure	83	3	0	0	3
Training and hiring staff	39	8	1	4	23

In the control of transformation programs, the CEO is primarily supported by the CDO—this is shown by a second evaluation of the mentioned study. In general, it can be observed that a CDO takes on a function that is strongly focused on supporting the CEO. He is therefore involved in the construction of structures that promote innovation, the communication of transformation in the company and also partly in the training of the staff. However, he is rarely involved in the allocation of financial resources, the modernization of the IT infrastructure and the control of the project portfolio. This study thus draws the picture of the CDO as a responsible person in the second row, who rarely acts as the main responsible person, but supports the CEO as a consultant and organizer on a broad front.

If distinguished between larger and smaller companies, one will notice some different nuances. For example, it can be observed that in larger companies, the CEO is largely responsible for the digital transformation. However, in larger companies, the other C-level positions are more responsible for their area, so the CFO for resource allocation, the CHRO for personnel training and recruitment, and the CIO for IT infrastructure and IT systems. It can also be observed that in medium and large companies, so-called digitalization boards are increasingly being used. In these boards, digitalization questions are discussed in more detail than in the line boards.

5.3.2 The CDO as a Supporting Role

5.3.2.1 Tasks of a CDO

The typical tasks of a CDO (who is often also found in companies under different titles, such as Head of Digital Transformation) can be well illustrated using the example of a publishing house from the media industry (Horlacher & Hess, 2016). This publisher offers learning solutions worldwide with great success, but paid too little attention to recent technological developments. The specific goal was therefore to develop the publisher from a pure print publisher to a modern, digital "education publisher" with many online offerings. To this end, a CDO was already appointed in 2012. He had previously worked in the strategy department of a media company. The first challenge for the new CDO, who reports directly to the CEO of the education division of the publisher, was to accompany the development of a comprehensive transformation strategy for the company. This was later an integral part of the publisher's strategy. Internally, the focus of the digital change was on the product, with the CDO primarily concerned with how the new digital products have to look in order to be future-oriented and successful on the market.

A central prerequisite for the implementation of the transformation strategy was the internal restructuring of the organization, such as the change in reporting structures. At the same time, the CDO had to keep an eye on the applications and infrastructure underlying the products and find out which (new) technologies the publisher needed to successfully produce and distribute new digital products. In this context, the entire product development was redesigned and significantly expanded. Lacking knowledge and experience outside of traditional publishing were integrated into the company by targeted recruiting. In production, many partial steps were standardized and a modular production adapted to the requirements of the digital world was introduced. An important part of the digital transformation of the publisher was also a so-called data-driven product development strategy. By evaluating the available data on product usage, a product should be adapted to customer wishes much faster than before. In 2015, the project was largely completed. The CDO then took over a line function in a large publishing group.

This example shows the typical tasks of a CDO. On the one hand, he is responsible for the fact that a transformation strategy arises, that it is based on the current technological development and that it is actually implemented by means of initiatives. For this purpose, he must in particular promote cross-company cooperation, which is not an easy task in many established companies. In addition, it is his task to arouse enthusiasm for the digital change in the company and thus to involve the employees in the creation of a transformation strategy—the more or less emergent character of transformation strategies makes this indispensable.

Nevertheless, CDOs can focus on different, possibly changing priorities over time, depending on the context of the company. For this purpose, three approaches have been established (Singh & Hess, 2017):

- CDOs as **entrepreneurs** explore innovations that can arise from the use of new digital technologies, formulate a corresponding digital transformation strategy and implement it in their company. CDOs of this nature initiate and design the controlled change of their company to a fully digital organization that uses new information technologies strategically for itself. In this role as entrepreneurs, CDOs occasionally change entire business models.
- As **digital evangelists** CDOs inspire the entire workforce of a company with regard to new technologies and their strategic use in the company. This usually requires a profound cultural change that the CDO drives

forward and thus also promotes cooperation across functions and hierarchical levels. For this purpose, such CDOs communicate their digital transformation strategy and the progress of digital activities throughout the company in order to take everyone on a common journey. Training also plays an important role in this cultural change, as the workforce has to deal with many new challenges and process changes during the digital transformation.

- In order to actively initiate and implement the change and the overall digital transformation strategy, CDOs can primarily act as **cross-departmental coordinators**. This is how they manage the controlled change from decoupled functions to cross-departmental cooperating organizations. CDOs of this nature network the entire company, do away with existing silo mentalities and control the digital transformation across departments.

In order to be able to successfully implement the respective role, it is necessary that the CDO, in addition to original transformation knowledge, also has sound IT knowledge and sufficient resilience. This resilience is particularly important for acting in cross-departmental projects. CDOs also benefit from visionary thinking in order to look beyond existing strategies and proven practices and shape the digital future of their companies. In addition, CDOs need to be inspirational in order to convince internal decision-makers and employees of their vision of digital transformation and to show the associated benefits.

CDO positions are currently being created in many companies, especially when the transformation pressure is high and the organization is complex. In a practice study by KPMG (2016) just under a third of media companies already said in 2016 that they had set up a CDO or a similar position. Not one of these companies wanted to roll back this position, rather almost half even thought about strengthening this position. Another practice study (etventure 2018) showed that in 15% of the companies surveyed in Germany from various industries, a CDO is already steering the digital transformation.

5.3.2.2 Delimitation of the CDO Role

The question of the delimitation of the role of the CDO to "neighboring" C-level positions (Horlacher & Hess, 2016) inevitably arises.

The closest points of contact are with the CIO and the Chief Strategy Officer (CSO). Of course, digital transformation is a strategically important task for companies. As a rule, strategic issues are the responsibility of the CSO. However, the CSO usually lacks dedicated digital expertise in terms of digital business models and, in particular, the potential of digital technologies for a company.

A CDO has different tasks than a CIO—topics such as developing new products are just as much a part of it as developing the culture of a company. Even if CIOs—as is increasingly expected of them—deliver digital innovations and thus strategic added value for the business on a point-by-point basis, they are nevertheless increasingly challenged by their classical business. On the one hand, the CIO is to further develop the system landscape and the infrastructure, and this is increasingly for a network of suppliers, with accelerating technology cycles and under growing cost pressure. With the increasing importance of IT, the requirements for availability and security of the IT landscape are also increasing. The CIO has the challenging role of a strategic IT specialist in the company, while the CDO is the digital transformation specialist of the entire company. This is also an important distinguishing feature between CDOs and CIOs: The digital transformation is the fundamental core of the work of a CDO, and not "just" an additional task among others. As a result, the CDO does not have a dedicated focus on technological aspects, but also takes into account the customer perspective in order to ultimately achieve value creation.

CDOs also do not replace innovation managers in a company. Chief Innovation Officers promote innovation and innovation readiness in companies, but not only in the digital sector. Nor is the CDO to be confused with a Chief Data Officer, as has already been installed in some companies. A Chief Data Officer focuses on the identification and use of a company's data stocks and is therefore clearly focused, unlike the CDO with its rather broad range of tasks.

In Table 5.3 the main tasks of the management roles mentioned above are contrasted with the tasks of the CDO.

Finally, two more aspects will be briefly discussed. Typically, a CDO is installed for the entire company. However, if it is a very large company with very heterogeneous business areas, it can make sense to install CDOs at the level of business units or even selected functional areas, which in this case often have specialized roles (e.g. digital marketing specialists). This is particularly obvious when the group management is more of a financial than a management holding. In addition, it can be observed that the idea of a CDO is also increasingly being taken up in the public sector. Thus, in the spring of 2018, Bavaria appointed a Minister of Digitalization for the first

Table 5.3 Tasks of the CDO Compared with Adjacent Management Roles

Chief Digital Officer	Chief Strategy Officer	Chief Information Officer	Chief Innovation Officer	Chief Data Officer
Accompanying the definition of a digitalization strategy Initiation of concrete digital initiatives Digital motivation of the entire company	Accompanying the definition of the company strategy Accompanying the implementation of the strategy M&A	Development of an IT strategy Provision of the appropriate IT systems and IT infrastructure	Promoting innovative approaches in the company Cooperation with innovative providers outside	Identification of data sets Improving possibilities for data exploitation and data analysis

time, whose central task is to further develop, implement and bring the topic into the other ministries—just like a CDO in a company.

5.3.3 Conditions for the Deployment of a CDO

CDO positions are currently being created in many companies. However, it is now also becoming clear that the installation of a CDO can be an adequate response to the challenges of digital transformation, but CDOs do not have to be part of a successful digital transformation in all contexts. Firk et al. (2021) show that the decision to centralize responsibility for digital transformation in the position of the CDO depends essentially on two factors.

The **transformation pressure** indicates how important it is for companies to switch to digital business models. From the perspective of individual companies, the importance of digital transformation varies. From an internal perspective, the inherent characteristics of the respective business models can lead to a significant change in value creation through the emergence of digital technologies. In particular, information- and knowledge-based business models, such as those of media or service companies, are susceptible to being replaced by digital substitutes. Such companies can particularly benefit from CDOs accelerating digital transformation by designing new digital business models and building the required digital skills. In terms of transformation pressure, however, external factors also play a role—in the form of new competitors who can endanger established market positions. New and agile companies that use digital technologies efficiently are increasingly penetrating established competitive contexts. In the automotive industry, for example, companies such as Uber are putting traditional players under pressure by building digital platforms that offer mobility as a service. In this context, companies can particularly benefit from CDOs who anticipate the strong threats posed by emerging digital companies and take appropriate countermeasures.

The need for a CDO in the TMT is also influenced by the internal and external **coordination needs** of digital transformation. The internal coordination needs for digital transformation are particularly large in highly diversified companies, as they are prone to the emergence of business silos that pursue digital initiatives decoupled. CDOs can bring together such decentralized digital activities and identify and realize synergies in the development and application of digital technologies across the product or geographic departments. Since digital transformation often changes organizational power structures in diversified companies, a CDO can also help to counteract the political tensions that arise from this. On the external side, a coordination need arises above all when the regional environment lags behind in digital infrastructure. This infrastructure includes both technical and legal conditions. For example, the implementation of digital transformation in a certain region depends on the existing technical framework conditions, such as the speed and coverage of broadband Internet access. A lag in the necessary infrastructure can prevent companies from introducing digital innovations—such as those based on the Internet of Things—into the respective markets. In addition, legal framework conditions can either facilitate digital change by adapting regulations to the characteristics of digital innovation, or hinder progress by creating additional obstacles. CDOs can point to resulting problems of inadequate infrastructure through communication with relevant stakeholders and negotiate an improvement.

Figure 5.5 summarizes the two sketched framework conditions for the implementation of a CDO in companies by means of a subdivision into four quadrants. In doing so, the transformation pressure and the coordination requirements of digital transformation are distinguished according to internal and external aspects. Below the quadrants, the contribution that a CDO can make in each dimension is represented.

It is worth mentioning the result of Firk et al. (2021), that the influence of the coordination needs increases over time, while the influence of the transformation pressure decreases. On the one hand, this can be explained by the fact that with the increasing penetration of various industries and company departments by digitalization, the coordination needs between

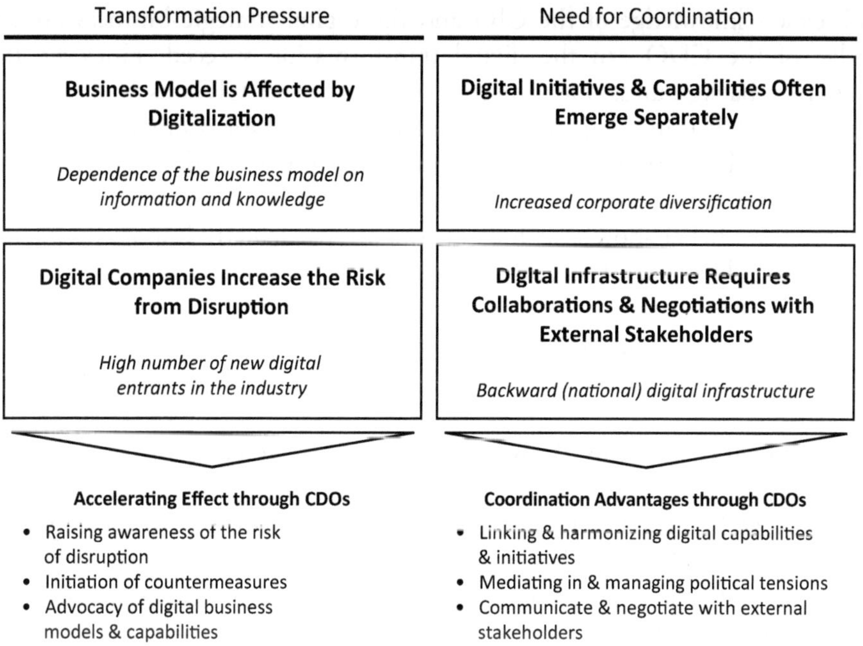

Fig. 5.5 Framework Conditions for the Implementation of a CDO (Firk et al., 2021)

different projects and units within the company increase. On the other hand, ideas and knowledge are more widespread and increasingly seen as self-evident with advancing digitalization. As a result, the need for change and the possible ways of digital transformation become more and more clear, so that the influence of the transformation pressure on the CDO presence decreases over time.

5.3.4 Successful Cooperation Between CDO and CIO

Without the adaptation of IT systems and IT infrastructure, any digital transformation is doomed to fail. But this also applies if the digital transformation is limited to the technical level only. Therefore, in part, CIOs claim to deal with new processes, products or even new business models in addition to the introduction of technical systems—even though this is usually limited to new processes in practice. For companies, this means that they should pay special attention to a functioning relationship between CDO and CIO and actively promote it, because only in the interplay between the

IT expert knowledge of the CIO and the digital strategic business knowledge of the CDO can the digital transformation succeed. However, the different backgrounds and expertise of CDOs and CIOs as well as some history of CIOs in companies contain the potential for conflict, as they can quickly lead to very different views and thus to the blockade of digitalization programs.

Studies (2017) show that four factors are particularly important for the interaction between CDO and CIO:

- a shared understanding of what the goals of digital transformation are,
- specialization,
- trust,
- coordination in terms of concrete cooperation (see Fig. 5.6).

Taken together, the latter three aspects lead to a reduction in the cognitive overload of CDO and CIO, as both specialize in different areas of knowledge, trust the knowledge and skills of the other, and focus on different aspects of a shared task.

In terms of specialization within CDO-CIO teams, the first step is the knowledge of the other's specific expertise. Good communication facilitates knowledge transfer in the next step. At least as important are well-defined roles that make it easier to distribute tasks between CDOs and CIOs. If, for example, CDOs are responsible for management tasks and CIOs for technological tasks in connection with digital transformation, the roles are usually clearly defined, which reduces potential friction. The prerequisite for this is, in turn, the acceptance of these roles by both parties.

The third factor, trust, also plays a particularly important role in the latter aspect. If CDOs and CIOs focus on different areas of responsibility, they must be able to trust each other's expertise. Mutual mistrust and constant (mutual) control would hinder and delay cooperation. In general, of course,

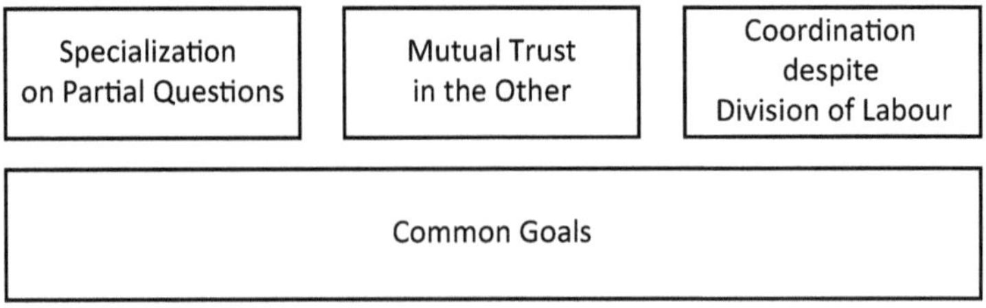

Fig. 5.6 Requirements for Good Cooperation between CDO and CIO (Singh et al., 2017)

a good fit of personalities also contributes to mutual trust, as this is usually associated with similar views and goals. Political competition, on the other hand, prevents mutual trust, which is why open and intensive task-related communication is essential in this context to strengthen mutual trust and thus cooperation in a constructive way. This can prevent political differences and strengthen team spirit. Similar work experience and knowledge in both IT and digital strategy and projects are also advantageous in order to strengthen the (mutual) trust in each other's expertise.

In terms of coordination, CDOs and CIOs need to aggregate and integrate their specialized expert knowledge. If activities are well coordinated, the goal of digital transformation can be achieved more efficiently, since both parties already know from the outset how tasks can be best distributed between them. Here too, clear role definitions and allocation of responsibilities are advantageous. In order to ensure these in turn permanently, it is important that the CEO also has an eye on it and is aware of how important clear role definitions are for cooperation. Thus, CEOs can also contribute to avoiding political differences between CDOs and CIOs. CDOs and CIOs themselves can, for example, positively influence coordination through regular formal meetings, because the good organization and structuring of their cooperation is another key element of efficient cooperation. This includes, for example, the prioritization of projects and the joint focus on the selected core projects, even if CDOs and CIOs are confronted with a multitude of tasks and construction sites. Especially in large companies, where regular direct communication between CDOs and CIOs is not always possible, intermediaries can strengthen communication and task integration between CDO and CIO.

Preceding the factors of specialization, trust and coordination is a shared understanding of the goals of digital transformation. This leads to faster decision-making and more effectiveness. Two aspects play a particularly important role here, namely personal similarities and mutual exchange of knowledge. Interactions for exchanging business and strategic IT knowledge support the shared understanding as well as regular informal communication. Personal similarities in the form of similar demographic and experience-technical characteristics lead in turn to similar attitudes. These have a particularly positive effect if both the CDO and the CIO have gathered business experience, IT knowledge and experience with entrepreneurial change or change processes during their careers, with it appearing particularly important that CIOs have gained a certain degree of business experience and CDOs a certain degree of IT knowledge over the course of their careers.

5.4 Maturity Models as a Tool?

Before developing a transformation strategy, it makes sense to take stock and thus to capture the status quo of a company in digital transformation. For this purpose, maturity models are always being advertised (Chanias & Hess, 2016a).

5.4.1 The Concept of Digital Maturity

In recent years, a number of maturity models have been proposed in this context to analyze the status of the digital transformation of a company. The majority of these approaches have been derived and developed by management consulting firms within a practice-oriented context. At first glance, many of the models seem to use similar approaches for assessing the digital maturity of a company and are based on the ideas of classical maturity models. On closer inspection, however, some differences between the models become apparent.

Maturity models are common instruments in areas such as development or project and quality management. They are always used when the object of observation is difficult to capture and a basis is needed for entrepreneurial or strategic decisions. The best-known example is the **Capability Maturity Model Integration** (CMMI), which can be applied to several areas: product and service development (CMMI for Development, CMMI-DEV), service set-up and management (CMMI for Services, CMMI-SVC) as well as product and service acquisition (CMMI for Acquisition, CMMI-ACQ). The main idea of these comprehensive models is to establish processes to avoid ad-hoc approaches and at the same time to introduce standardized procedures for processes in order to formalize and optimize them. In this context, "maturity" describes the degree of process control and improvement and refers—somewhat more generally formulated—to a state that is complete or perfect.

The term **Digital Maturity** can be interpreted in two different ways.

- On the one hand, the term can describe to what extent the tasks and information (or information flows) of a company are carried out or processed by IT. According to this technological interpretation, a company would be fully digital if it used IT exclusively for the execution of all tasks and the storage of all information. Although this definition is an

interesting interpretation from a technological point of view, it seems to be less relevant for management questions—see also Sect. 2.6.
- From a management point of view, it is therefore much more important to interpret the term Digital Maturity as the status of the digital transformation of a company, which describes what a company has already achieved in terms of (digital) transformation efforts. These efforts can, for example, include comprehensive changes from an operational point of view—such as changes to products or processes—as well as acquired metafunctions with regard to mastering the organizational change process.

5.4.2 Two Typical Maturity Models

In order to illustrate the diversity of existing models for determining digital maturity, two quite different but typical maturity models for digital transformation are presented below.

The MIT Center for Digital Business and Capgemini Consulting (Capgemini Consulting, 2011) have proposed an approach for the singular assessment of the digital maturity of companies using a **Digital Maturity Matrix** relatively early on. This approach allows companies to be evaluated according to two dimensions which are then brought together in a matrix.

- The first dimension, Digital Intensity (the "What"), describes a combination of strategic assets, digital elements, digital capabilities and investments.
- The second dimension, Transformation Management Intensity (the "How"), addresses management aspects which influence digital transformation and, for example, includes a digital vision or a specific leadership and organizational structure for digital transformation.

Together, these two dimensions represent the digital maturity of a company. A comprehensive digital transformation that creates value for all stakeholders can only be achieved if the company is fully mature in both dimensions. Four different digital maturity levels or company archetypes are distinguished in this context (see Fig. 5.7).

The maturity assessment according to this approach is based on a self-evaluation with ten leading questions for each of the two main dimensions. The intensity for each main dimension is therefore determined by evaluating the leading questions with values between 1 and 7. This means

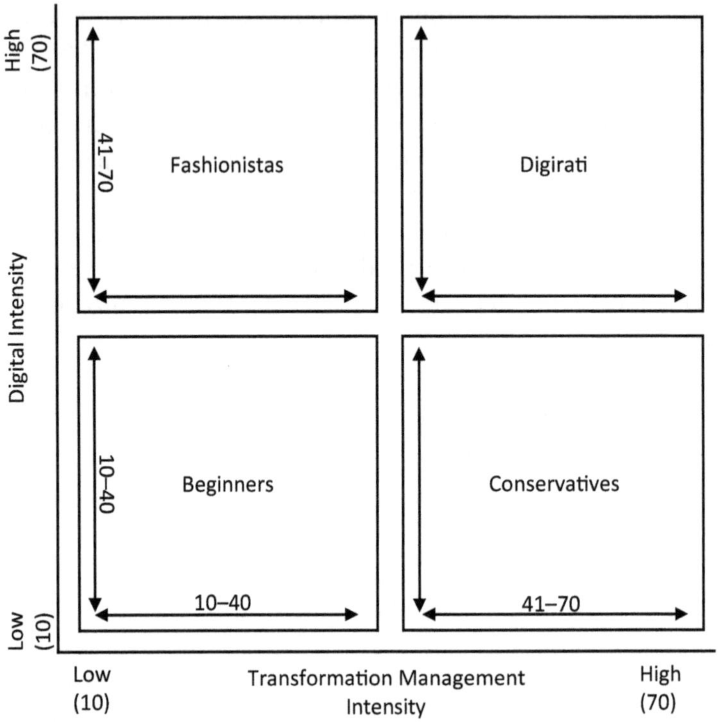

Fig. 5.7 Digital Maturity Matrix (Capgemini Consulting, 2011)

that the value 10 represents the lowest possible score per dimension and the value 70 represents the maximum. This also means that there is no weighting of the questions. The digital maturity of a company therefore represents the combination of the two main dimensions, with the value 41 being the threshold for each dimension.

The second model, the **Digital Maturity Model** (IWI-HSG & Crosswalk, 2015), comprises nine dimensions consisting of maturity criteria which in turn are measured by several best practice indicators. The main aim is to classify companies into five ascending maturity levels from "testing", "building", "consolidating", "structuring" to "optimizing".

To assess the digital maturity of a company, an online questionnaire must be filled out—as part of a comprehensive evaluation that includes a larger number of companies during a certain assessment period and typically covers up to nine topic areas, from "Customer Experience" to "Transformation Management". For each of the best practice indicators, participants must enter a rating on a five-point scale. Each indicator is then dynamically assigned to a certain level of difficulty. Subsequently, the indicators are divided into five maturity levels by means of a cluster analysis, with the simplest indicators being classified as maturity level one and the most demanding as maturity level five. In order to ensure that a company is not classified as maturity level five without meeting the requirements of the lower levels, a company can only move up if it also meets the criteria of the lower levels. In addition, a company is rated on the basis of its percentage maturity, which takes into account all indicators fulfilled in total. For this purpose, each indicator is assigned a certain maximum number of points on the basis of its difficulty. Thereafter, the percentage of points achieved is calculated in relation to the maximum number of points, which leads to the percentage maturity of a company. The overall maturity is derived from the calculation of the mean of the two levels.

The questionnaire of the "Digital Maturity Model" with the best practice indicators and a detailed description of the methodology is basically available free of charge, which makes it possible to trace the assessment to a certain extent. However, due to the design of the model, which requires a larger number of participating companies for the dynamic indicator assessment and a complex mathematical-statistical calculation, it is not possible to carry out the assessment independently and to understand the exact composition of the result without the support of the publisher of the model.

5.4.3 Design Parameters for Maturity Models

The two approaches presented have a number of similarities, but also differ in a number of ways. Based on a broad analysis of existing approaches (Chanias & Hess, 2016a), seven important design parameters can be delineated:

- Number and orientation of dimensions: The main feature of digital maturity models is the number and variety of dimensions that represent the competence areas and form the basis for the subsequent determination of maturity. The number and focus of these dimensions can differ to some extent; the range of dimensions can range from two to sixteen. From a content point of view, typical dimensions cover aspects of (strategic) transformation management, the core business including the digital product and service offering, the digital transformation of internal processes and procedures, digital customer interaction and IT use and development. In most cases, however, only the internal perspective is considered, while external perceptions such as customer feedback are not taken into account. In addition, there are hardly any models that take into account further performance indicators of a company, such as existing digital revenues or financial investments.

- Adaptability: Only a few models offer the possibility to adapt the method to the specific context of the company, such as the industrial background or other peculiarities of the company. Thus, most of the existing models use a standardized approach to assess digital maturity. However, some models are regularly revised by their publishers to reflect the current state of technological development. The latter aspect is particularly important with regard to the constant change of digital maturity assessment, as (technological) possibilities develop over time. When assessing the digital maturity of a company, therefore, almost all models take into account current and foreseeable possibilities both in terms of the changes already achieved (e.g. in what extent customers can be reached via mobile channels) and the expected challenges.
- Evaluation and data capture: The majority of the models studied do not offer the possibility of self-evaluation, as they are not described in detail or the necessary tools are not publicly available. As a result, in most cases, a consultancy has to be commissioned to carry out the assessment for the company. Nevertheless, there are some models that allow for manual or assisted self-evaluation, usually through broad guidelines or an online questionnaire. These models break down their main dimensions by using or considering certain areas, key questions or specific indicators, which in turn have to be assessed by company representatives.
- Determination of maturity: There is a wide range of qualitative and quantitative approaches to determine the digital maturity of companies. Qualitative models, for example, can be based on semi-structured management interviews and carry out their evaluation on an interpretative basis. Quantitative models usually use structured questionnaires with rating scales and can be very simple, for example by using a consolidated score for each dimension, or very complex, for example by combining different mathematical-statistical evaluation methods to determine a score. Some quantitative models are also based on a (dynamic) weighting of dimensions and underlying indicators.
- Assessment of maturity: The majority of the models carry out an assessment using four to five maturity levels. While some models use status levels that describe the internal digital penetration, others use certain archetypes or clusters of companies that each have common features. Again, different perspectives can be taken: either by looking at the

company as a whole or by looking at individual areas. In addition, either a single company can be evaluated or several companies can be compared with each other.

- Results presentation: To present their results, quantitative models use numerical scores that are calculated and expressed as absolute numbers or percentages. In some cases, however, these values only serve as an intermediate step, mostly to assign them to ascend maturity clusters, thus generating further but generic information about the overall status in digital transformation. Most of the qualitative and also some quantitative models also use a graphical representation of their results, e.g. by using a matrix or a spider diagram.
- Benchmarking and gap analysis: Only a few models offer the possibility to compare the results with those of other companies. The general importance and significance of benchmarking also depends on the availability of data on direct competitors with the same industry background. Furthermore, some models, which are based on best practices, enable the gap analysis to be carried out in order to identify improvement areas. However, none of the existing models provides concrete assistance in building digital transformation capabilities or in deriving concrete measures to close the identified gaps.

In Table 5.4 these seven parameters are summarized in three groups.

5.4.4 Limitations of Maturity Models

Maturity models are often used in practice. They serve—as described above—often as a starting point for management in increased efforts to digitally transform the company. In addition, statements about the degree of maturity are used at internal events such as strategy workshops, for example, to derive specific strategic measures such as the initiation of digital projects or larger digital programs. On the other hand, questions about the degree

Table 5.4 Design Parameters of Maturity Models (Chanias & Hess, 2016a)

General aspects	
Number and orientation of dimensions Adaptability	
Data collection and analysis Evaluation and data capture Determination of maturity	**Data presentation** Assessment of maturity Result presentation Benchmarking and gap analysis

of maturity can also arise in the external environment of a company, for example, as part of an inter-company comparison by analysts in the capital market.

The latter can often not be avoided, the internal use already. Especially in medium-sized and large companies, a generic classification of companies is often too vague and does not do justice to the size and complexity of the organization—unlike the typical areas of application of maturity models in narrowly defined areas. In addition, there is still no theoretical basis for the determination of a degree of maturity—see the considerations on an optimal degree of digitalization in Sect. 2.6. There is also a lack of further analytical tools that could help management to identify and derive specific areas for improvement and measures. Further challenges include the ensuring of the currency of maturity models or the too one-sided consideration of certain aspects (e.g. technologies) in the complex and therefore less transparent approaches of some models.

It should be mentioned that the majority of existing models were developed by or in cooperation with management consulting firms. On the one hand, this is understandable because consulting companies have a broad knowledge and are not only familiar with transformation management, but also with current (technological) developments in practice. On the other hand, representatives of companies must be aware that some consulting firms may see projects to determine digital maturity as a way to commission further work and therefore take a biased perspective.

References

Capgemini Consulting. (2011). Digital transformation: A roadmap for billion-dollar organizations. https://www.capgemini.com/wp-content/uploads/2017/07/Digital_Transformation__A_Road-Map_for_Billion-Dollar_Organizations.pdf. Accessed 23 Sept 2018.

Chanias, S., & Hess, T. (2016). How digital are we? Maturity models for the assessment of a company's status in the digital transformation. *WIM Management Report,* (2), 1–14.

Chanias, S., & Hess, T. (2016). Understanding digital transformation strategy formation: Insights from Europe's automotive industry. In *Proceedings of the 20th Pacific Asia Conference on Information Systems (PACIS 2016),* Chiayi.

Chanias, S., & Hess, T. (2016c). Vergleichsstudie zu Digitalisierungsstrategien in der europäischen Automobilindustrie: Digitale Transformation erfolgreich gestalten: Gemeinsame Studie von Berylls Strategy Advisors und dem Institut für Wirtschaftsinformatik und Neue Medien.

Chanias, S., Myers, M., & Hess, T. (2019). Digital transformation strategy making in pre-digital organizations: The case of a financial services provider. *Journal of Strategic Information Systems, 28*(1), 17–33. https://doi.org/10.1016/j.jsis.2018.11.003

Deutsche Bahn. (2018). Supplier innovation award. https://www.deutschebahn.com/de/geschaefte/lieferantenportal/supplier_award-1194354. Accessed 1 Sept 2018.

Facebook. (2012). Stay focused and keep hacking. https://www.facebook.com/notes/facebook-engineering/stay-focused-and-keep-hacking/10150842676418920/. Accessed 1 Sept 2018.

Firk, S., Hanelt, A., Oehmichen, J., & Wolff, M. (2021). Chief digital officers: An analysis of the presence of a centralized digital transformation role. *Journal of Management Studies,* 1–32.

Hess, T., Matt, C., Benlian, A., & Wiesböck, F. (2016). Options for formulating a digital transformation strategy. *MIS Quarterly Executive, 15*(2), 123–139.

Horlacher, A., & Hess, T. (2016). What does a chief digital officer do? Managerial tasks and roles of a new C-Level position in the context of digital transformation. In *Proceedings of the 49th Hawaii International Conference on System Sciences (HICSS 2016, January 5–9)* (pp. 5126–5135). Koloa.

IBM. (2018). IBM Research Zurich. https://www.zurich.ibm.com/. Accessed 1 Sept 2018.

IWI-HSG & Crosswalk. (2015). Digital transformation report 2015. https://aback.iwi.unisg.ch/kompetenz/digital-maturity-transformation/. Accessed 1 Sept 2018.

KPMG. (2016). *Der Chief Digital Officer – Phantom oder Wegbereiter? Studie zur Steuerung der digitalen Transformation in der Medienbranche.* Managementstudie der KPMG AG.

Lego Ideas. (2018). Lego ideas. https://ideas.lego.com/#all. Accessed 1 Sept 2018.

Matt, C., Hess, T., & Benlian, A. (2015). Digital transformation strategies. *Business & Information Systems Engineering, 57*(5), 339–343. https://doi.org/10.1007/s12599-015-0401-5

Mintzberg, H., & Waters, J. A. (1985). Of strategies, deliberate and emergent. *Strategic Management Journal, 6*(3), 257–272. https://doi.org/10.1002/smj.4250060306

Schroll, W. (2007). Kollaborative Innovationsprozesse – Hackathons in Theorie und Praxis. In T. Knoll (Hrsg.), *Veranstaltungen 4.0* (pp. 135–153). Gabler.

Singh, A., & Hess, T. (2017). How chief digital officers promote the digital transformation of their companies. *MIS Quarterly Executive, 16*(1), 1–17.

Singh, A., Barthel, P., & Hess, T. (2017). Der CDO als Komplement zum CIO. *Wirtschaftsinformatik & Management, 9*(1), 38–47. https://doi.org/10.1007/s35764-017-0004-7

Tavakoli, A., Schlagwein, D., & Schoder, D. (2017). Open strategy: Literature review, re-analysis of cases and conceptualisation as a practice. *Journal of Strategic Information Systems, 26*(3), 163–184. https://doi.org/10.1016/j.jsis.2017.01.003

von Hippel, E. (2001). Perspective: User toolkits for innovation. *The Journal of Product Innovation Management, 18*(4), 247–257. https://doi.org/10.1111/1540-5885.1840247

Walcher, D. (2010). Steering digital transformation strategically. In A. Picot, R. Reichwald, E. Franck, & K. Möslein (Hrsg.), *Der Ideenwettbewerb als Methode der aktiven Kundenintegration*. Deutscher Universitäts.

Weinreich, U. (2016). *Lean Digitization: Digitale Transformation durch agiles Management*. Springer. https://doi.org/10.1007/978-3-662-50502-1

Wiesböck, F., Matt, C., Hess, T., & Richter, A. (2017). How management in the German insurance industry can handle digital transformation. *WIM Management Report, 2017*(1).

6

The Complete Approach at a Glance

The three-layer framework structures the tasks involved in a digital transformation. It addresses three central topic areas—changing value creation processes, creating conditions for digital transformation and developing a transformation governance. The most important concepts and instruments for these topic areas are described in the overview below. Furthermore, it is elaborated how to properly start in the management of digital transformation in a company.

6.1 The Most Important Concepts and Instruments at a Glance

The 3LDT framework introduced in Chap. 1 is a framework. This structures the tasks involved in the management of digital transformation, but is by definition initially empty. In the following sections, the most important of the concepts and instruments mentioned in this book will be summarized first, with which this framework can be "filled".

6.1.1 Change Value Creation Structures through Digital Transformation

Digital innovations can be based on the products and services, the customer interfaces supporting them, the processes or the business models. In all four cases, it is crucial that the technical and the expert solutions are two sides

T. Hess, *Managing the Digital Transformation*,
https://doi.org/10.1007/978-3-658-38424-1_6

of the same coin and are developed as such—otherwise, in particular, the potentials of new technologies cannot be fully exploited.

Digital products and services can be standalone, combined with an offline component or supplement an offline product as a value-added service. The embedding of digital offers in ecosystems as well as the reaction of customers to access to their privacy must be given particular attention. Agile approaches are particularly suitable for product development. The introduction of agile, typically product-oriented forms of organization in the product-related areas of companies is currently strongly debated.

Digital technologies can improve customer interaction and personalization, lead to more automation, and make it easier to test change ideas. The customer journey map has proven to be a valuable analysis tool for changes at the customer interface. In particular, the new gatekeepers who can powerfully position themselves between customers and their own company should be noted.

Technical innovations, directly or indirectly, e.g. in the form of new value-added services, can lead to significant improvements in performance, support and leadership processes, in particular more automation. For the analysis of business processes, there are well-developed process modeling techniques such as the BPMN approach. These tools as well as, if necessary, process mining support the in-depth analysis. The approach to process optimization is more phase-oriented. Oftentimes, the detailed analysis of the current state is dispensed with. Occasionally, there is a secondary organization structured by processes with a process manager at the top.

For the integrated consideration of changes, the creation of business models has established itself. Here, the desired changes are brought together in terms of products, customer interfaces and processes and supplemented by the consideration of revenue models and value creation structures. The business model canvas approach has established itself in particular for the description of business models. Since a business model is always reflected in the IT architecture, this also has to be restructured and adapted accordingly.

6.1.2 Creating Conditions for Digital Transformation

Digital transformation requires a quickly adaptable IT landscape, an innovation-promoting corporate structure and a "digitalization-affine" corporate culture as well as competencies in the field of digitization and digital transformation. Rarely are all these requirements already given in a company. As a rule, however, support projects are required that specifically supplement missing requirements.

There are two approaches available for creating a quickly expandable IT landscape, both of which have advantages and disadvantages. Using **cloud computing**, established, encapsulated solutions can be brought into a company from the outside—even into a complex IT landscape. The idea of **bimodal IT** takes a different approach. It provides for new systems to be deliberately separated from established systems and for new systems to be developed using the agile approach. Both approaches can also be combined.

Innovation-promoting corporate structures can be achieved by separating the new unit in the company, by opening up to external partners and by breaking down cemented structures. Incubators can be used by a company to deliberately bring in external expertise—the success of such programs, however, requires flexibility and a willingness to take risks. With corporate venturing, a company becomes involved in a start-up. For large companies, this provides access to technology, innovation and agility.

The systematic analysis of culture, the introduction of specifically selected IT systems and special further training for managers can support the move towards a market- and employee-oriented as well as agile culture that is needed for digital transformation. It is important that the introduction of these instruments is embedded in a project of cultural change—and that a lot of time is available. Culture changes slowly, especially in successful organizations.

A digital change requires two types of competence: for digitalization (i.e. for the implementation of technical systems) and for digital transformation (i.e. for the implementation of new business concepts). Both competences are indispensable. The competences for digital transformation have to be built up in the company. For this, both internal measures (such as widespread training as well as idea competitions) and externally oriented measures (such as cooperation with universities) are available. However, large parts of the more technically oriented digitalization competence can be purchased from specialized technology companies. There are only few constellations in which non-IT companies should deal with the original development of technologies. However, a company must not give up the ability to "orchestrate" IT solutions for a product or process.

6.1.3 Develop Transformation Governance

The transformation governance in particular defines the strategies and structures of digital transformation. A transformation strategy sketches the direction of the most important changes in the value creation and management structure of a company in the context of digital transformation, makes statements about the handling of the relevant digital technologies and defines the financial framework of digital transformation. It lies "across" to the other, typically existing strategies in a company, in particular also to the IT strategy; and is thus an important tool for the management of digital transformation. The DTS framework supports the formulation of a company-specific transformation strategy.

A purely centralized approach to formulating a transformation strategy is unlikely to be successful. Although this usually provides very radical ideas, it is more sensible to systematically collect the ideas already present in many places and at many levels in a company, to prioritize them according to the company's goals and to bring them together to form a consistent strategy—and to do this again and again.

The formulation of a transformation strategy should always be flanked by the creation of suitable structures for the management of digital transformation. It must be ensured that the topic is driven by the CEO—only then are there real chances of success. In complex organizations, it is usually helpful to create a specialized unit to support it, possibly with a CDO at the top. This unit can coordinate the formulation of a strategy and, in particular, the implementation of projects derived from the strategy.

The results are summarized in Table 6.1.

The intensive examination of the concepts and instruments of digital transformation has only begun in recent years. In the coming years, certainly more concepts and instruments will arise and displace some of today's suggestions. Therefore, it is worth staying up to date in this field!

6.2 The Right Entry

Chapters 3 , 4 and 5 describe a "toolbox" that supports digital change—especially digital transformation—with the help of concepts and instruments. Which concepts and instruments are relevant depends on the specific situation in a particular company—that means there can be no "blueprint" for it. However, for a structured entry of a company into the topic, such a

Table 6.1 Important Concepts and Instruments of Digital Transformation

Topic area	Important concepts and instruments
Value creation structures change through digital transformation	Develop digital products/services, hybrid products/services or digital value-added services, possibly embedded in an agile, product-oriented organization Improve customer interface using a customer journey map through digital offers Further automate performance, support and leadership processes, possibly flanked by a process-oriented secondary organization Integrative consideration of changes using the analysis of business models, reflected in the IT architecture
Create conditions for digital transformation	Make IT landscape quickly expandable through cloud computing or the bimodal IT approach Flexibility, separation of new units and the selective opening up to third parties are concepts that lead to an innovation-promoting organization Cultural analysis, new IT systems and the training of managers as part of a long-term project for cultural change Building transformation competence in the company, often (but not always) limiting the technical competence to the orchestration of existing solutions
Define transformation governance	Design transformation strategy according to the DTS framework Structuring the process of strategy development, supplemented by ideas from top management and supporting staff Anchoring digital transformation as a task of the CEO, supported by a "digitalization unit", possibly with a CDO at the top

blueprint can be outlined. Figure 6.1 shows a proposal that includes seven steps.

1. In the first step, the topic is to be anchored provisionally in the organization. Most companies set up a small staff team for this purpose. This team organizes and coordinates the first systematic steps in the context of

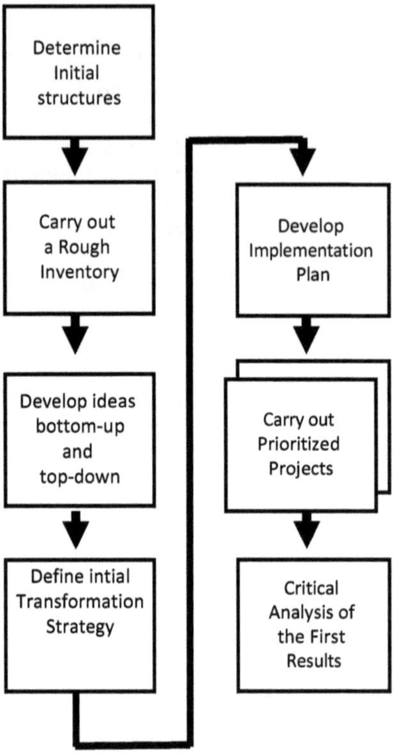

Fig. 6.1 Seven Steps for Getting Started with Digital Transformation

digital transformation. Sometimes the head of this unit is already referred to as CDO.

2. This unit carries out a rough inventory. For this there are two variants. Part of the companies tries to determine their own digital maturity with the help of one of the methods sketched in Sect. 5.4 . Others, rely on a rough analysis in the value-added area (i.e. at the products/services and their interfaces to the customer, at the processes and at the business models) in order to identify obvious weaknesses. As a rule, this also reveals deficiencies in the IT systems, the structures, the culture and the competencies.
3. In the third step, ideas for projects are developed, typically in a combination of bottom-up and top-down approach. Accordingly, many companies collect the ideas of the employees, for example, via an ideas competition. The newly created digitalization unit organizes this process and also gets down to developing new ideas in selected areas.

4. In the fourth step, a first version of the transformation strategy is developed from the collected ideas. Consideration is given in particular to the company strategy and the financial and technological possibilities.
5. In the fifth step, a first implementation plan is developed, i.e. the question is answered as to which project can be carried out with which budget at which time. Of course, the ideas for changing products/services, customer interfaces, processes and business models derived from the strategy are taken into account. But the possibly required changes in IT systems, structures and culture as well as in skills are also included.
6. In step six, these projects are then carried out.
7. A first conclusion is drawn in step seven.

In addition, a responsible manager is to be used for the entry into digital transformation, who ideally reports directly to the CEO. This project manager must have two essential qualities. On the one hand, he must be an expert in the field of digital transformation and know the central technical developments well. On the other hand, he should know the industry—only then will he quickly gain the necessary acceptance in the company.

6.3 Beyond the Digital Transformation: What Comes Next?

Digital transformation is a special management approach. It requires extensive investments, a matching structure and no less than the attention of top management. This is all necessary if new digital technologies fundamentally call a company into question. There must be constellations in a company where digital transformation no longer makes sense. For this, two cases must be distinguished.

For more than 40 years, companies have been dealing with digital innovations, for example, the changes in accounting in the 1970s or the gradual redesign of important processes in the 1980s and 1990s. In the literature, such companies are referred to as "IT-enabled Organizations".

Typically, the IT departments played an important role, they provided the IT infrastructure, they developed their own software solutions or adapted standard software to the needs of the company and were often the driving force behind the adaptation of the processes in the company. Specific structures, high investments and a lot of attention from top management were not necessary for this to work. In principle, it is conceivable that a company, after successfully completing digital transformation and no recognizable fundamental technical innovations, will fall back into this status. This is the first case.

However, the second case will be more typical. Again and again, new digital technologies become available that represent important opportunities or critical threats for a company. In this case, it would be disastrous to go back to the old state, which only allows companies to deal with smaller digital innovations. At the same time, however, it will also not work to permanently set a company in the "special state" of digital transformation. In this case, what is required is rather a "digital defined organization" oriented towards the constant challenges posed by digital technologies. Figure 6.2 describes these three states and the two cases that result from the digital transformation of a company.

How such a "digital defined organization" looks like can only be roughly seen today. On the one hand, there are a number of companies that have no analog past, i.e. companies that started with an online service or an online product. There are many examples, from Google to Tesla and Spotify, to countless regional providers such as Interhyp. But of course, the providers of IT products and services are also interesting, such as the software provider SAP or the IT service provider Bechtle. These are also "digital born", although in a different way. In addition, there are other companies that have been dealing with the digital transformation for over 20 years and for which the topic has accordingly already passed into the DNA. This group certainly includes some, but not all, media companies. The first change came here with the wide availability of the Internet as a bidirectional medium. Quite quickly, devices such as smartphones and tablets were added, which allow entirely new forms of presentation of content and interaction with the user. Currently, media companies are dealing with the question of to what extent current solutions of artificial intelligence are superior to humans in curating and even creating content.

The example of the media companies shows once again quite clearly: Digital transformation is a concept that can bring a company onto the path

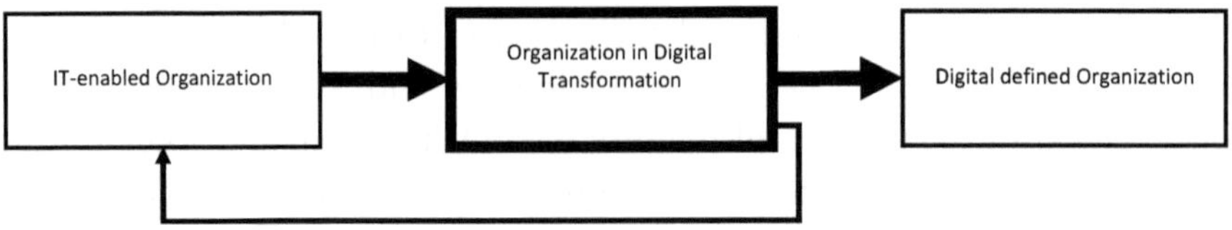

Fig. 6.2 Embedding of Digital Transformation

of systematic use of digital technologies—quite in the sense of an effort. If the need for digital change becomes a permanent necessity, then new concepts are required. These are only known in outline today. But to get started on the topic, it is enough to "only" deal with digital transformation in the sense of the mentioned effort. If this succeeds, then a lot has already been won. This effort is not a matter of course. The concepts outlined in this book are intended to help with the successful completion of this challenge.

MIX
Papier aus verantwortungsvollen Quellen
Paper from responsible sources
FSC® C105338

If you have any concerns about our products,
you can contact us on
ProductSafety@springernature.com

In case Publisher is established outside the EU,
the EU authorized representative is:
Springer Nature Customer Service Center GmbH
Europaplatz 3, 69115 Heidelberg, Germany

Printed by Libri Plureos GmbH
in Hamburg, Germany